So Idle
A Rogue

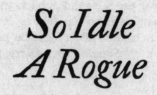

... this very morning the King did publicly walk up and down, and Rochester I saw with him as free as ever, to the King's everlasting shame, to have so idle a rogue his companion.

Samuel Pepys, Diary, 17 February 1669

I can as well support the hatred of the whole world, as anybody, not being generally fond of it.

Lord Rochester in a letter to his friend Henry Savile

So Idle A Rogue

THE LIFE AND DEATH OF LORD ROCHESTER

JEREMY LAMB

SUTTON PUBLISHING

For my parents

This book was first published in 1993 by
Allison & Busby

This edition first published in 2005 by
Sutton Publishing Limited · Phoenix Mill
Thrupp · Stroud · Gloucestershire · GL5 2BU

Reprinted 2005

British Library Cataloguing in Publication Data
A catalogue record for this book is available from the British Library.

ISBN 0 7509 3913 3

Typeset in 10/12pt Plantin.
Typesetting and origination by
Sutton Publishing Limited.
Printed and bound in Great Britain by
J.H. Haynes & Co. Ltd, Sparkford.

CONTENTS

ACKNOWLEDGEMENTS

More than any other reason, it is probably the sexually explicit nature of much of the Earl of Rochester's poetry which accounts for comparatively so little having been published about him over the years. At various times he has been *persona non grata* in polite circles and was by no means received by even his own society with open arms. He is now, however, widely and rightly recognised as one of the most important Restoration writers – as a satirist, perhaps second to none and, as a lyrical poet, up there with the best of them. In more recent times, both David Vieth (*Complete Poems of John Wilmot, Earl of Rochester*, 1968) and John Adlard (*The Debt to Pleasure*, which is a standard reference work for University students) have taken advantage of the relaxation in the obscenity laws and have duly published the Earl's more notorious work as well as his lyrical poems. I have used both books in quoting Rochester's poetry, sometimes changing the punctuation where it seemed to help make what can be fairly complicated language more accessible to the general reader.

Earlier this century, three other writers published major biographies of Rochester – all of them, in their different ways, excellent. Johannes Prinz paved the way with his 1927 book, *John Wilmot Earl of Rochester. His Life and Writings*, and the lack of previous detailed research made his task particularly hard. His book includes a number of Rochester's letters to his family, as well as the two letters to the Earl from the Duke of Buckingham, both quoted in *So Idle A Rogue*. Graham Greene then wrote the superb *Lord Rochester's Monkey* in the 1930s (though he did not have the book published until the 1970s), while Professor Vivian de Sola Pinto published his revised version of the poet's life, *Enthusiast in Wit*, in 1962. All these biographies express different interpretations of Rochester's highly complicated character; all of them proved invaluable to the writing of this book.

It is most unlikely that any startling new letters or poems about or by Rochester are still waiting to be discovered, and this book does not pretend to have uncovered hitherto unseen material. Where it is different from anything yet published about the Earl is the emphasis I have placed on the disease of alcoholism, which wrecked the man's life, destroying his health, friendships and happiness before killing him at thirty-three. In this sense, I would like to think of the interpretation as 'modern' and necessary for the 1990s. If Rochester was truly so idle a rogue, it was only because he was mentally and physically ill, and what helped me in my understanding of this was *Alcohol and the Addictive Brain*, published a couple of years ago by Professor Kenneth Blum and James Payne. I have quoted several passages from this work, in each case taking care to attribute Blum and Payne's findings. For anyone interested in learning more about the most recent research into the condition, their book (published by Macmillan) cannot be recommended too highly. Prinz, Pinto and Greene, meanwhile, cannot be accused of overlooking the Earl's alcoholism, since they were all writing at a time when it was regarded more as a wanton addiciton than a chronic (i.e. incurable) illness.

My fascination in Rochester was initiated by a study of his poetry at Goldsmiths' College, London University, where I first came across his work his work in 1987. I was especially lucky to have Professor Alan Downie as my lecturer. Rochester is one of his own specialist subjects and like all the best teachers he has the gift of instilling his enthusiasm for a topic in his students.

My thanks also go to His Grace the Duke of Marlborough, who allowed me to visit High Lodge, Rochester's country retreat, which is in the grounds of the Blenheim Palace estate. The Earl's death-bed, a relic of some importance, has suffered noticeable delapidation in the past twenty years (no doubt due to weathering) and is now very fragile indeed. His Grace will know best how it can possibly be preserved for as long as possible. I should also like to thank Philip Everett, land agent at Blenheim, and his assistant Jonathan, for kindly showing me round High Lodge.

Last but certainly not least I am extremely grateful for the hard work, encouragement and advice which I have received at all times from my publisher, Peter Day, and his assistant Petra Fergusson. I have also been able to benefit from the support of my agent, Patrick Walsh, to whom I am similarly grateful.

I should stress that I have made certain minor alterations to the punctuation of Rochester's letters, besides his poems, and also to the writings of his contemporaries. The book is aimed at the general reader with an interest in poetry, and it seemed important to make the language as easy to understand as possible without changing its meaning or spirit.

INTRODUCTION

SO USEFUL A PERSON

Sure there has not lived in many ages (if ever) so
extraordinary, and, I think I may add, so useful a
person as most Englishmen know my Lord to have been ...
for as he was both the delight and the wonder of men,
the love and the dotage of women, so he was a continual
curb to impertinence and the public censor of folly.

Robert Wolseley, one of Rochester's friends,
writing five years after the Earl's death.

October 1992. Pheasants are playing chicken in the back lanes of the Blenheim Palace estate as land agent Philip Everett drives me towards High Lodge, the country retreat of seventeenth-century England's most notorious, salacious rake. This gladed pocket of Oxfordshire was once Woodstock Park, and as we trundle through it under leaden skies and swirling branches, treetops dipping in the strong wind, my thoughts turn to the satisfaction its most infamous former keeper and ranger would have taken from knowing how unspoilt it has remained throughout his long absence. More than three hundred years have passed since the scourge of the Restoration age breathed his last in the house we have come to visit, but today he would surely recognise these surroundings in an instant. It was in one of these nearby clearings on an October afternoon in 1677 that John Wilmot, second Earl of Rochester, set tongues wagging yet again by running naked to dry himself after a swim. 'A frisk for forty yards,' he explained with characteristic nonchalance. It was through the trees somewhere around here that on another, more restrained occasion, an old women from Woodstock spied on the Earl and his young son Charles walking with the Duke of Monmouth who, so she told the antiquary Thomas Hearne, gave the child 'a present of a fine little horse'. How different that day was to the one which saw the park's tranquility shattered by the arrival of that archrogue George Villiers, second Duke of Buckingham, riding amidst his usual hullabaloo and 'the finest pack of hounds that ever ran upon English ground'.

A flash of stone through the overhanging branches ahead heralds the austere building granted to Rochester in 1674 by King Charles II and in which the Earl, unwilling to confine his debauchery to the mere perimeters of London, is said to have had several 'lascivious' pictures drawn. Inside these tall, grey imposing walls with their castellated tops, Rochester gave vent to the base desires which perversely caused him so much self-loathing by ravishing, 'among other girls', said Thomas Hearne, one Nell Browne of Woodstock. 'She looked pretty well when clean,' Hearne added, 'yet she was a very nasty, ordinary, silly creature.'

Rochester would probably have known the enormous oak which towers at the north end of the lodge, its uppermost branches now so aged that they stretch out, forever bare, like tortured fingers. Neither would the bricked-up windows in the south wall, though they give a clue to the changes the entire facade must have undergone during the centuries, be likely to fool the Earl today into mistaking this place for anything other than the sanctuary to which he would journey by carriage from London, perhaps having been banished from Court, perhaps ill from his latest debauch, and sometimes both. He made constructive use of his stays here too; for, according to Rochester's confessor, the historian and priest Gilbert Burnet, he would 'often go into the country and be for some months wholly employed in study, or the sallies of his wit, which he came to direct chiefly to satire. And this he often defended to me by saying there were people that could not be kept in order, or admonished, but in this way.'

High Lodge, which was recently renovated to the tune of several hundred thousand pounds, and, until a few years ago, housed the families of Blenheim Palace estate workers in its two wings, now stands empty. The large rooms, which echoed once to the clatter of cavalier boots and the clinking of goblets, today play host to falling dust, to silence, and, on the second floor, to an old and rickety four-poster bed. This, however, is not just any old four-poster. It is one of the more notable death-beds in English history and its presence as the solitary item of furniture in the whole house is as wonderful as it is eerie. Only the ruined remains of its once grand pelmet, or tester, are left to indicate the quality of person whose final, agonising weeks are believed to have been spent in it, and who, in the very throes of his death, sent a shock wave of rumour throughout the kingdom.

For in the spring of 1680, word reached London that the most celebrated sinner of the age, the terrible 'House of Heaven' whose vicious but brilliant satires had made him so hated and feared, was going to the grave not as a defiant atheist but as a Christian convert. As gossip spread through the capital's ale-houses, market places and dining rooms, those who thought they had known Rochester, from the prostitutes of Drury Lane to the elegant men and women who draped themselves around the rooms of Whitehall Palace, assumed he had finally lost his mind. It is an opinion shared by some to this day.

Rochester's enemies, including the sour-faced and unforgiving John Sheffield, Earl of Mulgrave, jealously regarded such a late change of heart and mind as a false act of contrition; a far too convenient get-out. Down from Windsor journeyed the disbelieving but nevertheless intrigued Will Fanshawe, who was one of the Earl's drinking companions and now had instructions from King Charles II's courtiers to report his findings back to them. What he found at the lodge and heard from the lips of its dying tenant had him leaving (according to one witness) trembling with shock, but he recovered enough composure to spread the news that so many wanted to hear: the Earl had definitely gone mad. 'Poor wretch!' declared Rochester, 'I fear his heart is hardened.'

At the bedside today and through the mind's eye, the ghosts of those dramatic final weeks can be seen assembling round the patient. While the numerous priests – Dr Burnet, Robert Parsons (the family's chaplain), Dr Marshall, Dr Price and the Bishop of Oxford – took it in turns to tend to his spiritual needs, the physicians – Dr Radcliffe, Dr Lower, Dr Browne and Dr Shorter – did their helpless best to meet his medical ones. For Dr Shorter, who was 'libertine in principles', the whole experience proved so overwhelming that he tunred to Christianity – in his case, Catholicism – shortly afterwards. Rochester had always found it easy to influence people but now he was leading them up quite a different path. Above him, fretting, fussing and instructing the servants, was the long-suffering and beautiful young women he called 'my more than meritous wife'. Now, under his guidance and reunited with her husband at last, Lady Rochester was back at prayer too, newly returned from Catholicism to 'her first love, the Protestant religion'. Meanwhile, hovering in the background was the intimidating figure of the Earl's puritanical mother, more convinced than she had ever been before about the power of God's mercy, emotionally declaring in letters which she sent to relatives and friends but wanted all the world to see, that her 'poor child' was not mad. 'Let the wicked of the world say what they please of him,' she wrote, 'the reproaches of them are an honour to him, and I take comfort that the devil rages against my son; it shows his power over him is subdued in him, and that he has no share in him.' The Earl's four young children were brought to him too and he duly urged them to follow the teachings of Christ. 'He called me once to look on them,' wrote Gilbert Burnet, 'and said, "See how good God has been to me in giving me so many blessings, and I have carried myself to him like an ungracious and unthankful dog."'

In this tattered deathbed the Earl of Rochester did no so much take his leave from the world as turn his back on it in disgust. When one of his physicians, hoping to please him, told him the King had only the other day drunk his health, Rochester (according to his mother) 'looked earnestly upon him and said never a word, but turned his face from him'. It is a poignant moment in our story, for the Earl's bitterness towards the world and his ultimate rejection of its values were, rightly or wrongly, directed more at King Charles II than at any other individual. He might have remembered the words spoken by Charles's father to Bishop Juxon shortly before his execution: 'I go from a corruptible crown to an incorruptible crown, where no disturbance can be, no disturbance in the world.' There was no disturbance in this bed either when, at about 2 a.m. on the 26 July 1680, Lord Rochester discovered what he had been seeking all his short and stormy life: in his own words, 'my everlasting rest'.

1

CIVIL BEGINNINGS

So I walked a mile and an half through very pleasant
country, in a good measure adorned with marvellous
pleasant woods, till I came against Ditchley House . . .
I think I was never better pleased with any sight
whatsoever than with this house, which hath been
the seat of persons of true loyalty and virtue.

The Oxford antiquary Thomas Hearne,
visiting Rochester's birthplace in June 1718

Even by the standards of the most swashbuckling cavalier,
Henry Viscount Wilmot's life was eventful. Born in 1612,
nine years into the reign of James I, this third but only
surviving son of Charles, first Viscount Wilmot of Athlone, Ireland,
was captain of a troop of horse in the Dutch service in 1635 and
commissary-general of horse in the King's army when the second
Scottish war was fought in 1640. The Scots battled with the
English at Newburn that August and Wilmot distinguished himself
in the fighting until he was captured and taken prisoner. After his
release he represented Tamworth in the Long Parliament, but in
June 1641 he was sent packing to the Tower of London (which
twenty-five years later would house his infamous son) for trying to
help his troubled monarch by plotting to bring up the army and
intimidate parliament. In December, parliament expelled him.

He was free again and with King Charles I at York the following
spring, and when civil war was signalled by the raising of the royal

standard at Nottingham on 22 August, Wilmot was in charge of a troop of horse and held the post of muster-master as well as that of commissary-general. Wounded at Worcester in September during one of the war's opening skirmishes, he recovered quickly enough to lead the cavalry of the King's left wing into the indecisive Battle of Edgehill the following month. In December, he seized the town of Marlborough.

King Charles did not particularly like the swaggeringly ambitious Wilmot – they were very different types of men – but he was impressed enough by his obvious military gifts to make him his lieutenant-general of horse in April 1643. In June, the thirty-one-year-old royalist was created Baron Wilmot of Adderbury in Oxfordshire and a few weeks later he celebrated his rising importance by being one of the senior officers who led the victory over Sir William Waller's parliamentary forces at Roundway Down. The next summer, at Copredy Bridge in Oxfordshire, he crushed Waller a second time. In this battle he was again wounded and taken prisoner, but his men rescued him almost immediately.

All this high adventure and success seem to have made Wilmot a little giddy, for he now disgraced himself with an alacrity which might even have tested his own son. The instincts of the upstanding Prince Rupert, who had always mistrusted the lieutenant-general of horse, were at last proved right. Convinced that the King was frightened of the consequences of peace, Wilmot decided it would be best to negotiate with the enemy, put pressure on Charles to abdicate, and set up the fourteen-year-old Prince of Wales in his father's place. Later events, culminating in Charles I's execution, suggest that this was by no means crackpot thinking – but Wilmot's over-confidence ensured that he broke the 'eleventh commandment' and was caught plotting by his superiors. A private message which he sent to the parliamentary commander, the Earl of Essex, aroused suspicion within his own camp and on 8 August 1644 he was arrested, deprived of his command and charged with endeavouring, with Essex's help, to impose terms on the King and parliament. He also lost the joint presidency of Connaught – an office in which he had succeeded his father earlier that year. What saved Wilmot from a worse fate (imprisonment again or perhaps even the death penalty) was his popularity with his fellow officers. They successfully petitioned the King to be merciful and he was duly allowed to retire to Paris.

The war's turning point came in June 1645 when, at Naseby, Oliver Cromwell's cavalry overwhelmed Prince Rupert's outnumbered forces. In September, the New Model Army pressed home its advantage by forcing Rupert to surrender the key city of Bristol and in May the next year the King gave himself up to the Scots at Newark. Although hostilities flared up again in 1648, the first and main Civil War ended with the capitulation of Oxford, the royalist headquarters, in June 1646. That summer saw the shamed Lord Wilmot languishing at home with his wife before departing to France. In the autumn he received the news that she was expecting a child.

✤ ✤ ✤

Anne Wilmot lived in the tranquil surroundings of Ditchley Park, Oxfordshire, about five miles north-west of Woodstock and some ten miles south-west of her husband's ancestral home, a 'magnificent mansion', at Adderbury, near Banbury. As the daughter of Sir John St John, of Lyddiard Tregoz, Wiltshire, she came from sound and strait-laced puritan stock. She had acquired Ditchley through her previous marriage to its owner, Sir Francis Henry Lee, who was Lord Warwick's stepson and therefore came from a notable parliamentary family. Sir Francis had died in 1639, just two years into the marriage, leaving her with two infant sons to bring up and a debt-ridden estate to manage. (This was Henry Wilmot's second marriage as well. In 1633, at the age of twenty-one, he had married Frances, daughter of Sir George Morton of Dorset. She, too, had almost certainly died.)

Perhaps one positive aspect of widowhood is that through necessity it tends to bring out strength of character and encourage resourcefulness. If Lady Lee had not needed to live on her wits before Sir Francis's death then she certainly did after it and, as manager of her own estate she now became, and remained for the rest of her life, a formidable businesswoman. In 1644, halfway throught the first Civil War, she took the politically expedient step of marrying Henry Wilmot. Since her own background was puritan and her previous marriage had been into a parliamentary family, it may at first seem that she was in danger of alienating herself from her origins, but this was not so. Such a marriage had the effect of bridging the parliamentary/royalist divide rather than jumping across it, for she now had connections with both the opposing factions instead of just one of them. Whatever the outcome of the war (and at the time of her marriage there was every reason to believe the royalists would win it) Lady Wilmot's joint political attachments would protect her land and ensure she kept her respected place in society. Thus, during Cromwell's rule she was able to defend her estate against his property-stripping officers by pointing out that it had come to her through her marriage to a good and honest parliament man, while the Restoration of the monarchy in 1660 held no fears for her either on account of her second marriage to a cavalier. The most notable example of this kind of cross-party union occurred in 1657 when one of the most prominent royalists, George Villiers, second Duke of Buckingham, managed to save his own estate from the clutches of Cromwell's Committee of Sequestration by marrying Mary Fairfax, daughter of the famous parliamentary general. (Since the Duke then proceeded to debauch himself into debts – according to Andrew Marvell – of £140,000 and let the estate run to ruin, one wonders why he ever bothered saving it in the first place. There was never an easy explanation for Buckingham, though, who only seemed to want things so that he could throw them away.)

There is much to admire about the bold and stalwart Lady Wilmot. She was a survivor in every sense, outliving both husbands besides the son she was then carrying, and it was not until that son came home to die thirty-three years later that her tough facade finally cracked open to reveal a mixture of simple and maternal emotions; despair at the prospect of his death and euphoria over his religious conversion. In the intervening years she was a powerful presence at Ditchley, summoning her faithful agent John Cary to issue him business instructions, asking for advice in letters written to her other chief mentor, Sir Ralph Verney of Claydon, Buckinghamshire, who was as highly principled and fastidious as she was herself, but otherwise running the estate with a firm hand and a decisive, no-nonsense mind of her own. From his mother, a 'Lady of equal parts and beauty', her son was to acquire the air of great authority and the sense of sheer command, which put his peers in awe of him.

It is interesting to note that the shrewd Lady Wilmot had begun nudging her way nearer to the royalists several years before her second marriage. She was anxious, whether or not she remarried, to strengthen her hand with them. In 1642, just as the war was staring, she sent some arms to the royalists and then turned up in Oxford to ask a favour (money?) of the Court. Cary Gardiner, a member of the Verney family, wrote of this in a letter home, explaining how Lady Lee had come to speak with Lord Saye 'concerning the arms she had sent to the King'. Saye, however, 'not being a courtier would not listen to her, so she returned away with a great blame the country laid upon her, her being a widow made her a little to be pitied . . .' For once she had not got her way. On another occasion that year Lady Lee gave refuge at Ditchley to Sir Edward Hyde, the future Lord Clarendon, who was on his way to join the King at York and had stopped off for fear of being arrested by parliamentarians ahead. The following dawn Lady Lee's own coach and horses smuggled Hyde out of the park and took him safely to a village just outside Coventry. It is clear, then, that even if she had not married Lord Wilmot, she would have done everything possible to ensure the royalists treated her well.

Lady Wilmot was always ambitious on behalf of her relatives – besides others whom she felt were deserving – and the Restoration of 1660 saw her sending out instructions (she was a prolific and excellent letter-writer) to Sir Thomas Yates, asking him to secure seats in the new Free Parliament for her adviser and friend Sir Ralph Verney and her son Sir Harry Lee. 'Good Mr Yates, next to my son Lee, let not Sir Ralph Verney fail of being chosen . . . what you shall say to the people of the place to encourage them to it, I shall leave to your prudence . . . if my brother St John be not chosen, I shall rather have him disappointed than Sir Ralph Verney.' She was then most indignant when Yates asked for quite a bit of money in return for his help. Mr Yates, she declared, 'expects much for his reward, more than he has reason for, though for the present it is my opinion the least notice is taken of it the better.' Her ambitious expectations of her own family not only had her pushing her son John Wilmot into Oxford University at the precocious age of twelve but led her to believe, much later, that her great-grandson Lord Norreys ought to be entering parliament at the age of thirteen. It was, she said, a good school for youth to be improved in. There is no arguing with that.

With a timing which would later seem appropriate, John Wilmot was born at Ditchley Park on April Fools' Day 1647. (He was his mother's fourth son; an earlier child by Lord Wilmot had not survived). According to the astrologer Gadbury, the boy, born under the sign of the Ram, arrived at 11.07 a.m. and was endued with a noble and fertile muse. 'The sun governed the horoscope, and the moon ruled the birth hours. The conjunction of Venus and Mercury in M. Coelie, in sextile of luna, aptly denotes his inclination to poetry. The great reception of Sol with Mars and Jupiter posited so near the latter, bestowed a large stock of generous and active spirits, which constantly attended on this native's mind, insomuch that no subject came amiss to him.' Cynics of astrology (the child became one himself) might be glad to learn that this horoscope was published eighteen years after the poet's death, allowing plenty of time to get the facts right.

He was born at a time of renewed unrest, for the armies were now amassing for the brief second Civil War. Abroad, his father – who had predicted that peace would not last under King Charles I – was soon involved in a fight of his own: a duel in Paris with his arch-enemy, Lord Digby.

❧ ❧ ❧

While the stringency of the mother was to nurture within the boy a fiercely puritan and critical streak, we need look no further than the father if we are to begin to understand why John Wilmot's conduct would one day be so dramatically at odds with the standards of behaviour he always claimed to admire. The great historian of the age, the Earl of Clarendon, wrote a detailed profile of Henry Wilmot's character, and when we consider that John Wilmot hardly knew his father – indeed might, just conceivably, never have met him – the description is uncanny. At times Clarendon could be writing about the son.

As his involvement in the plot to threaten parliament by bringing up the army had indicated in 1641, and as his plan to set up the Prince of Wales confirmed, Lord Wilmot loved intrigue. He was a meddlesome, interferring man who spent as much time scheming against his colleagues as he did working out battlefield strategy against his foes. (His son's love of intrigue would express itself in amours, his relish of scandal and his interest in gossip. He even posted a sentinel to spy at the doors of courtiers and ladies suspected of having affairs, and the information gained would then be put into libels and satires.) The Civil War enabled his father to carry out intrigue on a much grander scale than this, and we have already noted how wary Prince Rupert was of him. Clarendon called Wilmot 'a man of haughty and ambitious nature, of a pleasant wit and an ill-understanding, as never considering above one thing at once'. Headstrong, then, and something of a table-thumper too: 'He was positive in all his advices in council and bore contradiction very impatiently.'

A picture of the restless son who one evening declared to King Charles II: 'I hate still life' begins to emerge with Clarendon's comment that the father was not only proud and ambitious but 'incapable of being contented', and the alarm bells really start ringing with his observation that Henry Wilmot 'drank hard, and had a great power over all who did so, which was a great people'. The son's encouragement of others to drink and his power over them would be strong enough to earn a mention at his funeral. Clarendon added that the father 'had a more companiable wit even than his rival Goring [Henry Wilmot's successor as lieutenant-general of horse], and swayed more among the good fellows'. In other words, he preferred the camaraderie of the low life and the companionship of drinkers. His son was often to land himself in trouble through socialising with incorrigible rogues and rakes.

Whether the father was alcoholic is open to question, for Clarendon stated: 'Wilmot loved debauchery, but shut it out from his business and never neglected that, and rarely miscarried it.' Unquestionably this debauchery included heavy drinking bouts, for Clarendon noted how hard Wilmot drank; on the other hand it should be said that ambition, a quality Wilmot never lost, is one of the first casualties of active alcoholism. However, it is possible to be alcoholic and not let the condition interfere with work. This is achieved by simply 'going on the wagon' whenever duty calls, and the finality of the phrase 'shut it out from his business' could suggest a man who did not trust himself to drink moderately once he had started and therefore never touched the stuff when there was work to be done. This is the real test of alcoholism: whether or not a light, controlled intake can be sustained at length. It has nothing to do with being able to go for weeks or months without having a drop. Many alcoholics do exactly that. To say Wilmot was an alcoholic is admittedly speculative, but the point is that his son was, as we shall see, predisposed to alcoholism and he clearly did not inherit the condition from his mother. Modern-day research shows that such a predisposition can come from further up the family tree than from the parents, but Henry Wilmot's apparent love and weakness for drink is surely likely to have been a huge factor in the chronic condition acquired by his son.

There can be no doubt that soldiery and war provided Wilmot with badly needed discipline. How might he have behaved had he not lived through times of crisis? Like his son, perhaps? The similarities they shared as drinkers even went as far as their wittiness whilst under the influence. Clarendon said Henry Wilmot's wit was 'inspired' when he was 'in the very exercise of debauchery'. A characteristic which helped his son's early downfall was the fact that alcohol fuelled his muse and sharpened his tongue. John Wilmot was never funnier than when he was drunk and was therefore never without encouragement from his peers to 'have another'.

An accusation which plagued the son in adulthood was that of cowardice. It was unjustified and yet understandable. In his teens, John Wilmot proved himself capable of immense courage, but his increasingly worsening alcoholism in later years accounted for behaviour which *appeared* cowardly. It is interesting to see that Clarendon accused the father of cowardice too. Henry Wilmot, he said, 'saw danger in the distance with great courage' but he 'looked upon it less resolutely when it was nearer'. Danger was something he 'commonly prevented' and 'warily declined'. Cowardice seems an odd charge to level at a man whose body was so heavily battle-scarred; who, for want of any real action, was duelling in Paris with Lord Digby and picking up yet another wound; and who, when he was being chased across southern England in 1651 by Cromwell's soldiers, was too proud to wear a disguise. Perhaps the more a man has a reputation for bravery, the more others try to find a chink in his armour. The son's patronage of London's leading playwrights in the 1670s has given rise to the accusation of fickleness in his friendships, and Clarendon is far from complimentary about the father's loyalty to others. Neither

Lord Wilmot nor Lord Goring, he wrote, 'valued their promises, professions or friendships, according to any rules of honour or integrity; but Wilmot violated them less willingly, and never but for some great benefit or convenience to himself'. Finally, we are reminded of John Wilmot's conversion to God by Clarendon's remark that the father 'had more scruples from religion to startle him' than his successor Goring, and 'would not have attained his end by any gross or foul act of wickedness'.

Even if Lord Wilmot had been able to live with his wife after the Civil War and be the father his son never knew (rather than be forced to live in exile with the other leading royalists as a 'malignant' of Cromwell's state), it would still have been remarkable if the boy's character had managed to embrace such diametrically opposed personalities as those of his young parents: the upbraiding, strict and principled mother who had no time for fools and the archetypally cavalier father, fast-living, hard-drinking and volatile. Yet that is precisely what the infant in the cradle at Ditchley Park was destined to do.

Henry Wilmot was in many ways a child of fortune; a gambler and an opportunist who chased glory when it surfaced and was there for the taking but who was content, when fate dealt him a bad hand, to reminisce in candlelit taverns; to amaze the 'good fellows' who drank in his company with tales of derring-do at Edgehill, victory at Roundway Down and triumph at Copredy. By the winter of 1648 he was probably at the Hague, where the Prince of Wales and his Court were helplessly awaiting the news from London which their worst instincts told them was inevitable. On 5 February 1649 it came. Six days earlier, King Charles I, wearing two shirts to prevent him from shivering in the cold and giving the impression that he was frightened, had stepped out onto the scaffolding at Whitehall. Before kneeling, he had handed to Bishop Juxon the George, the insignia of the Garter, with instructions that it be passed on to the Prince of Wales along with one word: Remember. The axe-head fell and the crowd groaned.

Wilmot's star was in the ascendant again.

✤ ✤ ✤

Suddenly, the onus was upon 'the young gentleman', as Cromwell liked to call the exiled Charles Stuart, to capture the crown that was his by right of inheritance but which, according to parliament, was now and forever obsolete. Among those urging Charles into action was a man whose botched career had effectively been resurrected by the late King's execution. Wilmot had never fallen foul of the nineteen-year-old Charles, who, besides being in need of all the advice and assistance he could muster, was also free to pick the men he wanted to provide it. At some stage – preferably sooner than later – Charles, if he was to restore the monarchy, would have to face Cromwell on the battlefield. Who better to have at his side than his father's former lieutenant-general of horse? In spite of his youth at the time Charles had attended the Battle of Copredy Bridge in June 1644 and had seen for himself Wilmot's natural authority as a military commander, as well as his flair for soldiery. True, the disgraced viscount had proved dangerously untrustworthy shortly afterwards, but had he not expressed his penitence repeatedly and served out his sentence? And had his folly, though serious, not at least been committed in good faith? After all, it was the young Charles himself whom Wilmot had wanted to see on the throne. It was time to make fresh beginnings. Just two months after his father's execution, Charles appointed Wilmot Gentleman of the King's Bedchamber.

The position sounds menial, but carried considerable status. Gentlemen of the Bedchamber, who were almost always members of the nobility, took it in turns to wait upon the King in his quarters for one week out of every three months. Duties included sleeping on a pallet-bed in the King's bedchamber, helping him to dress in the morning whenever the groom of the stole was absent, and waiting at his table when he ate in private. The job was worth the handsome salary of £1,000 a year. Wilmot's appointment shows the surprising degree of trust Charles was prepared to place in him at a very uncertain time. The royalists had not ruled out the possibility that the parliamentarians would attempt to assassinate the King, and any Gentleman of the Bedchamber was privy to Charles's entire itinerary. When he visited Jersey eight months after his father's death, the fear of assassination was such that Charles's attendants were all armed with swords and sentries were posted throughout the royal quarters. Yet Wilmot quickly became a confidant in other ways too and, though he was not a member of the privy council, he was regularly consulted by the King on policy matters. All this renewed faith did not turn out to be misplaced: in the coming months Wilmot proved to be one of his sovereign's most valuable servants.

With the monarchs of Europe being either unable or unwilling to help Charles with the money and troops he would need if he was to take the throne, and with Cromwell decimating Ireland's forces at Drogheda, north of Dublin, and at Wexford in the south-east, the eyes of the royal Court turned to Scotland for salvation. Only on one condition would the Scots help, though: Charles would first have to sign the Presbytarian Oath of the Covenant. The very idea of him swearing to impose Presbyterian worship on the whole of Britain, as well as promising to practise it himself, would in normal circumstances have been laughable – but what alternative routes back to Whitehall were there? None. He duly gave his signature.

This whole grubby episode even embarrassed one of the leading convenanters, Alexander Jaffray, who later confessed:

We did sinfully both entangle and engage the nation and ourselves and that poor young prince to whom we were sent, making him sign and swear a covenant which we knew from clear and demonstrable reasons he hated in his heart. He sinfully complied with what we most sinfully pressed upon him; where I must confess, to my apprehension, our sin was more than his.

In the context of the bitterly disappointed view of the world which John Wilmot was to have, this was a significant moment. Charles's motives in signing the covenant were wholly practical but entirely unprincipled. What would his father, who went to the block rather than yield an inch over his beliefs, have thought? To make the business even more unsavoury, Charles's signature effectively sacrificed the life of the dutiful Marquess of Montrose, who was despised by the covenanters and was campaigning in the north of Scotland oblivious to the fact that his sovereign was agreeing to their demands. The upshot of this was that Montrose was captured by the triumphant covenanters, paraded through the streets of Edinburgh, hanged, drawn and quartered and had his limbs stuck up in various public places as a warning to anyone who was thinking of trifling with the Kirk.

The signing of the Oath of the Covenant (done with the approval of Wilmot, among others) was the first indication that an era of idealism was to be replaced by one of cynicism. The age of Faith, celebrated by the divine right of kings, was giving way to that of Reason, which incurred such things as compromise and political expediency. Meanwhile, a small child was being brought up in Oxfordshire on all the old values of honour and incorruptibility. He would never forgive society for the rude shock it had in store for him.

When Charles arrived in Scotland to organise his forces with the help of a party that included Wilmot, he was forced to endure the horribly self-satisfied smiles of the Presbyterians and made to sit through sermon after yawn-inspiring sermon. He hated this period of his life to the extent that he was never to look upon the Scots with much kindness again. During one service of yet more confession, repentance and beating of breasts he was heard to murmur: 'I think I must repent me ever being born.' It was with a considerable feeling of relief that Charles, Wilmot and the other royalist leaders crossed south of the border on 5 August 1651 at the head of a 16,000-strong Scottish army and made for Worcester, which had been the first city in the early days of the Civil war to declare loyalty to the crown.

What the royalists had not expected was the reluctance of Englishmen everywhere to swell their marching ranks. They simply had not appreciated the firmness of parliament's grip on the country: a stranglehold which was already turning England into a primitive form of police state. Many people who had been fervent royalists during the Civil War were now dissilusioned with the cause, too cynical from bitter experience to do anything about it, too frightened of the consequences, or had simply come to know and prefer the benefits of peace. Not even the spirit was willing. Charles and his army had twelve days at Worcester in which to recover from their exhausting journey and organise themselves for the impending battle, but what they really needed was a minor miracle. They met the onslaught of parliament's vastly superior forces with hopeless bravery instead, and Cromwell was impressed enough to call the Battle of Worcester 'as stiff a contest as ever I have seen'. Charles himself, clearly prepared to die if it meant Cromwell's defeat and revenge for his father's death, fought and commanded with distinction. Because his reign is always associated with *joie de vivre*, it is often forgotten that Charles was a man of considerable and proven physical courage. He had attended his first battle – Edgehill – at the age of twelve, where he is said to have come close to being captured as he flourished a pistol, yelling: 'I fear them not!' Nevertheless, on 3 September 1651 the hopes any royalist might have entertained of a swift return to the monarchy were buried alongside more than 2,000 Scottish troops. Cromwell's losses were a tenth of that. By dusk the royalists' most urgent objective was to prevent a disaster from becoming a catastrophe: namely, to get Charles out of the city before it was overrun and he was captured. There then remained the enormous task of smuggling him back to the sanctuary of mainland Europe. That took six weeks to achieve, and nobody played a greater part in its success than Lord Wilmot.

The story of Charles's escape from Worcester and the ensuing chase which took place across southern England is one of the most extraordinary and romantic chapters in the history of the monarchy. Charles, who on the eve of the Restoration related the whole adventure to a wide-eyed Samuel Pepys, never grew tired of retelling it in the years ahead, even though it meant putting up with the mock yawns of his celebrated Court wits. The image of him hiding in an oak tree while Cromwell's soldiers frantically searched the undergrowth beneath him is the stuff of legend and yet it did happen. While he was travelling in disguise from one safe house to another, the parliamentarians were desperately issuing 'WANTED' notices for 'a tall, black man, six feet two inches high', and a £1,000 reward was offered for information leading to his arrest. During these weeks Wilmot was closer to Charles than anybody else in their tiny party, advising him on the route they should take the following dawn, organising lodgings at night and, eventually, securing the fishing boat which they boarded at Shoreham, near Brighton, just as Cromwell's troops were arriving to search the coastline. An instance of Wilmot's vanity was that during the chase he had initially refused to wear a disguise on the grounds that he would 'look frightfully' in it. Later he made the rather ridiculous gesture of sporting a hawk on his wrist – a see-through disguise if ever there was one. If, at the time, Charles had felt like throttling his stubborn companion then on their safe return to Paris hs was more inclined towards rewarding him – and soon did so. On 13 December 1652, Henry Wilmot was created Earl of Rochester.

❖ ❖ ❖

It is most unlikely that Wilmot had either the time or opportunity to visit his wife and son during those hair-raising weeks in England, and it was now clear to Lady Rochester that if she and her children were ever to see her husband again they would have to travel to the continent. The four of them duly crossed the Channel in the summer of 1653, but if Lady Rochester was expecting her husband to be in Paris when the family arrived then she was disappointed. In fact, during this visit, he appears to have given her the run-around. Not for the first time, one suspects this marriage would not have been particularly close even if different circumstances had enabled the couple to live under the same roof. Although mother and children stayed in Paris for at least nine months, it is not even certain that they saw Lord Rochester at all. In August Edward Hyde, to whom Lady Rochester had given refuge at Ditchley eleven years earlier and who was now in Paris too, wrote to her husband – who was in Germany, trying to raise money for Charles – and encouraged the Earl to come and see his family. The six-year-old John Wilmot, wrote Hyde, was an excellent child and loved to receive letters from his father. Whether or not Rochester showed up is unclear, but in May the following year Hyde wrote again to tell the Earl that his wife would not return to England until she had seen him. That letter definitely got no response, for Hyde's next one, written just two weeks later, sounds irritated. Lady Rochester, he said, was heartily weary of Paris, and Henry, one of the Earl's stepsons, was even more so. They were ready to believe the place stood in the worst air in the world.

Perhaps Rochester arrived before his family left, perhaps not. But it is rather hard to believe that his prolonged and possibly complete absence was entirely due to the business he was conducting on Charles's behalf; one is tempted to think that in his spare time he preferred to 'sway more among the good fellows' than be confronted by his austere wife. His son's later sentiments about marriage seem to have reflected his own:

Marriage, thou state of jealousy and care,
The curse of wife, what flesh and blood can bear?
She ever loads your head, and stuns your passive ear,
And still the plague you feel, or still you fear.

Back in England, romance was the last thing on Lady Rochester's mind when Cromwell's officers started nosing around Ditchley Park in 1656 and then ordered her husband to send in particulars of his estate for its decimation. The defiant Lady Rochester now played the trump card of her first marriage. She strongly objected to her own property, acquired through Sir Francis Lee, being included in any considerations of her present husband's over at Adderbury. Her husband, she said in her petition, 'hath no interest in her said jointure lands' and she begged the Lord Protector Cromwell to put a stop to 'all further proceedings touching or concerning the same and to discharge your petitioner from further trouble or attendance'. It saved Ditchley, but the puritans almost certainly decimated Lord Rochester's land at Adderbury. Gilbert Burnet said the first Earl 'left his son little other inheritance but the honour and title derived to him' and, when John Wilmot married, Samuel Pepys remarked that it was a 'great act of charity' by his young wife, for 'he hath no estate'.

Lord Rochester, meanwhile, was not resting upon his laurels. He had now risen high enough in his sovereign's estimation to be one of the committee of four which Charles consulted in exile on all affairs. The year before his family visited Paris he had been sent on several diplomatic missions, and during their stay he had been to see the Elector of Brandenburg in an attempt to extract finances to further the uprising of the Scottish royalists. Then, in February 1655, when his family were probably back in Oxfordshire, Rochester volunteered to go to England and oversee another royalist conspiracy against Cromwell. He was given powers to authorise it or prevent it, as he saw fit. He landed at Margate, broke through Cromwell's ring of coastal spies and sanctioned the conspiracy only to discover some one hundred Yorkshire cavaliers gathered at Marston Moor when he had been banking on nearer 4,000.

Having abandoned the whole hopeless enterprise, his task now was to get back out of the country in one piece – something he only just managed. Although he rode south posing as a Frenchman and sporting a yellow periwig (his son was to be brilliant at disguising himself, and once avoided arrest by dressing up as a self-invented and outlandish character called Doctor Alexander Bendo), Rochester was stopped at Aylesbury and detained by a suspicious county justice for further examination. He escaped overnight by bribing the innkeeper who was supposed to have kept him under lock and key. Cromwell had known the Earl was somewhere in the country but when he bolted from Aylesbury the rabbit finally showed itself to the dog. Thorough searches were made of all Rochester's favourite watering holes in London, but the fugitive somehow managed to break back through the network of spies and agents along the coast and take a boat to the Hague, where he had safely arrived by June. After the Restoration it became clear that he had been saved by Colonel John Hutchinson, former parliamentary Governor of Nottingham, whose wife was related to Lady Rochester. Hutchinson had tipped Rochester off when Cromwell's men were about to close in on him. In 1660, Lady Rochester was one of ten people to petition Chales II to remove Hutchinson's name from the Act of Indemnity and Oblivion (he had been one of those who signed Charles I's death warrant) partly on the grounds that he 'gave the Earl of Rochester notice and opportunity to escape when Cromwell's ministers had discovered him the last time he was employed in his Majesty's service here in England'.

Rochester's three-month adventure in England was his last throw of the dice. In 1656, Charles, now staying in Bruges, founded the King's Regiment of Guards (years later it became the Grenadiers) and made the Earl colonel of one of its three regiments. But the fast-living days of action, danger and intrigue, compounded by the long nights of carousel and debauchery, had taken their toll. On 19 February 1657 the forty-five-year-old royalist died in Sluys, having played his supporting role on the stage of history for every ounce it was worth. He was buried in Bruges by Lord Hopton but, after the Restoration, his body was brought back to England and laid to rest at Spelsbury Church in Oxfordshire, where his wife and son were eventually interred alongside him.

That son, not yet ten years old, was now the second Earl of Rochester, Baron Wilmot of Adderbury and Viscount Wilmot of Athlone in Ireland. If he thought that all he had inherited from his father was a series of titles, he was to prove himself tragically wrong.

2

SHINING PARTS, DREAMING SPIRES

When he was at school he was an extraordinary
proficient at his book: and those shining
parts which have since appeared with so much
lustre began then to show themselves . . .

Gilbert Burnet

By the time her husband died, Lady Rochester had been living the life of a widow for a decade. It is difficult to imagine that the news of his demise greatly affected her. Supported by her able agent John Cary and with the guidance of her adviser Sir Ralph Verney, she had long since made the management of the Ditchley estate and the upbringing of her children her twin personal missions, and in both she had satisfied her own high standards. Her youngest child in particular was showing signs that he would reward his own and her endeavours well, and now that the father was dead she appointed Sir Ralph Verney – notably strict on all matters of principle and morality – as the boy's guardian.

First as the baby of the household and then as a future Earl, there can be little doubt that John Wilmot had always held a privileged place in his mother's proud and ambitious heart. His two stepbrothers, eight and nine years older than him, had left home some years before he inherited his father's titles, and since they had never been of the same playing age as him anyway, John Wilmot had much in common with any only child. As an adult he not surprisingly associated the country with solitude, also viewing it as a sanctuary from the noise, smell and sheer danger of life in London:

> Dear solitary groves, where peace does dwell,
> Sweet harbours of pure love and innocence!
> How willingly could I forever stay
> Beneath the shade of your embracing greens,
> Listening to harmony of warbling birds,
> Tuned with the gentle murmurs of the streams.

The tranquility of Ditchley had proved in every way conducive for the young Earl to study and he had used the advantage well. The absence of playmates to distract him and the demanding but encouraging mother who stood over him also combined towards shaping John Wilmot into a model pupil. Books gave him solace and compensated for any lack of company. The atmosphere within the house breathed an austerity which complemented scholasticism, and visitors to Ditchley were always struck by its imposing mood and beautiful setting.

The diarist John Evelyn visited Ditchley one afternoon in October 1664 to dine with Lady Rochester and her son Sir Henry Lee and described the manor house (which no longer stands) as a 'low, ancient timber house, with a pretty bowling green'. Adorning the walls inside were pictures of ancestors which Evelyn thought 'not ill painted', and there were also portraits of a pope and of Christ. The atmosphere, it seems, was quasi-religious. Another visitor – albeit much later, in 1718 – was Thomas Hearne, who recalled passing through the kitchen into a great hall nine yards by eight-and-a-half yards. 'I was mightily delighted with the sight of this old Hall, and was pleased the more because it is adorned with old stags' horns . . . I saw this date (1592) upon one of the leaden spouts of the house. The house itself was built before that year. But I cannot tell how old it is. It seems to have been done in the time of K. Hen. VIII.' Beneath the antlers and the watching figures painted by Van Dyck and Cornelius Janson, Rochester read poems by Cowley, Donne and Boileau, ploughed through Shakespeare's plays, heard the wind blow through the rafters above, thought of his father in service to the King abroad and dreamt of his own golden future. . . .

Lady Rochester appointed Francis Giffard, a young clergyman in his mid-twenties, as her son's tutor. A graduate of Queen's College, Cambridge, Giffard also became chaplain to the Countess herself. In 1711, long after Rochester's death, Thomas Hearne reported the elderly Giffard telling him that his infamous former pupil 'was then a very hopeful youth, very virtuous and good natured . . . and willing and ready to follow good advice'. Giffard told Hearne he was to have continued as the Earl's tutor when the boy went up to Oxford, but that he was 'supplanted'. (Rochester's tutor at Oxford was Mr Phineas Bury, 'a very learned and good-natured man'.) 'His Lordship had always a very good opinion of Mr Giffard,' wrote Hearne, presumably having been told this by Giffard himself. 'Mr Giffard used to lie with him in the family, on purpose that he might prevent any ill accidents . . . Mr Giffard says that my Lord understood very little or no Greek, and that he had but little Latin, and that therefore 'tis a great mistake in making him . . . so great a master of classic learning.' On another occasion Hearne recounted Giffard, who must have been in his late seventies, telling him that 'the said mad Earl was then very hopeful and ready to do anything that he proposed to him, and very well inclined to laudable undertakings'.

Describing Giffard as a 'pompous cleric', Graham Greene suggested in his biography of Rochester, *Lord Rochester's Monkey*, that the poet's former tutor was bitter enough about having been supplanted to be guilty of distorting the truth in his recollections, setting out to depict himself as the only man who had ever been able to control the 'mad' Earl. Certainly, Giffard must have enjoyed the look on people's faces when he told them that the Rochester he knew had been virtuous, but this does not mean he was not telling the truth. John Wilmot had already been described in Paris by Sir Edward Hyde (who became Earl of Clarendon in 1660) as an 'excellent youth', and it is hard to believe that the son of the authoritative Lady Rochester was a born tearaway. How would he have been such 'an extraordinary proficient at his book' if he had been anything other than the diligent student recalled by Giffard? With regard to the extent of Rochester's mastery of the classics, if Giffard's recollections had been purely self-serving then would he not, far from dismissing the poet's classical learning out of sight, have acknowledged it as a result of his own excellent teaching? It is my guess (and guessing is what Graham Greene was doing) that either the Earl's appreciation of the classics improved significantly during his grand tour of Europe after leaving Oxford, or Giffard's memory was proving genuinely unreliable. He was, after all, talking of a time of more than fifty years earlier.

Greene also scoffs at Giffard for having told Hearne that he went to see Rochester 'some time' before the Earl died and had a conversation with him which Hearne described as follows: 'Says his Lordship, "Mr Giffard, I wonder you will not come and visit me oftener. I have a great respect for you and I should be extremely glad of your frequent conversation." Says Mr Giffard (who could say anything to him), "My Lord, I am a clergyman. Your Lordship has a very ill character of being a debauched man and an atheist, & 'twill not look well in me to keep company with your Lordship as long as this character lasts, and as long as you continue this course of life." "Mr Giffard," says my Lord, "I have been guilty of extravagances, but I will assure you I am no atheist."'

Greene, tongue firmly in cheek, describes this conversation as 'amazing', but to me it sounds convincing. If, towards the end of his life, Rochester asked the priest Gilbert Burnet to come and counsel him, and if he held philosophical discussions with the deist Charles Blount – both of which we know he did – then why should he not have wanted his first tutor, a clergyman, to come and see him as well? It was a time when he was desperately trying to rediscover his religious roots. What lends further credibility to Giffard's account is the phrase 'I am no atheist'. Rochester came to recognise his agnosticism a long time before he finally converted, and he would have been at pains to point this out as a step in the right direction. Finally, it might be 'pompous' of Giffard to claim that he could 'say anything' to Rochester, but it is also very much in keeping with the almost parental and sometimes presumptuous manner in which many teachers do address their old pupils. Most of us are familiar with at least one former teacher who can still make us feel uncannily adolescent, and if Rochester did not entirely appreciate Giffard's frankness then neither would it have come as a shock to him. Pompous or not, Mr Giffard, I feel, had been a little harshly judged by Mr Greene.

While Rochester's translations of verses by Seneca, Horace, Lucretius and Ovid bear witness to his flair for Latin, the extent of his understanding of Greek remains less certain. According to Burnet, 'he acquired the Latin to such perfection that to his dying-day he retained a great relish of the fineness and beauty of that tongue: and was exactly versed in the incomparable authors that writ about Augustus's time, whom he read often with that peculiar delight which the greatest wits have ever found in those studies'. Both the Reverend Robert Parsons (who succeeded Giffard as Lady Rochester's chaplain) and Anthony Wood acknowledged the Earl's mastery of Greek too. Wood said he was 'thoroughly acquainted with the classic authors, both Greek and Latin; a thing very rare (if not peculiar to him) among those of his quality'.

Lady Rochester soon supplemented her gifted son's academic progress by sending him to the Free School at Burford, which had the reputation of being the top school of its day. Rochester learnt under the 'noted master' John Martin and lodged, like the other boys, in the town. He contined to be tutored during his holidays by Mr Giffard, who had remained at Ditchley.

Life at Burford was a hard slog: pupils went to school at 6 a.m. in the summer and 7 a.m. in the winter, left for dinner at 11 a.m. and, upon returning, studied until 6 pm. in the summer and 4 p.m. in the winter. Moreover, the strong religious upbringing which John Wilmot had been given by his pious mother and clergyman-tutor was now intensified for, when school ended for the day, it was time for the boys to go to church with their master, or, 'if there are no prayers, to sing psalms and to read a chapter in the school'. Every Sunday the pupils had to report to the schoolmaster by 8 a.m. to say prayers before leaving for church, and four times a year they were exhorted to give thanks to God and recite the names of all the school's founders and benefactors before singing a psalm. On 23 January 1660 the young Earl – still officially Wilmot, since Cromwell had refused to acknowledge all titles bestowed by either Charles I or 'the young gentleman' after the Civil War – entered Wadham College, Oxford, as a nobleman or fellow commoner. This allowed him to mingle with the dons and wear a gown distinguishing him from lower-ranking undergraduates. Still two months short of his thirteenth birthday, the precocious Wilmot was for the first time, but not the last, entirely in the heady company of elders.

He could not have picked a more exciting time to come to Oxford, for the city, Charles I's stronghold during the Civil War, was buzzing in anticipation of a possible restoration of the monarchy. Cromwell's death in September 1658 had signalled the beginning of the end of the puritan revolution; his son, Richard, who had nothing like the ambitious zeal of the father, summoned a parliament in the first few weeks of 1659 which fell out with the army. First ordering the army to obey parliament, then giving in to the army and sanctioning parliament's dissolution, the hapless Richard finally decided to resign. The army took power, restored the Rump Parliament, argued with it, dissolved it and then reinstated it. As the people began to grow aware that a state of political chaos existed, their muted and long-suppressed resentment of living under the stringent, joyless rule of the puritans, God's self-appointed and self-righteous Christian soldiers, started to make its voice heard. 'Boys do now cry "Kiss my Parliament" instead of "Kiss my arse" so great and general contempt is the Rump come to among all men, good and bad,' wrote Pepys.

The man who seized the initiative was General George Monck, commander of the army in Scotland and later first Duke of Albermarle. On New Year's Day, 1660, he began to march south with the might of his forces behind him to sort out the political wrangling and restore parliament's sovereignty. 'We went walking all over Whitehall, whither General Monk [sic] was newly come,' wrote Pepys on 3 February, 'and we saw all his forces march by . . . the town and guards are already full of Monk's soldiers.' Three days later the diarist was at Westminster, 'where we found the soldiers all set in the Palace Yard, to make way for General Monk to come to the House. I stood upon the steps, and saw Monk go by, he making observance to the judges.' The General successfully persuaded the Rump to readmit the royalist MPs who had been expelled from the House in 'Pride's Purge' in 1648, and the following month parliament dissolved itself to make way for the election of the Free Parliament. By now it had become a common sight in London to see symbolic rumps of beef being roasted on the bonfires which are traditionally lit to celebrate royal occasions, and the royal arms even began to reappear above schools and in churches. In Oxford, the undergraduates threw rumps and sheep's tails into a bonfire at the gate of Queen's College, and the young Earl of Rochester joined in with the excited chatter about the dawning of a new and golden age. At Ditchley, his mother was scribbling her instructions for the forthcoming election to Sir Thomas Yates. On 1 May, widespread rejoicing greeted the news that the House of Commons had passed a resolution inviting Charles Stuart to govern the nation. There was dancing around paypoles – in Oxford a maypole was set up in Cornmarket Street to 'vex the Presbyterians and independents' – and the taverns were packed with noisy crowds. 'Great joy all yesterday at London,' wrote Pepys on 2 May, 'and at night more bonfires than ever, and ringing of bells, and drinking of the King's health upon their knees in the streets, which methinks is a little too much.' On 26 May Charles stepped ashore at Dover from a landing barge which he shared with four others: a footman, a dog, a Mr Mansell and the ubiquitous Samuel Pepys.

'Infinite the crowd of people and the gallantry of the horsemen, citizens, and noblemen of all sorts,' wrote Pepys, to whom the King had related, during the crossing, the tale of his escape after Worcester. 'The Mayor of the town came and give him his white staff, the badge of his place, which the King did give him again. The Mayor also presented him from the town a very rich Bible, which he took, and said it was the thing that he loved above all things in the world . . . The shouting and the joy expressed by all is past imagination.' John Evelyn described Charles's entry into London 'with 20,000 horse and foot, brandishing their swords and shouting, with inexpressible joy; the ways strewed with flowers, the bells ringing, the streets hung with tapestry, fountains running with wine . . . I stood in the Strand and beheld it, and blessed God.' There were sore sights for puritan eyes in Oxford too, where undergraduates passed more wine to their new young friend who was the son of a famous cavalier general. The unrelenting discipline of Ditchley and the rigours of school life at Burford had suddenly found a happy but disastrous substitute. The boy who lurched back to his rooms at the end of that head-spinning day and night had discovered the spirit of his dead father. It was a revelation he could have done without.

✤ ✤ ✤

'When he went to the University the general joy which over-ran the whole nation upon his Majesty's Restoration, but was not regulated with that sobriety and temperance . . . produced some of its ill effects on him: He began to love these disorders too much,' wrote Gilbert Burnet. 'The humour of that time wrought so much on him, that he broke off the course of his studies; to which no means could ever effectually recall him,' he added. The Earl's former tutor Mr Giffard also said that Rochester 'soon grew debauched' once he was at Oxford. The reason for this is fundamental. The boy's predisposition to alcoholism made drink taste like nectar from the first sip on.

In America the most recent research into alcoholism has identified a chemical imbalance in the brain of the alcoholic which produces a craving temporarily satisfied by drink. An increasing amount of evidence is showing this to be genetically influenced. Professor Kenneth Blum and Mr James Payne, who revealed their findings in the book *Alcohol and the Addictive Brain* (1991) to the widespread attention of the medical world, say alcoholics can be divided into two very general types: those who inherit a predisposition to compulsive drinking, and those who 'develop a habit of excessive drinking as the result of long-continued stress or long-term social drinking'. They state that genetic alcoholics are rarely able to achieve and sustain sobriety without professional help (where was that in the 1660s?), and that even if they do succeed through willpower alone, they will continue to display the behavioural characteristics of the alcoholic, such as anger, deceit, arrogance and depression. Such reformed drinkers become known as 'dry drunks'. (Rochester's alcoholic characteristics are listed, with examples, on pp. 221–2). Whichever type the alcoholic is, Blum and Payne stress that 'the environment acts as the trigger initiating the actual onset of the disease'.

Royalist Oxford in the year of the Restoration was the Earl of Rochester's trigger, and the fact that his father appears to have had a certain degree of control over his own drinking does not stand in the way of the son's rampant alcoholism being genetically induced. As we all know, the traits of a parent can reappear in the child in exaggerated form. The extent and effects of the first Earl's drinking remain uncertain anyway, and he may have displayed any number of the characteristics commonly found in alcoholics. One of these is impetuosity, which certainly seems to apply to the man who Clarendon said 'bore contradiction very impatiently'.

Given that Rochester had not drunk alcohol in any quantity to speak of before going to Oxford, the magnetic appeal it held for him was far too quickly pronounced once he got there for it to have been the result of the 'long-term social drinking' associated with the second type of alcoholic. He graduated after less than two years, by which time he considered drink to be his trademark. Hence his choice of parting gift to Wadham: four silver pint-pots. From his first mouthful, the Earl's drinking was never normal – particularly for someone barely in his teens. By the time Rochester was twenty-four, drink had started damaging his eyesight.

It would be wrong to think, however, that he was a helpless drunk at the age of thirteen. Quite the opposite. Like many alcoholics, he was fooled by his apparent ability in the early days to handle drink better than others – an ability which is, in itself, all part of the problem. The teenager who is fond of alcohol but is weaving and swaying after four pints has nothing to fear compared to the one who appears to be totally sober after eight pints. It would be years yet before the worst symptoms – the physical illness, the dreadful bouts of depression and the continuous drunkenness itself – struck home. (In the most chronic cases of genetic alcoholism these symptoms can and do appear from the first drink onwards.) Meanwhile, he would regard drink as his best friend – and even to observers it would seem as though it was just that. The capacity which alcoholics have for self-deception is virtually limitless, and for most of his life the Earl would deceive himself into believing he was master in charge of his own pleasures. Pleasure was to become a crucial word for him; a pursuit which he justified on intellectual grounds but which simultaneously hid him from both his addiction and his real, puritan core. As a genetic alcoholic, the adolescent Earl drinking in the taverns of Oxford can be seen as a young man who was now rowing out to sea: the further he went on, the harder it would be

to make it back to shore. By the time he really did try to stop
drinking, in 1678, he was lost over the horizon.

To make matters worse, Rochester was starting to drink just as
it was becoming a fashionable pastime. There was more to the
drinking-on-knees in the streets which Pepys so disliked than sheer
joy at the King's return; it was an expression of defiance in the
faces of those sanctimonious puritans who for eleven long and
dreary years had been preaching against the wickedness of
inebriation. Never has alcohol been more of a pivatol and political
symbol for a nation's feelings than it was at the Restoration and in
the years which immediately followed. Even the legendary (and
factual) hedonism of Charles's Court can be seen (in part) as a
backlash against the years of moral correctitude under the
Calvinistic Cromwell. There would be very few rules of the house
at the party which was starting now at the Palace of Whitehall and
which would last a whole reign. As Burnet wrote:

> With the restoration of the King, a spirit of extravagant joy
> spread over the nation, that brought on with it the throwing
> off the very professions of virtue and piety. All ended in
> entertainments and drunkenness which over run the three
> kingdoms to such a degree, that it very much corrupted their
> morals. Under the colour of drinking the King's health, there
> were great disorders, and much riot everywhere.

Abraham Cowley, the English poet most admired by the
undergraduate Rochester, penned a poem about drinking which
summed up the attitude of a people fed up with puritan
moralising:

> The thirsty earth soaks up the rain,
> And drinks and gapes for drink again,
> The plants suck in the earth, and are
> With constant drinking fresh and fair;
> The sea itself (which one would think
> Should have but little need of drink)
> Drinks ten thousand rivers up,
> So filled that they o'erflow the cup.
> The busy Sun (and one would guess

By's drunken fiery face no less)
Drinks up the sea, and when he's done,
The Moon and Stars drink up the Sun:
They drink and dance by their own light,
They drink and revel all the night:
Nothing in Nature's sober found,
But an eternal health goes round.
Fill up the bowl, then, fill it high,
Fill all the glasses there – for why
Should every creature drink but I?
Why, man of morals, tell me why?

Rochester had his own experiences of puritanism to rebel against; he may not have spent more than a decade in exile as the leading royalist had done, but he had known the joylessness of a puritannical upbringing, and now the same spirit which had once belonged to a hunted man stealing out of Aylesbury in disguise, a spirit which the boy had not previously realised he possessed himself, broke free. It was not just releasing itself from the social constraints of life at Ditchley and Burford, but from physiological containment too. The study of alcoholism tells us that if he was predisposed to the disease, Rochester may have suffered high levels of anxiety as a child. The odds are on him having been of a nervous disposition; a worrier and a fretter; serious and introverted. Problems of little significance would have caused him undue concern. This would certainly fit with Mr Giffard's recollection of him being an obedient and willing pupil. Anxiety might even have been to blame for an alarming and surely painful problem which Giffard also remembered the young Earl suffering. Thomas Hearne recounted the former tutor telling him that Rochester 'had a natural distemper upon him which was extraordinary . . . which was that sometimes he could not have a stool for 3 weeks or a month together'. In adulthood Rochester told Giffard that his childhood constipation had been 'a very great occasion of that warmth and heat' he always expressed, his brain having been 'heated by the fumes and humours that ascended and evacuated themselves that way'. (It is tempting but probably unfair to imagine Giffard nodding sagely at this.) Given alcohol's often unwelcome potency as a laxative, constipation was presumably one health problem from which the Earl now managed to 'relieve' himself. He was to replace it with a whole range of others.

If Rochester was using alcohol as an emotional release following his strict and isolated childhood then it is possible to qualify still further what type of alcoholic he was. In 1960, Dr E.M. Jellinek published his revolutionary medical book, *The Disease Concept of Alcoholism*, establishing five types of alcoholic under the first five letters of the Green alphabet. Alpha alcoholism, he said, meant a psychological dependence which leads the drinker to rely on alcohol to relieve physical or emotional pain. While the drinking is heavy enough to violate accepted rules of behaviour, it does not lead to loss of control. But Jellinek also noted that in certain circumstances this type of alcoholic (which describes the teenaged Rochester) could turn into the Gamma type, which is the most serious of the five in terms of physical and psychological damage. This is precisely what happened to the Earl. We will deal with the nature of Gamma alcoholism when Rochester reaches it.

There should be no underestimating the obsessional view of alcohol which Rochester held from the moment he discovered it. It would have seemed to him the most important, wonderful finding of his life so far: the key which unlocked the door of his personality and allowed him to express himself. It gave him a confidence he had never known, removed all the anxiety he had ever had and, above all, made life seem, for the very first time, fun. And there was an increasing amount of fun to be had in Oxford. The local antiquary, Anthony Wood, was appalled at the behaviour of the undergraduates now that puritanism had gone. Their aim, he wrote, was 'not to live as students ought to do, viz. temperate, abstemious and plain and grave in the apparel; but to live like gents, to keep dogs and horses, to turn their studios and coalholes into places to receive bottles, to swash it in grey coats with swords by their sides.' A group of All Souls' College fellows were even found trying to print an edition of Aretino's erotic postures on the newly founded Clarendon Press.

The discovery of drink led to a dramatic change in the company Rochester kept, for he quickly swapped the sober conversation of dons for the camaraderie of 'the regulars' in taverns like The Saracen's Head and The Split Crow, where he enjoyed celebrity status as the son of the great cavalier Wilmot. Good fellowship is one of the rewards on offer in the low life, and Rochester would always be a sociable and garrulous drinker. In Robert Whitehall, his guide at Oxford, he also found the perfect foil for the corrective guardians who had governed him so far. A physician, fellow and 'useless member' of Merton College whose ruddy features were 'loined with sack and faced with claret', Whitehall it was who initiated the young Earl into the world of pleasure. According to Anthony Wood, Whitehall, who had previously published verses upon Richard Cromwell's installation as Chancellor of the University, 'absolutely doted' on Rochester and pretended to instruct him in the art of poetry. Together they sent a verse of praise under the Earl's name to the King, *To his Sacred Majesty on his Restoration*, which so lacks Rochester's hallmark of easy vigour (even accounting for his age) that one suspects that Whitehall was chief author:

> And though my youth, not patient yet to bear
> The weight of arms, denies me to appear
> In steel before you; yet great SIR, approve
> My manly wishes, and more vigorous love;
> In whom a cold respect were treason to
> A father's ashes, greater than to you;
> Whose one ambition 'tis for to be known,
> By daring loyalty, your Wilmot's son.

Two more verses were sent to Charles in 1661 – one in English, one in Latin – mourning the death of his sister, Princess Mary of Orange. Nudging the King into remembering that one of his subjects was a servant-in-waiting with the surname of Wilmot was not a bad idea, but it was probably unnecessary. One of Charles's most appealing characteristics was his genuine gratitude to those who were good to him, and his continued generosity towards Rochester throughout the 1660s and '70s may well have resulted from giving assurances in Bruges to the dying father that he would look after his son. He had Rochester's father to thank as much as anyone for the fact that he was still alive, let alone King. He spoilt the Earl as a rich aunt keeps heaping presents on an ungracious nephew. The result was disastrous, fuelling Rochester's licence at Court and hastening his dissipation. The first gift, a £500 annual pension, arrived in February 1661. Drinks all round.

❧ ❧ ❧

When it came to carousal, young Rochester more than held his own with Robert Whitehall and the other sparks who made up their Oxford coterie. Graham Greene believed the Earl's youth probably restricted his misbehaviour at this stage to mere buffoonery, but Professor Pinto was surely nearer the mark when he suggested that Rochester might have contracted the venereal disease, which plagued him in the years ahead, during his time at Oxford. There is in fact no evidence for believing this to be the case, but neither is there any reason for thinking that Rochester's general precocity did not embrace sexual adventure at an early age as well. He was nearly fourteen-and-a-half years old when he graduated, which is certainly old enough for him to have been sexually fully active, if not fully mature. Sex would have been as uppermost in his mind as it is in that of any pimply male youth, and Rochester never knew the meaning of self-restraint. A verse-letter which Whitehall sent to him some years later, together with a self-portrait, indicates that the Earl dodged Oxford's prowling proctors during nocturnal rambles by wearing his guide's more senior gown. The portrait showed Whitehall

> . . . not in vest, but in that gown
> Your Lordship daggled through this town
> To keep up discipline and tell us
> Next morning where you found good fellows.

Just as sixth-form boys have been known to wear university scarves in order to impress the girls, so Rochester might have misled impressionable young serving-wenches with the fellow's gown which belonged to Whitehall. It is the first hint we have of the dressing in disguise that was to be one of his life-long predilections.

It is Rochester's most famous disguise, that of the self-invented Doctor Alexander Bendo, in 1676, which suggests that during his

Oxford days he drank in The Saracen's Head. The mysterious Dr Bendo, an Italian quack, dispensed his strange and 'miraculous' medicines from Tower Hill in 1676 when his alter-ego, the Earl of Rochester, was in serious trouble with authority and therefore keeping out of sight.

In his 'factional' *A Journal of the Plague Year*, Daniel Defoe provides us with some idea of just how naive the general public was in medical matters. When London's plague broke out in 1665, the 'posts of houses and corners of streets were plastered over with doctors' bills and papers of ignorant fellows, quacking and tampering in physic, and inviting the people to come to them for remedies'. In particular, people were greatly impressed by anyone who lent themselves an air of foreign mystery by claiming to be, for example, a 'High Dutch physician' or an 'Italian gentleman'.

Goodness knows what rubbish was used to concoct the various ointments and lotions on sale (Dr Bendo used anything from soot to urine), but one of the first conmen to realise that it was a surefire method of earning quick and easy money was a James Themut, who arrived at Oxford in February 1660 and lodged at The Saracen's Head. Claiming to be a Dutch doctor from Vienna (the more exotic the background the better), he boasted of being able to rid his patients of 'falling sickness, madness, Phrenzie and Giddiness in the head' and cure 'stinking breath, rotten Teeth, scurvey, or Water-canker'. Having duped his gullible customers for a whole month, including the taking of advance payments, the enterprising Mr Themut vanished as suddenly as he had arrived. Did he, during those weeks, talk about his work in The Saracen's Head to an interested young man wearing a college fellow's gown? If he did then Rochester never forgot him.

Wadham College, which had been rechristened 'Sodom' by the undergraduates, played an important part in developing Rochester's rebellious attitudes even though he spent little or virtually no time poring over books. As the newest of the Oxford colleges, Wadham encouraged radical thinking. The Earl arrived there just after Doctor Blandford – later Bishop of Oxford – had succeeded Cromwell's brother-in-law, Doctor Wilkins, as Warden. During his ten years in charge, Wilkins had established the college as a centre of the English Enlightenment – the scientific movement of the times – and his lodgings were used as a meeting place for the Experimental Philosophical Club. This later became The Royal Society and boasted the membership of such great men as Sir Christopher Wren and Sir Isaac Newton. Although Wadham's reputation for radicalism related specifically to its promotion of mathematics, physics and mechanics, the provocative spirit spilt over into other areas too, encouraging undergraduates like Rochester to challenge conventional behaviour. Nothing is more conventional than sobriety, and another of Wadham's brightest and most famous students, Sir Charles Sedley, who preceded Rochester at the college and later befriended him at Court, was hardly known for temperance either.

On 9 September 1661, Rochester graduated as a Master of Arts and was admitted 'very affectionately into the fraternity by a kiss on the left cheek' from Lord Clarendon, Chancellor of the University, who had spoken of the six-year-old Earl in glowing terms but was so critical of the father. The worldly young man who left Oxford that summer was a far cry from the innocent boy who had arrived little more than a year-and-a-half earlier, but the angel in him still so outshone the devil that nobody could have been blamed for thinking that his prospects were very bright indeed. The King now arranged for Sir Andrew Balfour, a thirty-year-old, widely travelled physician and naturalist, to polish the Earl's education by acting as his tutor on a three-year grand tour of Europe. If the journey was to be anything other than a glorious waste of time, Balfour was going to have to discipline Rochester and change his reckless thinking. Amazingly, he did just that.

✤ ✤ ✤

Rochester never forgot the debt of gratitude he owed Sir Andrew Balfour for persuading him to make his tour of French and Italian cities, towns, palaces, libraries, colleges, churches, rivers, cathedrals and castles so educationally beneficial. Balfour induced the recalcitrant Earl to do all the studying he had singularly failed to undertake at Oxford, thus providing him with the learning he needed if he was to make his mark upon the Restoration age as a writer of import. As I have suggested, it was on this journey that Rochester vastly improved his understanding of the classics, which is why his old tutor Mr Giffard was always puzzled that people should consider the Earl such a master of them.

In between the wildest and worst of his alcoholic 'benders', those times when remorse set in along with a hopeless but avowed intent of changing his ways forever, Rochester always turned to the books gathering dust on the tables at High Lodge and rediscovered the academic hunger which had first been instilled in him by Mr Giffard and compounded by Sir Andrew Balfour. In his last years in particular, as his determination to stop drinking became increasingly desperate, he read more and more voraciously, winding up, of course, with the Bible. Not surprisingly then, Balfour's name was frequently on the grateful Earl's lips during the conversations with Gilbert Burnet which were conducted in the final months and weeks of his life.

Burnet wrote: '. . . he often acknowledged to me, in particular three days before his death, how much he was obliged to love and honour this his governor, to whom he thought he owed more than to all the world, next after his parents, for his great fidelity and care of him, while he was under his trust'. Balfour, added Burnet, 'engaged him . . . to delight in books and reading: so that ever after he took occasion in the intervals of those woeful extravagancies that consumed most of his time to read much: and though the time was generally but indifferently employed, for the choice of the subjects of his studies was not always good, yet the habitual love of knowledge together with these fits of study, had much awakened his understanding, and prepared him for better things when his mind should be so far changed as to relish them'.

So how did Balfour succeeded where Oxford had failed? Burnet again: '. . . by many tricks'. This, according to the priest and historian, was the Earl's own phrase, and it is not difficult to see what it means: bribery. Balfour made Rochester promises of places they could visit, people they could meet and permission to go off alone *on the one condition* that he first did as he was being asked – which usually meant studying. It is the way most parents persuade reluctant children to do their homework and it tends to be an effective ploy.

Burnet even said that during these three years abroad, Rochester 'so entirely laid down the intemperance that was growing on him before his travels that at his return [to England] he hated nothing more'. It is a crucial remark to remember when considering the bitterness which grew inside him as he was sucked into the debauchery of life at Court. The young man who returned to England with Balfour was the Rochester who rediscovered himself through God at the end of his life; a man who hated nothing more than drunkenness. On the tour itself it was easy for him to abstain completely from alcohol for the simple reason that he had not been drinking that long. He was also obviously still capable of restricting himself to occasional light drinking, for the pair certainly visited several famous vineyards and wine cellars. It was excessive drinking which would prove lethal to him and would inevitably pull him right in once he started it. Clearly, and with Balfour at the helm, he avoided that throughout his time abroad.

Most significantly – and Charles II would have done well to take note of it – Balfour's disciplining of Rochester showed just how easily he could still be manipulated. He was not a born rebel at all, but a highly impressionable and unstable youth; a ship with no rudder who could easily be shifted onto a different course by whoever happened to be in his company. In France and Italy this was a good thing; at the Palace of Whitehall it would be the opposite.

The two journeymen set sail for France on 21 November 1661. Far from being a cloistered academic, Balfour was a worldly man 'of an excellent wit, and of ripe judgement, and of a most taking behaviour'. In short, a great travelling companion. He was an outstanding scholar, having studied at Oxford, Paris, Montpelier and Padua, and had graduated as MD at the University of Caen only two months before this tour began. He had also acted once before as a tutor on a grand tour. Years later Balfour, who became a celebrated physician in his native Scotland, wrote a book about travel in France and Italy and described a grand tour in detail. Unfortunately he does not mention his travelling companion by name, so we cannot be sure it was this particular tour he was describing. All that is certain is that Rochester visited and stayed in all the great French and Italian cities, including Paris, Lyons, Marseilles, Toulouse, Venice, Florence, Rome, Pisa, Naples, Verona. . . . The following passage from Balfour's book shows just what a discerning and knowledgeable guide he was:

Although a traveller cannot be altogether sure of his times, there being so many contingencies that may force him either to arrive too soon or too late; yet it were to be wished that a man might happen to be at Venice in the time of Carnival, because of the operas and fine shows that are to be seen, and the extraordinary music at that time. In the summertime the great divertisement is to go in gondol upon the Great Canal, where towards the evening one may see five or six hundred gondols touring up and down, full of ladies and gentlemen, & several of them with music, both vocal and instrumental; which is one of the greatest gustos imaginable.

You cannot miss to meet with a great many curiosities here, both natural and artificial, because of the great resort that strangers have to this place, especially from the Levant; you will find medals, intaglios, cameos &c. amongst the goldsmiths. I have seen several curiosities to sell in the Place of St Mark, and sometime within the Court of the Palace, and in many other corners throughout the city. You may meet with many curiosities of glass that are both useful and delightful. It will be worth your while to visit the booksellers' shops, for besides many curious books that you may light upon here, and particularly of botany, you may likewise find very many books that are prohibited in many other places of Italy . . .

The two journeymen re-entered France in the summer of 1664 by crossing the Alps on mules – dismounting at the highest point of the pass to be wheeled across in barrows by their guides – and eventually they reached Paris. There, Rochester bowed deeply before Charles II's beloved and favourite sister, 'Minette', or Henrietta, Duchess of Orléans, who presented him with a letter to take back to her brother in London.

Reformed, sober and ambitious, Rochester set sail for England with Sir Andrew Balfour having more than compensated for his wasted days at Oxford. His mind now was fixed upon impressing his peers at the Palace of Whitehall and advancing his career as quickly as possible. In particular he needed to secure financial stability through marriage into a wealthy family. He was also aware that war was looming between Britain and the Dutch. Service at sea could provide him with the reputation for valour which was sought by all courtiers. The dashing and richly dressed young Earl who strode through Whitehall's great corridors on Christmas Day 1664 to present himself at Court was still only seventeen years old, but his confidence, experience, manners and charm belied his years. All of his education – Burford, Oxford and the continent – had been geared towards this day of proud arrival.

Five months later, he was a prisoner in the Tower of London.

3

COURTING DISASTER

The lewdness and beggary of the court . . .
will bring all to ruin again.
Samuel Pepys, August 1661

Describing a Sunday evening at the Palace of Whitehall,
John Evelyn once wrote:

I can never forget the inexpressible luxury and profaneness,
gaming, and all dissoluteness, and as it were total
forgetfulness of God . . . the King sitting and toying with his
concubines . . . a French boy singing love-songs, in that
glorious gallery, whilst about twenty of the great courtiers
and other dissolute persons were at Basset round a large
table, a bank of at least 2,000 in gold before them.

To Englishmen with long memories and moral consciences (the
most eminent at the time of Rochester's arrival being Lord
Chancellor Hyde, Earl of Clarendon, whose disapproval cast a
shadow over the Court's fun until his convenient dismissal in
1667), conduct at Whitehall was a matter of grave concern and
regret. The contrast between the palace run by the promiscuous
Charles and the one ruled by the uxorious father whose command
to his son from the scaffold had been 'Remember' could not have
been more stark. During the years of exile, Charles, who as early
as 1652 was reported to have taken up with his seventeenth

41

mistress abroad, wrote: 'We pass our lives as well as people can do that have no money, for we dance and play as if we had taken the Plate Fleet.' After the Restoration this hedonism became not so much a way of keeping hopelessness at bay, but a celebratory creed which embraced the philosophy of Thomas Hobbes.

Hobbes's *Leviathan*, which appeared in 1651, rejected the idea of conventional morality and propounded the theory that man's behaviour was, and therefore always should be, governed by his senses, desires and passions. God was a supreme first (effectively, the Big Bang), a creator not to be worried about. The soul, as Christians think of it, did not exist, for 'that which is not body, is no part of the universe'. He depicted men and women as living bodies whose senses – sight, hearing, smell, taste and touch – were continually undergoing a bombardment of 'motion in matter'. He dismissed imagination, for example, as like ripples moving across water long after the stone has hit the surface and sunk. It was, he said, a 'decaying sense'. Conceptions and apparitions are nothing really, but motion in some internal substance of the head,' declared Hobbes.

This sensual brand of atheism gave free licence to the fulfilment of every kind of appetite. According to Hobbes, people who condemned the pleasures to be had from the gratification of the senses were priests and teachers with a vested interest in illusions inherited from the age of monkery and superstition. Such critics lived in the 'Kingdom of Darkness'. Constancy – in love or in anything else – was not necessarily to be expected either, since the different impressions being made on our senses through motion in matter subjected as to continual *change*. (This obviously becomes significant when considering the attitudes towards love expressed by Rochester in much of his early lyrical poetry.)

For a generation of courtiers who had seen religion form the basis of a civil war and who had suffered personal deprivation at the hands of God-fearing puritanism, Hobbism was a very easy medicine to swallow. It also acted as a perfect backdrop to an age committed to scientific experiment (Rochester was only five years younger than Isaac Newton) and, as the Earl's poetic idol Cowley pointed out, it was a marvellous excuse for having a rollicking good time:

Fill the bowl with rosie wine,
Around our temples roses twine
And let us cheerfully awhile
Like the wine and roses smile.
Crowned with roses we contemn
Gyges' wealthy diadem.
Today is ours; what do we fear?
Today is ours; we have it here.
Let's treat it kindly, that it may
Wish, at least, with us to stay.
Let's banish business, banish sorrow;
To the Gods belong tomorrow.

Nobody in the court practised Hobbism with more ease than the King. It was as though it had been tailor-made for him. 'All appetites are free and God will never damn a man for allowing himself a little pleasure,' he remarked to Burnet. He was not being flippant. He meant it. The trouble was, 'a little pleasure', in Charles's dictionary, meant a platoon of mistresses. Anthony Wood called the Earl a 'perfect' Hobbist only because Rochester practised Hobbism so loudly, so excessively and with such apparent conviction. He did not know about the poet's deeper doubts (not even Rochester confronted them until the last year of his life) and could not see how much emotional dissatisfaction lay behind the intellectual front. At times – those moments Burnet referred to as 'sad intervals' – it was an effort for the Earl to believe in Hobbism at all.

Effort was alien to the King. The delight of his company had much to do with his sheer *easiness*. Fundamentally indolent yet also restless, graceful, languid, charming, witty, cultured, sensual and sexually insatiable, King Charles II was arguably the greatest playboy the western world had ever seen. Burnet observed that: 'He has a strange command of himself; he can pass from business to pleasure and from pleasure to business in so easy a manner that all things seem alike to him; he has the greatest art of concealing himself of any man alive, so that those about him cannot tell when he is ill or well pleased.' But it was pleasure that the King sought, not business, and he really did believe (unlike Rochester) that life was worth living for its own sake. There was absolutely no aspect of this luxuriant, Frenchified and hedonistic Court which was not infected by his charismatic personality. With the possible exception of Queen Victoria, no British monarch has ever had more influence over manners, taste and fashion. In 1660, Whitehall's Court became Charles's creation.

His favourite (and therefore everybody's favourite) social pastime was the theatre, which the puritans, regarding it as immoral and likely to encourage immorality, had banned. Three months into the Restoration Charles had issued patents to Thomas Killigrew and Sir William Davenant to form two licensed theatre companies, and early-afternoon visits to watch the latest offerings at the Theatre Royal in Drury Lane (King's Players) or Lincoln's Inn Fields (Duke's Players) were made by many people with a regularity we would today find obsessive. Between 6 September and 11 September 1661, for example, Samuel Pepys watched *The Elder Brother* (by Fletcher and Beaumont), *Bartholomew Fair* (Jonson), *'Tis Pity She's a Whore* (Ford) and a 'new play', *Twelfth Night*. As the 1660s wore on there was such a proliferation of new plays that revivals of old ones became unnecessary. (Shakespeare was not popular at this time anyway.) Following the Cromwellian ban the pendulum really had swung to the opposite extreme, for women were now being seen on the stage for the first time. The sexually charged atmosphere in these playhouses, with the young gallants and fops preening themselves unashamedly in front of the ladies, coyly fluttering their fans, was summed up by Dryden thus:

> But as when vizard mask appears in pit,
> Straight every man, who thinks himself a wit
> Perks up; and managing his comb with grace,
> With his white wig sets off his nut-brown face.

Charles's courtiers enjoyed their own tightly knit society and tended to live either in the palace itself or in apartments close by in Whitehall and St James's. (Rochester took lodgings in the latter.) As with any closed group, in-jokes, gossip and petty scandals abounded. The dastardly Lord Southesk caused much hilarity, for example, when he tried to take revenge on his wife's lover, the Duke of York. 'He went to the most infamous places, to seek for the most infamous disease, which he met with; but his revenge was only half completed; for after he had gone through every remedy to get quit of his disease, his Lady did but return him his present, having no more connection with the person for whom it was so industriously prepared,' reported Anthony Hamilton, author of the *Memoirs of Count Grammont*.

In its entirety the Court stretched to scores and scores of men and women; ministers, privy councillors, lords, ladies, knights, gentlemen, ladies-in-waiting, fops, rakes, courtesans, secretaries and a whole host of lesser functionaries who all enjoyed the lavish entertainment of life at the palace. Anthony Hamilton described the Court as 'an entire scene of gallantry and amusements . . . the beauties were desirous and charming, and the men endeavoured to please . . . some distinguished themselves by dancing; others by show and magnificence; some by their wit, many by their amours, but few by their constancy'. Fantastic banquets, masques and balls liberally dotted the calendar, while in the summer evenings the Court sometimes took to the Thames in a flotilla of boats to the accompaniment of music and fireworks. During the less socially hectic hours, the earthier courtier who did not wish to join in with the interminable games of charades or blind man's buff (the favourite game of Charles's unrequited passion, the coquettish Miss Frances Stewart), and who could no longer stand the sound of somebody playing that new-fangled contraption the guitar, might find plenty of amusement beyond the palace precincts. At the Bear Garden, John Evelyn once saw a bull toss a dog clean out of the pit into a woman's lap, and the ever-inquisitive Samuel Pepys faithfully recorded the atmosphere of a cock-fight at a pit in Shoe Lane for us:

Lord, to see the strange variety of people, from Parliament men to the poorest prentices, bakers, butchers, brewers, draymen and what not; and all these fellows one with another in swearing, cursing and betting. I soon had enough of it, and yet I would not have but seen it once, it being strange to observe the nature of these poor creatures, how they will fight till they drop down dead upon the table, and strike after they are ready to give up the ghost.

The thirsty courtier would retire to Chatelain's, a fashionable drinking house in Covent Garden, or to The Bear, or to 'Oxford

Kate's' hostelry, The Cock Tavern, where, in the year before Rochester came to court, an inebriated Sir Charles Sedley had caused quite a stir. Pepys reported that he strode

> in open day into the balcony and showed his nakedness . . .
> and as it were from thence preaching a mountebank sermon
> from the pulpit, saying that there he had to sell such a
> powder as should make all the women in town run after him,
> 1,000 people standing underneath to see and hear him, and
> that being done he took a glass of wine, and drank it off, and
> then took another and drank the King's health.

Both he and Lord Buckhurst, who was standing naked alongside him, were forced to beat a retreat under a shower of stones and bricks. Pepys later recorded that when the shamed Sir Charles appeared before the bench, Lord Chief Justice Foster said it was 'for him, and such wicked wretches as he was, that God's anger and judgements hung over us,' and, added Pepys, he called him 'sirrah many times'. Unfortunately for the Lord Chief Justice there was no offence of indecent exposure in 1663, and so Sedley was merely bound over to be of good behaviour in the sum of £5,000. (This has often been referred to as a fine, but Sedley did not have to part with the money unless he misbehaved in public again.)

Other popular watering holes among the dozens to choose from included The Rose – or 'Long's' – in Russell Street, Locket's Ordinary at Charing Cross, or the Pillars of Hercules and the Dog and Partridge, both in Fleet Street. A visit to Will's Coffee-House often afforded the unctuous sight of sycophants hanging on to the coat-tails and every word of Mr John Dryden, while a dip in the seedier side of London life could always be accommodated (along with the pox) by Mother Temple's girls at Drury Lane, Madame Bennet's at Moorfields, or any of their cousins at Whetstone Park, Lewkenor's Lane and Dog-and-Bitch Yard.

The most fashionable place in which to be seen was St James's Park, which Charles redesigned in the French style with avenues and a rectangular lake with an island in the middle. He also had an aviary built containing various species of exotic bird. Wrestling matches were staged in the park and croquet, bowls and pall-mall (similar to croquet) were all popular games. Early in the mornings

– usually about 6 a.m. – the tall figure of the King himself could often be seen striding around the park's perimeters as he took his 'physic' with a pack of sniffing, yelping spaniels running ahead of him. On warm summer evenings the park was full of couples strolling together, and as the young fops bowed and posed in their dandy costumes the ladies would stop to compliment each other on their beautiful new silk or satin dresses. Vanity prevailed in this arena to such an extent that when, shortly after Rochester joined the Court, Count Grammont presented Charles with a magnificent calash affording a full view of the occupants, the King had to settle a heated argument between Lady Castlemaine, his official mistress, and Frances Stewart, his unattainable one, as to who could be seen riding in the wretched thing first. Castlemaine, who was pregnant (again), threatened to miscarry if she was not given preference, while Stewart implied that if her own claim was not granted the King would never be in a position to make her pregnant in the first place. Castlemaine's atrocious temper won the day, Stewart stomped off in a huff and a few months later the palace corridors were echoing to the cries of yet another bastard child. Observing all this nonsense was a young man who had come to Court expecting to find substance, honour and high ideals.

The long years of adversity prior to 1660 had left the King extremely cynical of human nature and essentially melancholic. Burnet said: 'He has a very ill opinion of men and women and so is infinitely distrustful; he thinks the world is governed wholly by interest.' While his own hedonism gave Charles one means of escaping this gloomier side of his character, the light-hearted company of others represented another. The Court wits, a group of men whose continuous lampoonery and good-natured mockery of each other was delivered with a remorseless stream of repartee, entertained their monarch almost as much as they pleased themselves. Dryden believed that even this verbal dexterity, which characterises all the Restoration comedies, was attributable to Charles. 'If any ask me whence it is that our conversation is so much refined, I must freely and without flattery ascribe it to the Court, and in it, particularly to the King, whose example gives a law to it,' declared the great playwright and poet.

Charles was fully aware of the influence he wielded upon style, and when he felt that the fashion in men's clothing was becoming too diverse and in some cases eccentric, he decided in 1666, to set an example for all to follow. Up until then men's dress was more varied and every bit as spectacular as women's, and frequently bordered on the ridiculous. 'It was a fine silken thing which I spied walking the other day through Westminster Hall,' wrote the diarist John Evelyn, 'that had as much ribbon about him as would have plundered six shops and set up twenty country pedlars. All his body was dressed like a May-pole or Tom-o'-Bedlam's cap'. Charles's new style of an embroidered coat, to be worn over a tight-fitting waistcoat plus knee-length breeches, not only, predictably, caught on but it remained the standard men's wear well into the 1700s. Nevertheless, the appearance of many a more ambitious young fop continued to give the Court wits something to laugh about.

Head of the wits – also known as the Ballers or the Merry Gang – was the extraordinary George Villiers, Duke of Buckingham, orphan of the assassinated favourite of James I. As childhood friends, he and Charles had both been tutored in mathematics by Thomas Hobbes, and in spite of the Duke's outlandish behaviour they remained close throughout their lives.

Boisterous, unstable and yet hugely talented, Buckingham it was who went on a dirty underwear strike when Charles denied him command of the army at the Battle of Worcester in 1651. In 1667 he exceeded even his own standards of outrageousness. His lover at the time was the Countess of Shrewsbury, and when her husband discovered the affair the inevitable duel was fought. Having mortally wounded his opponent, Buckingham took his mistress back home only to be confronted by an irate Lady Buckingham. 'I refuse to endure the presence of that woman under this roof!' she cried. 'Quite so madam,' replied the Duke, 'which is why I have ordered a carriage to convey you to your mother's.' Later he had the gall to decide that his illegitimate son by Lady Shrewsbury should be chistened in Westminster Abbey.

Famously labelled by Alexander Pope as 'this lord of useless thousands', he was, it need hardly be said, a thoroughly dangerous character. But he could also be terribly funny, and his wit did not even let him down on his deathbed in 1687, two years after the reign had ended. Asked if he required a priest he snorted: 'No!

Those rascals eat God! But if you can find someone who eats the devil, I should be glad to see him.'

Buckingham, thirty-seven years old when Rochester came to Court, was a ferociuos drinker and debaucher, and when he became a minister upon the honourable Clarendon's dismissal in 1667, it was a final confirmation of the direction in which the Court had been travelling since 1660. Perhaps the Duke's most striking characteristic was his apparent contempt for his own talent. He excelled at everything he turned his hand to but soon lost interest in whatever it was and, like a sparrow in a tree, hopped onto something different. His play *The Rehearsal*, for example, written in 1671, was an ingenious attack on the kind of heroic drama mastered by Dryden (it formed the basis of Sheridan's The Critic) and yet the Duke was soon bored of writing. Dryden wrote of him in *Absolom and Achitophel*:

> A man so various, that he seemed to be
> Not one, but all mankind's epitome:
> Stiff in opinions, always in the wrong;
> Was everything by starts, and by nothing long.
> But, in the course of one revolving moon,
> Was chemist, fiddler, statesman and buffoon;
> Then all for women, painting, rhyming, drinking,
> Besides 10,000 freaks that died in thinking.

As they had indicated on Oxford Kate's balcony, Sir Charles Sedley, who was twenty-six years old when Rochester arrived, and Charles Sackville, Lord Buckhurst, who was four years younger, were both men who knew how to unwind. Sedley was another talented drinker who wrote several plays and had his lyrics set to music by Henry Purcell. Like Buckingham, his wit did not let him down even in the direst circumstances. When the theatre roof fell in during a performance of his play *The Mistress*, injuring Sir Charles and a number of others, his friend Fleetwood Shepherd tried to console him with the suggestion that the play had been so full of fire it had blown up the poet, theatre and audience. 'Nonsense,' said Sedley, 'it was so heavy it brought down the house and buried the poet in his own rubbish.'

Lord Buckhurst (later Lord Dorset) had earnt himself a stretch in Newgate for murder. In February 1662 he, his brother Edward and three other men had killed a tanner called Hoppy at Stoke Newington. They mistook him for a highwayman, set upon him and then made off with his money, thinking it was stolen anyway. Burnet described Buckhurst as a generous, good-natured man. 'He was so oppressed with phlegm, that, till he was a little heated with wine, he scarce ever spoke.' In 1667 he ran an ale-house at Epsom with his lover, a seventeen-year-old actress called Nell Gwyn.

Of the other wits, the tubby and jovial Henry Savile, who by Christmas 1664 was twenty-two years old, drank as heavily as any. Clarendon called him 'a young man of wit and incredible confidence and presumption'. Although he once made an indiscreet (and most unwelcome) foray into Lady Northumberland's bedroom in the dead of night, Savile did not allow alcohol to jeopardise his career and by the late 1670s he was a trusted ambassador of the King's in Paris. William Wycherley, the playwright whose comedy *The Plain Dealer* earnt him that nick-name among the wits forever afterwards, cast a rather sorrier figure who drifted through a discontented life without seeming to be aware of just how very talented he was, and spent seven years in Fleet Prison for debt. George Etherege, or 'Gentle George', knighted at the end of the 1670s, was the easy-going and good-humoured playwright who immortalised Rochester as Dorimant, the suave and witty hero of one of the best of the Restoration comedies, *The Man of Mode*.

Other courtiers included Baptist or 'Bab' May, Keeper of the Privy Purse, who was almost as well known for his love of art, particularly paintings, as he was for his drunkenness; Tom Killigrew, the playwright who had founded the King's Players, and was one of the most outspoken wits at Whitehall, where his unrestrained comments often carried near-the-knuckle moral overtones; and Henry Bulkeley, who was a sharp critic of all things foppish and affected. Sir Carr Scrope and John Sheffield, Earl of Mulgrave, both had squints, which suited Rochester perfectly when he came to satirise them. Mulgrave was a particularly arrogant man who wore a supercilious sneer and earnt himself the nick-name 'King John'. He was the only one of the wits who, by a few months, was younger than Rochester. To varying degrees, all of them drank more than was good for them. Even General

George Monck, who had set up the Restoration and was now Duke of Albermarle for his troubles, was celebrated by the wits for his astonishing capacity for drink. It was, said Dryden simply:

> A very merry, dancing, drinking,
> Laughing, quaffing, and unthinking time.

Just as ready in the arts of wittiness and revelry was Charles himself – and as a lover he had no equal in the age. Being King did rather help in this department, but he also had many personal qualities which made him extremely attractive. Quite apart from his generosity, charm and wit, he had one tantalising characteristic: nobody knew what made him tick. There was something impenetrable about Charles; he had learnt to protect his sensibilities from a world which had abused his family, and the one person who had access to his innermost emotions was his adored sister 'Minette'. She was the only woman who was capable of seriously influencing him and when she died in 1670 of suspected poisoning by her husband, the King was beside himself with grief.

It would be easy for a female biographer of Charles II to become a little dewy-eyed about him, but it should be stressed that while he liked women and treated them well (which is more than can be said for several of his wits), his cynicism embraced the issue of love and he viewed women ultimately as sexual toys. The father of fourteen bastard children, Charles's remarkable feats of sexual athleticism earnt Whitehall Palace the nickname among the wits of 'the Augean stable'. Like any good Hobbist he had no intention of practising the fidelity which would have come unnaturally to him anyway, and, being a reasonable man, he did not see, why his mistresses should have to be faithful to him either. When, in the 1670s, his lover Jane Roberts asked him to take her back following a brief spell with Rochester, he agreed without so much as a shrug of the shoulders. This apparent indifference provoked the famous observation by Lord Halifax that 'his inclinations to love were the effects of health and a good constitution, with as little mixture of the seraphic part as ever man had; and though from that foundation men often raise their passions, I am apt to think his stayed as much as any man's ever did in the lower region'.

His constitution was certainly extraordinary, for no matter what time he crawled into bed he would be up at dawn, sometimes playing tennis as early as 8 a.m. At six feet two inches he dwarfed most of his courtiers and was a supreme athlete and horseman. Fishing, hunting, walking and hawking were all favourite pastimes and by the end of the 1660s his enjoyment of horse racing had become a passion. He established Newmarket at British racing's headquarters, rode winners there himself (including one as late as 1684, when he was in his fifties), and was nick-named 'Old Rowley' after a prodigious sire of that name stabled in the Suffolk town. (The Rowley Mile at Newmarket commemorates the horse to this day.) Always remarkably tolerant of those who teased or mocked him, he caused a maid at Whitehall to blush when he overheard her singing one of the many ballads about 'Old Rowley the King' as she was working in a room. 'Who is it?' she called out, when he knocked. 'Old Rowley himself madam,' he replied, popping his head round the door.

In the eyes of the wits a large number of offspring was not the only thing Charles had in common with the stallion, for, as Lady Castlemaine indiscreetly told a number of people, he was formidably well endowed. This snippet of information soon became a joke throughout the Court and in 1663 even Samuel Pepys got to hear about it. He recorded Sir Thomas Carew telling him 'that the King doth mind nothing but pleasures and hates the very sight or thoughts of business; that my Lady Castlemaine rules him; who he says hath all the tricks of Aretine that are to be practised to give pleasure in wich he is too able having a large ——'.

Charles did regard much of his business as a chore but even so did not shirk his duties. A series of notes passed between him and the paternal Clarendon during council meetings have survived and they testify to his boredom on such occasions. Judging from one of them the Lord Chancellor sometimes even had to keep him awake. 'This debate is worth three dinners, I beseech you be not weary of it, but attend it with all patience, the benefit that will follow, is greater than you will yet see,' wrote Clarendon.

Anxious to present to his subjects that sacred image of kingship in which his father had believed so passionately, Charles had revived the ritual known as Touching for the King's Evil. This involved those who were ill with scrofula coming to the palace and kneeling to be touched or stroked on the head by their monarch while a chaplain murmured: 'He put his hands upon them and he healed them.' In reality Charles was as cynical about religion as he was about everything else, remarking about one priest: 'He is a very honest man, but a very great blockhead, to whom I gave a living in Suffolk that was full of Nonconformists; he went about among them from house to house, yet I cannot imagine what he could say to them, for he is a very silly fellow; but I believe his nonsense suited their nonsense; for he has brought them all to Church.'

Hobbism's rejection of anything which was not fact, and which could not be proved, naturally extended itself in Charles's case to a fascination in science, and he must be given great credit for the crucial steps in scientific discovery which were made during his reign. He founded the Greenwhich Observatory (designed by Wren), from which Greenwich Mean Time is calculated; and the Royal Society received the Royal Charter in July 1662. While many of the discoveries made by the likes of Newton, Halley, Boyle and Hooke established essentail principles for modern scientific understanding, some of the experiments seemed so bizarre to the outside world that the poet Samuel Butler was moved to write:

> These were their learned speculations,
> And all their constant occupations,
> To measure wind, and weight the air,
> And turn a circle to a square;
> To make a powder of the sun,
> By which all doors should be undone;
> To find the North-West passage out,
> Although the farthest way about . . .

In other respects the King had set the tone of his reign by spending the first night of the Restoration with his twenty-year-old mistress Barbara Palmer. In 1661 he ensured the nobility of any illegitimate children she bore him (six eventually) by making her husband Earl of Castlemaine. In May 1662, Charles had married Catherine de Braganza of Portugal, but this union, which ironically was childless, made no difference to his taste for sexual adventure. Although Castlemaine successfully warded off all rivals to her position of official mistress until 1670, there is no way of telling how many casual female visitors were shown up the backstairs by Charles's secretary, spy and 'pimp', Thomas Chaffinch, or Chaffinch's brother William who succeeded him in 1666.

Castlemaine, a cousin of Rochester's on his mother's side, was sexually insatiable herself – or in Gilbert Burnet's words, 'enormously vicious and ravenous'. Her flagrant infidelities are said to have included flings with her own footmen and when her indiscretions became too much for even Charles to tolerate he pensioned her off, in August 1670, as Duchess of Cleveland, Countess of Southampton and Baroness Nonsuch. By that time she had consoled herself with the athletic attentions of Jacob Hall the rope dancer. Stunningly beautiful, she was, in spite of her renowned temper, Samuel Pepys's pin-up girl. In 1665 he wrote of having had the best dream that ever man dreamt,

> which was that I had my Lady Castlemaine in my arms; and then dreamt that this couldn't be awake, but that it was only a dream: but that since it was a dream, and that I took so much real pleasure in it, what a happy thing it would be if when we are in our graves (as Shakespeare resembles it) we could dream and dream but such dreams as this, that then we should not need to be so fearful of death.

At the time of Rochester's arrival Castlemaine was battling for survival against the attentions Charles was paying 'La Belle Stewart'. When Frances Stewart presented herself at Whitehall aged about fourteen in January 1662 even Pepys became momentarily diverted, calling her 'the greatest beauty I ever saw, I think, in my life'. Whether the King was in love with Stewart herself or with her elusive and very irritating chastity is highly debatable. It can easily be argued that he never truly fell in love once, and it is significant that the only other woman who drew helpless sighs from him was Louise de Kéroualle, later Duchess of Portsmouth, who held on to her virginity for more than a year after coming to Court in 1670. Stewart, the model for Britannia on British coins, did even better than that. She never surrendered to Charles at all. While some of his closest friends, including Buckingham, founded a Committee for the Getting of Mistress Stewart for the King, the girl herself – vain and empty-headed –

on one occasion had the gall to lift up her skirts and give the court an agonising glimpse of her stupendous legs. For Charles, who was notably partial to a good pair of legs, it was all simply too much to bear, and he said as much in these verses:

I pass all my hours in a shady old grove,
But I live not the day when I see not my love;
I survey every walk now my Phyllis is gone,
And sigh when I think we were there all alone.
Oh, then 'tis I think there's no Hell
Like loving too well.

But each shade and each conscious bower when I find
Where I once have been happy and she has been kind;
When I see the print left of her shape on the green,
And imagine the pleasure may yet come again;
Oh, then 'tis I think that no joys are above
The pleasures of love.

While alone to myself I repeat all her charms,
She I love may be locked in another man's arms,
She may laugh at my cares, and so false she may be,
To say all the kind things she before said to me!
Oh then 'tis, oh then, that I think there's no Hell
Like loving too well.

But when I consider the truth of her heart,
Such an innocent passion, so kind without art,
I fear I have wronged her, and hope she may be
So full of true love to be jealous of me.
Oh then 'tis I think that no joys are above
The pleasures of love.

When Frances suddenly eloped with the Duke of Richmond in 1667 and married him she had the decency to return to Charles all the jewellery he had given her, but he was nevertheless both shocked and angry. He subsequently allowed the couple back, forgot about the whole business and was gracious enough to make the Duke his ambassador in Denmark. The truth was that Frances was never terribly interested in love or in men, and when her husband died prematurely she devoted the rest of her life to her cats and never married again.

This, then, was the powdered and periwigged jungle awaiting the young man who upon his return to England hated nothing more than intemperance. Hedonism thrives on selfishness, and behind the apparent friendliness of this noisy, colourful Court, there lay little help for those who could not stand up on their own. For someone still three months short of his eighteenth birthday, entering the palace must have required a deep breath. From Sir Andrew Balfour to the Duke of Buckingham was a very big step indeed.

❧ ❧ ❧

Even amidst this gathering of 'beautiful people', the new boy turned heads from the start. Burnet said Rochester

. . . appeared at Court with as great advantages as most ever had. He was a graceful and well shaped person, tall and well made, if not a little too slender. He was exactly well bred, and what by a modest behaviour natural to him, what by a civility become almost as natural, his conversation was easy and obliging. He had a strange vivacity of thought and vigour of expression: His wit had a subtilty and sublimity both, that were scarce imitable. His style was clear and strong: When he used figures they were very lively, and yet far enough out of the common road: he had made himself master of the ancient and modern wit, and of the modern French and Italian as well as the English. He loved to talk and write of speculative matters, and did it with so fine a thread, that even those who hated the subjects that his fancy ran upon, yet could not but be charmed with his way of treating them. Boileau among the French, and Cowley among the English wits, were those he admired most. Sometimes other men's thoughts mixed with his composures, but that flowed rather from the impressions they made on him when he read them, by which they came to return upon him as his own thoughts, than that he servilely copied from any. For few men ever had a bolder flight of fancy, more steadily gathered by judgment, than he had. No wonder a young man so made and so improved was very acceptable in a Court.

One of the Court's French guests, Charles de Marguetel de Saint-Denis, Seigneur de St Evremond (hereafter referred to as just St Evremond), gave an equally enthusiastic description of the youthful Rochester and also noted his powers of animated conversation:

> His person was graceful, tho' tall and slender, his mien and shape having something extremely engaging; and for his mind, it discover'd charms not to be withstood. His wit was strong, subtle, sublime, and sprightly; he was perfectly well-bred, and adorned with a natural modesty which extremely became him . . . he drew a conversation so engaging, that none could enjoy without admiration and delight, and few without love.

The references to his height place him somewhere around five feet ten or eleven inches, which for the age was tall. As we have noted, at six feet two inches the King was a comparative giant. Rochester was also extremely good-looking, Thomas Hearne describing him as 'one of the handsomest persons in England'. To Anthony Wood he was a 'noble and beautiful count'. Paintings and line drawings of him all emphasise an outrageously sensual set of lips and hooded, suggestive eyes. By appearing to be constantly on the brink of breaking into a broad smile he transmitted a seductive but strangely innocent air of naughtiness, and it was this paradox which caused Sir George Etherege to have a character say of Dorimant, 'I know he is a Devil, but he has something of the Angel yet undefac'd in him.' The gracefulness mentioned by both Burnet and St Evremond reflects a manner of standing (one hand on the hip, one leg leading away from the body, head held high) and moving (gently, exposing the inside of the thigh by swinging the leg outwards and back round in a smooth circular motion with each step) which all Charles's courtiers adopted but which Rochester had clearly acquired before his arrival. All his features were refined, particularly his long, slender-fingered hands.

The few recorded occasions on which Rochester was outdone in wit may well refer to his early months at Court when he was less prepared for the fast-thinking punchlines of his contemporaries. Bumping into Doctor Isaac Barrow one day he smiled: 'Doctor, I am yours to my shoe tie.' 'My Lord, I am yours to the ground,' replied Barrow. 'Doctor, I am yours to the centre,' added Rochester. 'My lord, I am yours to the antipodes,' came the answer. 'Doctor! exclaimed the Earl, 'I am yours to the lowest pit of hell!' '*There*, my lord,' said Barrow, calmly turning on his heel, 'I leave you.'

Burnet said Sir Charles Sedley had a 'sudden and copious wit, which furnished a perpetual run of discourse; but he was not so correct as Lord Dorset [Buckhurst], nor so sparkling as Lord Rochester'. The Earl's ability to make up impromptu lines astonished the older courtiers, never more so than when Charles asked him to compose a verse about the assembled company of himself, his brother James, Duke of York, the Duke of Monmouth, Laurendine, and the royal physician, Frazier. One of Rochester's skills as an satirist was to home in on genuine weaknesses rather than simply throw irrelevant insults, and in recording this anecdote Thomas Hearne pointed out that while the King was known to be 'negligent and careless', the Duke of York 'would not take a jest', Monmouth was 'half witted', Laurendine was a 'deformed person' and Frazier was a 'mean empty physician'. Rochester lampooned all of these characteristics by declaring to Charles:

> Here's Monmouth the witty,
> Laurendine the petty,
> And Frazier the great physician;
> But as for the rest,
> Take York for a jest,
> And yourself for a great politician.

The most famous exchange between the two men ended in Charles reminding Rochester that he had a sharp wit of his own which would take some beating. Having invited his courtiers to make up his epitaph, the King added that they should feel free to say anything they wanted, since he would take nothing amiss. Rochester seized this opportunity to declare with a grin:

Here lies our Sovereign Lord the King
Whose word no man relies on;
He never said a foolish thing
But he never did a wise one.

''Tis easily explained,' replied Charles, 'for my words are my own but my acts are my ministers'.' Cheeky the Earl certainly was, but it was all good-natured fun and no one could have predicted in these early days the salacious turn his wit would eventually take. Having proved himself so quick at thinking on his feet he showed an equal flair for doing it on his backside. When he tried to steal a kiss from Lady Castlemaine as she stepped from her carriage, she knocked him to the ground and he laughed:

By Heavens! 'twas bravely done,
First to attempt the Chariot of the Sun
And then to fall like Phaeton!

Such exuberance gave him instant popularity at the court and especially among the wits. So, was he immediately lapsing back into the debauchery and hedonism of his days at Oxford? No. Burnet wrote that 'falling into company that loved these excesses, he was, though not without difficulty, and by many steps, brought back to it again'. We have Rochester's word, given to his confessor at a time when lying would have contradicted the entire purpose of their discussions, that his dissipation happened gradually. Sir Andrew Balfour's three years of influence did not vanish overnight and the Earl was particularly conscientious in the self-discipline he applied to his drinking.

During the Christmas of Rochester's arrival, the Court's chatter was never far away from two topics, one of them being a puzzling comet which was described a perfect arc in the night-time skies over London. On 16 December the King, who was fascinated by astronomy (but dismissive of astrology, which was so popular at the time), sat up with Queen Catherine to observe it and later wrote to his sister Minette of 'no ordinary star'. Having been frustrated by cloud cover the evening after, Pepys's patience was finally rewarded on Christmas Eve:

I saw the comet, which now, whether worn away or no I know not, appears not with a tail, but only is larger and duller than any other star, and is come to rise betimes, and to make a great arch, and is gone quite to a new place in the heavens than it was before.

After the plague, the Great Fire of London and the war with the Dutch, many people cast their minds back superstitiously to the comet.

Unofficial warfare with Holland, England's traditional and commercial seventeenth-century rival, had been rumbling on throughout the year and overall the English had been enjoying the better of it. In America they had seized the New Netherlands along with a usefully positioned Dutch town on the east coast called New Amsterdam, which was immediately re-christened New York. Samuel Pepys, Clerk of the Acts at the Navy Office, had received letters on 9 December telling of 'our bringing in great numbers of Dutch ships' from the Channel to add to the Hollanders' Bordeaux fleet which had been brought into Portsmouth during November, but Pepys was being as shrewd as ever when he spoke of forthcoming war with dread: an unfashionable though far more realistic sentiment than the one of nationalistic fervour sweeping both the Court and London generally. His supicion that the Dutch would be no pushover was confirmed when, on Christmas Eve, he went

. . . to the Coffee-house; and there heard Sir Richard Ford tell the whole story of our defeat at Guinea, wherein our men are guilty of the most horrid cowardice and perfidiousness, as he says and tells it, that ever Englishmen were.

The insult of a Dutch victory only served to increase the pressure being put on Charles by the popular mood, but a chronic shortage of cash (always a problem for him) and a waiting game to try and see what Louis XIV would do in the event of England committing herself (France eventually supported the Dutch) postponed the inevitable declaration of war until February of the New Year.

✤ ✤ ✤

While the war was looming, Rochester's attention was already focused on a woman – though not, as one myth implies, the teenaged Nell Gwyn. It was inevitable that the scandalmongers of the eighteenth century would try to match the Earl up with his monarch's most famous mistress, and in the mid-1700s one unknown editor duly published a 'Poetical Epistle from the Earl of Rochester to Nell Gwyn' which, he claimed, had been copied from manuscript volumes of the Earl's work presented by Charles II to Louis XIV. He said they had been found in Louis's library. The idea of Charles sending the French monarch a work as scandalous as this, describing his mistress's every pore and crevice, seems preposterous to say the very least. The 'Epistle' begins with the line: 'Nelly, my life, tho' now thou'rt full fifteen', and Nell reached that age a few weeks after Rochester arrived at Whitehall. However, while the Earl may well have made Nell's acquaintance by the time the 'Epistle' purports to have been written, and though he was certainly back in England by her fifteenth birthday, it is inconceivable that he was already using the kind of language the 'Epistle' contains.

The rumour of a sexual liaison between Rochester and Nell had already been fuelled by the publication, thirty-six years after Rochester's death, of Captain Alexander Smith's tawdry book, *The School of Venus* which included verses (allegedly written by Rochester's friend Etherege) charting Nell's ascent to the royal bed. The following lines are among them:

> To Buckhurst thus resigned in friendly wise,
> Our glaring lass begins to rise,
> Distributing her favours very thick,
> And sometimes witty Wilmot had a lick.

Smith went further, claiming that Nell became the Earl's lover shortly after *she* arrived in London. Hardly. Aged fourteen, she was acting for the King's Players in 1664 (while Rochester was still abroad) and before that she worked as one of the theatre's orange-sellers. Although she hailed from the Welsh borders – possibly Hereford – Nell had also previously worked as a serving-maid in her mother's London 'merry house'. She had therefore been living in the capital for some time, possibly several years, when Rochester entered court.

Neither is there any evidence to suggest that Nell ever distributed 'her favours very thick'. She became established as a royal mistress in 1669 and was never known to be unfaithful to Charles, so any fling with Rochester must have happened sooner rather than later in their lives. The 1708 edition of John Downes's *Roscius Anglicanus* contained the *Memoirs of Nell Gwyn* and poured cold water on all the gossip with the observation that it in no way appeared Rochester had 'ever been enamoured' of her. 'Mrs Barry was his passion, and Mrs Boutel [another actress] antecedently to Mrs Barry, at the time when Mrs Gwyn trod the stage.'

What gave the gossips encouragement though was the fact that Rochester and Nell not only knew each other but were firm friends. He acted as her trustee as late as 1677 (which actually would seem to be further evidence of a long-standing *platonic* relationship), and in a letter to Henry Savile he described the advice he used to give her concerning her relationship with the King. It sounds more like the advice of an avuncular mentor than a lover. There is no doubt that Rochester liked Nell more than he did most of the royal mistresses; and although he includes her in some of his bawdiest satires he does not launch direct attacks on her personality in the way he did with both Lady Castlemaine and Louise de Kéroualle, Duchess of Portsmouth. One reason he was never cruel to Nell is that she was wholly unpretentious: there was little for him to knock down. One of her celebrated declarations was made in the late 1670s around the time of the Popish Plot, when an aggressive crowd mistook her for the Catholic royal mistress, Louise de Kéroualle. 'Good people!' yelled Nell from her carriage, 'this is the *Protestant* whore!' She is also said to have secured a title for her royal son by calling him 'you little bastard' in front of the King. When Charles ticked her off she asked him, wide-eyed with innocence, what other name there was to use. She was tough, funny and possessed a quality essential for anyone who wanted to be liked by Rochester: the ability to laugh at herself. Another reason he was not cruel to her in his writing is that she was not promiscuous. The man who all his life long loved morality in others admired fidelity when it was natural and not the result of self-restraint. If Nell had been promiscuous in the years before she met the King, then the Earl could have been more sceptical of her fidelity as a royal mistress – but she had never been fickle. One of her first lovers, in the mid 1660s, was the actor Charles Hart and another was Charles Sackville, Lord Dorset. Both these relationships were committed and not casual; the King, she explained, was her Charles III.

Johannes Prinz implied that it was possible Rochester had written the 'Poetical Epistle' tongue-in-cheek. 'Piqquant personal illusions of this sort are nothing uncommon in Rochester's work, but must not be taken too literally,' he wrote. It is, though, most unlikely that the Earl would have written something so scandalous about somebody he liked. He saved that for himself and for his enemies. The 'Poetical Epistle' is almost certainly as fake as an affair between Rochester and Nell is mythical, and when he did come to give his verdict on her it was both kind and protective:

> . . . much more her growing virtue did sustain
> While dear Charles Hart and Buckhurst su'd in vain.
> In vain they su'd; cursed be the envious tongue
> That her undoubted chastity would wrong;
> For should we fame believe, we then might say
> That thousands lay with her as well as they.

Besides, in 1665 Rochester's desires lay elsewhere. Recently arrived at Court was a beautiful young heiress from Enmore in Somerset called Elizabeth Mallet. Upon her mother's death she would be worth the handsome sum of £2,500 a year – five times Rochester's annual pension – and her mother kept little back from her anyway. Probably aged fourteen or fifteen, she was now being touted for marriage at Whitehall by her stepfather, Sir John Warre, sheriff of Somerset and a member of parliament, and her grandfather, Lord Hawley. As a suitor Rochester faced two problems: he had no wealth and he had not arrived back in England early enough to be first on the scene. Ahead of him in the queue were the highly eligible Viscount Hinchingbrooke, son of Lord Sandwich, the commander of the English fleet, and Lord John Butler, son of the Duke of Ormonde. The latter's claim was being considered first.

Rochester, of course, had no father to make his proposals for him as was the custom – so he very sneakily tried to turn this to his advantage by asking the King to recommend him instead. He even went one better than that: he asked his cousin Castlemaine to have a word with Charles on his behalf. In so much as this made his rivals nervous, the plan worked. Henry Bennet wrote a worried letter to Lord Sandwich saying that Lady Castlemaine had 'rigged' the King to recommend Rochester and was being seconded by the Earl of Clarendon. However, he had been told that Elizabeth was declaring she would choose for herself. 'If she hold to it, the game is upon equal terms at least.'

Bennet must have been right about the lady insisting that she would choose for herself, for it is unlikely that her socially ambitious guardians would have stalled for long once they had been approached by the two most powerful men in the country, Charles and Clarendon. According to Pepys the King 'spoke to the lady often' about marrying Rochester, 'but with no success'. It is not surprising, for Elizabeth was a wonderfully spirited girl who had no intention of giving herself up without some fun and games first.

She got more than that from Rochester. On the night of Friday, 26 May he kidnapped her.

After eating supper with Frances Stewart at the palace, Elizabeth and her grandfather were trundling back to her lodgings by coach when they were brought to a halt at Charing Cross by a gang of men on foot and horseback. One of the latter was Rochester. She was pulled from the bewildered Lord Hawley, her grandfather, and ordered into another coach in which two women were waiting to receive and reassure her. With six horses pulling it for extra speed, this coach then rattled through London's narrow cobbled streets. Rochester was galloping along a different route in an apparent attempt to draw any followers off the main scent. Pepys said an 'immediate pursuit' took place – by whom is not clear – and after a long chase the Earl was finally caught at Uxbridge. The carriage carrying Elizabeth was nowhere to be seen.

While the news went through the Court like a gunshot, the King was furious, or, in Pepys's words, 'mighty angry'. It is easy to see why. He had gone out of his way to recommend Rochester to Elizabeth's guardians as a responsible and mature young man who would make the lady an excellent husband. By abducting her the Earl had not only publicly undermined Charles's authority but had made his judgement look faulty. The fact that Charles was such a placid man only made this burst of temper more frightening, and Rochester was brought down to earth with a hard bump. The following morning a warrant for his imprisonment was issued to Sir John Robinson, Governor of the Tower of London, and he was locked up.

Meanwhile a proclamation went out asking all 'his Majesty's men and loving subjects whom it may concern' to hunt down 'all persons who shall appear guilty of the misdemeanour'. Once apprehended, the culprits were to be detained in safe custody 'until further order'. So where was Elizabeth? Two days later, on Sunday afternoon, Pepys told the whole story to a fascinated Lady Sandwich, mother of the suitor Hinchingbrooke, and noted in his diary that night that Elizabeth 'is not yet heard of'.

Rochester had nothing to gain by not co-operating with the search except for an even longer stretch in the Tower than was otherwise going to be the case. The likeliest scenario is that his lackeys, realising their leader had been caught, were moving from safe house to safe house in a blind panic as to how to return the captive prize without being caught themselves. A search of any address given by Rochester certainly proved fruitless, and whether Elizabeth was surrendered by his men or recaptured by the King's troops is not known. One way or another, though, she was restored to safety, unharmed.

The experience may not have been as frightening for her as it would be for a young girl today. Abductions by desperate lovers were not unheard of in the mid-seventeenth century and the moment Elizabeth was stopped at Charing Cross and saw Rochester on horseback, she knew what was happening: she was being taken into the country where, away from her restrictive guardians, the Earl intended to persuade her to marry him. Elizabeth's family were as angry as the King and at the time she was hardly impressed herself. Less than two weeks later Pepys paid another call on Lady Sandwich and wrote:

> She tells me my Lord Rochester is now declaredly out of hopes of Mrs Mallet, and now she is to receive notice in a day or two how the King stands inclined to the giving leave for my Lord Hinchingbrooke to look after her, and, that being done, to bring it to an end shortly.

But Elizabeth was an intensely romantic girl – she wrote poetry to prove it – and once her anger had subsided then the excitement of that night, combined with Rochester's sheer gall, would weigh heavily in his favour. It did not seem so to anybody at the time, but his move had instinctively been the right one.

The most striking aspect of this whole episode is that Rochester had approached what was really a business transaction with a diabolical romanticism. Among the aristocracy, wives were chiefly sought for dowries and heirs: love had much more to do with mistresses. Yet when he petitioned Charles for his release, the Earl said 'passion' had been his motivation. Drink was certainly not responsible for his extravagant action (though it should be remembered that alcoholics are notoriously impetuous by nature), but what certainly had gone to his head was the excessive atmosphere at Court. This was already a different young man from the one who had sat in libraries abroad poring over Greek and Latin texts. While impetus for the abduction had come from Rochester's awareness that Hinchingbrooke was due back from the continent in the coming weeks, the influences of Whitehall's Hobbism seem to have played a part too. In 'A Satire Against Reason and Mankind' Rochester tells us:

> But thoughts are given for action's government;
> Where action ceases, thought's impertinent.

Instead of pining for Elizabeth while the families of Hinchingbrooke and Lord John Butler negotiated with her guardians, why not take a leaf from Thomas Hobbes's book and *do something about it*? Hobbism, as we have observed, dictated that passion is instilled in us not to be restrained but to be used.

At the Tower of London, away from the solace which the laughter of the wits would have offered, the Earl felt, for the first time in his life, bitter.

> Oh why am I, of all mankind,
> To so severe a fate designed?
> Ungrateful! Why this treachery
> To humble, fond, believing me,
> Who gave you privilege above
> The nice allowances of love?

In the context of his satire 'A Ramble in St James's Park' those questions are asked sarcastically, but in the Tower they were put with an innocent and aggrieved sincerity. Not only had he been rejected by Elizabeth – punishment enough in his own view – but nobody had warned him that the rules at Court were made up as the King went along. Getting drunk in public and exposing oneself from a balcony, for example, did not merit imprisonment, but having the bravery to protest love did. Naive, maybe, but injustice is a strong theme in the Earl's poetry and that is how he felt. And who was the King to lecture him on proper behaviour anyway? The King was not even faithful to the Queen!

The heat wave of June only added to Rochester's discomfort, while outside on the streets – in Drury Lane to be exact – Samuel Pepys, on 'the hottest day that ever I felt in my life', came across a frightening sight:

> . . . two or three houses marked with a red cross upon the doors, and 'Lord have mercy upon us!' writ there; which was a sad sight to me, being the first of the kind that, to my remembrance, I ever saw.

The arrival of the plague quicky spread throughout the capital. Those who could afford to leave their businesses packed their bags and headed for the country. The plague's stranglehold tightened gradually but steadily, and in one week at the end of June it accounted for more than a hundred lives. Rochester, meanwhile, ironically safer than most from infection, had decided how to recover his reputation once he was released. The answer was not so much staring him in the face as reaching his ears, for the thudding of cannon fire at the Battle of Lowestoft – the first major engagement against the Dutch – could clearly be heard in London.

He would go to war.

4

WAR HERO

. . . during the whole action, the Earl of Rochester showed as
brave and as resolute a courage as was possible: a person of
honour told me he heard the Lord Clifford, who was in the
same ship, often magnify his courage at that time very highly.

Gilbert Burnet, describing Rochester's conduct
at the Battle of Bergen

'Victory over the Dutch', announced an excited Samuel
Pepys in his diary, when news of the triumph at Lowestoft
reached him. '. . . we have taken and sunk, as is believed,
about twenty-four of their best ships; killed and taken near 8,000
or 10,000 men, and lost, we think, not above 700. A greater
victory never known in the world.' It suddenly seemed to the
imprisoned Rochester, as it did to most, that the Dutch ships
represented easy pickings; that this war would be a quick and
famous victory for the English. Burnet tells us that Rochester
'thought it necessary to begin his life with . . . demonstrations of
his courage in an element and way of fighting, which is
acknowledged to be the greatest trial of clear and undaunted
valour'. If it sounds a cynical and self-serving reason for a man to
go to war, the Earl was hardly alone. Some might argue that it is
the motivation most teenagers have had for enlisting in wars
throughout the centuries. Moreover, Rochester's bitter poem 'The
History of Insipids', written in the 1670s, shows that loot from
captured ships and his own reputation were not the only reasons

he wanted to fight: he cared deeply, in 1665, about his country's fortunes and the success of this new and supposedly golden age.

The petition he sent from the Tower asking for his release was too endearing for even the doubting Charles to withstand. Rochester assured his monarch that the petition showed

> That no misfortune on earth can be so sensible to your petitioner as the loss of your Majesty's favour.

> That inadvertently, ignorance in the law, and passion were the occasions of his offence.

> That had he reflected on the fatal consequences of incurring your Majesty's displeasure, he would rather have chosen death ten thousand times than done it.

> That your petitioner in all humility and sense of his fault casts himself at your Majesty's feet, beseeching you to pardon his first error, and not suffer one offence to be his ruin.

> And he most humbly prays that your Majesty would be pleased to restore him once more to your favour, and that he may kiss your hand.

On 19 June, after just over three weeks of imprisonment, he was discharged on the two conditions that he gave 'good and sufficient security' and promised to 'render himself to one of his Majesty's principal Secretaries of State' on the first day of the forthcoming Michaelmas Term. In spite of the plague's mounting death toll, Charles and his Court were still in London (later in the summer they moved to Oxford via a spell at Salisbury), but Rochester, aware that his only chance of winning Elizabeth was to leave her alone and gain her respect, had no time for dalliance at Whitehall. When the King gave him a letter on 6 July to take to Lord Sandwich, father of Hinchingbrooke (his chief rival for Elizabeth's hand in marriage), he headed for Lowestoft where the fleet had been refitted, and set sail in the *Success*. He then transferred to Sandwich's ship and delivered the letter, which recommended 'the bearer my Lord Rochester to your care, who desires to go a volunteer with you'. Sandwich replied to the King on 17 July: 'I have accommodated him the best I can and shall serve him in all things that I can.' He told Charles that the aim now was to intercept and capture the Dutch East Indies Fleet – laden with immense riches – which was on its return voyage home.

Sandwich and his officers had blockaded the Dutch coast so effectively that they expected the East Indies fleet to opt for sanctuary in the neutral Danish port of Bergen. A deal was therefore struck with Frederick III, King of Denmark and Norway: that, in return for a share of the captured booty he would allow the English fleet to enter the harbour and attack the Dutch vessels. Sir Gilbert Talbot, England's Copenhagen envoy, confirmed that King Frederick had not only approved the deal but had ordered the governor of Bergen to seem highly offended by the English intrusion (thus the Dutch would not think they had been betrayed) but not to shoot anything at them except powder. In other words, no cannon fire. When the Dutch duly sailed straight into Bergen as expected, the English licked their lips and Sandwich sent a score of frigates off under the charge of Vice-Admiral Sir Thomas Teddiman. Rochester boarded Teddiman's own ship, the *Revenge*.

Just as the English were about to pounce, they realised that Bergen's governor was either unwilling or unready to betray the Hollanders. For twenty-four hours, while Rochester and other young, inexperienced volunteers endured a nerve-racking wait, desperate negotiations took place between the English and the Danes – allowing the Dutch, who were now fully aware of the plan, to organise themselves for battle. Rochester angrily remembered this critical delay in 'The History of Insipids':

> The Bergen business was well laid,
> Though we paid dear for that design:
> Had we not three days parling staid,
> The Dutch Fleet there, Charles had been thine.
> Though the false Dane agreed to sell 'um
> He cheated us, and saved Skellum.

He had another reason to feel bitter, for perhaps the most frightening part of battle is the agony of waiting for it to start. The longer this goes on, the more thoughts tend towards death. It is remarkable that it was on the eve of a sea battle against the Dutch that Rochester's friend Sir Charles Sackville, Lord Buckhurst, was high-spirited enough to pen the most famous ballad prompted by the war:

> To all the ladies now at land
> We men at sea indite;
> But first would have you understand
> How hard it is to write:
> The Muses now, and Neptune too,
> We must implore to write to you –
>   With a fa, la, la, la, la.
>
> For though the Muses should prove kind,
> And fill our empty brain,
> Yet if rough Neptune rouse the wind
> To wave the azure main,
> Our paper, pen, and ink, and we,
> Roll up and down our ships at sea -
>   With a fa, la, la, la, la.
>
> Then if we write not by each post,
> Think not we are unkind;
> Nor yet conclude our ships are lost
> By Dutchmen or by wind:
> Our tears we'll send a speedier way,
> The tide shall bring them twice a day -
>   With a fa, la, la, la, la.

On the eve of the Battle of Bergen, while the diplomatic wrangling continued, Rochester's frame of mind was morbid enough to account for an incident which had a tremendous impact on the rest of his life. Two of his more eminent colleagues in the *Revenge*, Edward Montagu and a Mr Wyndham, told him they had strong premonitions of dying in the fighting. Montagu was quite convinced about it; Wyndham a little less so. According to Burnet, Rochester and Wyndham 'entered into a formal engagement, not without ceremonies of religion, that if either of them died, he should appear and give the other notice of the future state, if there was any. But Mr Montagu would not enter into the bond.'

The true intent of Bergen's governor became clear to the English when it was realised that he was allowing the Dutch to move their own cannons into the Bergen forts. His 'negotiations' had been aimed at helping the Dutch and buying them time. An angry Sir Thomas Teddiman gave the signal to open fire at 5 p.m. on 2 August and at last Rochester, Montagu, Wyndham *et al.* sprang into action.

The result was an English disaster, mitigated only by the fact that no more than one ship out of twenty-two was lost. Whilst coming under fire from both sea and land, the English ships were cramped for room, could not manoeuvre properly, were in danger of being dashed on the rocks and could not even send out their fire-ships since a hard wind was blowing off the land against them. Four hundred men died, including five commanders. Rochester's own ship, the *Revenge*, escaped lightly: only four men were killed.

Two of them were Montagu and Wyndham.

That they were killed by the same cannon ball only increased the deep and superstitious doubt which underlined Rochester's subsequent atheism – or professed atheism. The two men who had told him they would die not only did so before his eyes but virtually in each other's arms. The Earl never forgot this moment, and on his deathbed, as he lay struggling to believe in God, the memory came back to haunt him. He recounted the story to his confessor and Burnet later wrote:

When the day came that they thought to have taken the Dutch Fleet in the port of Bergen, Mr Montagu, though he had such a strong presage in his mind of his approaching death, yet he generously stayed all the while in the place of greatest danger. The other gentleman signalised his courage in a most undaunted manner till near the end of the action, when he fell on a sudden into such a trembling that he could scarce stand: and Mr Montagu going to him to hold him up, as they were in each other's arms, a cannon ball killed him outright and carried away Mr Montagu's belly, so that he died within an hour after. The Earl of Rochester told me that these pressages they had in their minds made some impressions on him, that there were separated beings and that the soul, either by a natural sagacity or some secret notice communicated to it, had a sort of divination. But that gentleman's never appearing was a great snare to him during the rest of his life.

Rochester did admit that in hoping Wyndham's ghost would materialise, he was expecting a little too much:

. . . he could not but acknowledge it was an unreasonable thing, for him to think that beings in another state were not under such laws and limits that they could not command their own motions but as the Supreme Power should order them: and that one who had so corrupted the natural principles of Truth, as he had, had no reason to expect that such an extraordinary thing should be done for his conviction.

The effect of this bizarre episode was twofold and, as ever with Rochester, conflicting. The premonition of death, indicating that the soul might have 'a sort of divination', left the mind's religious door ajar enough for God to steal in at the end of the Earl's life. The hope the incident offered therefore eventually overcame its darker aspect – which was that Wyndham never appeared as he had said he would if there was an after-life. Until 1679 it was the latter element – what Burnet called a 'great snare' – which weighed uppermost in his mind. Atheism seemed more likely to represent certainty, and Hobbism placed an emphasis upon not speculating. God was just a supreme first cause. Life after the war seemed as eternal to Rochester as it does to most young people, and so the business of seriously contemplating religion could be put off until tomorrow. Meanwhile, for a man who claimed to be dismissive of religion, he did write, as we shall see, a suspicious amount about it.

In fact, owing to the crowded scenes beneath the decks of these ships during battle, and because of the horrific effects of splintering wood, it was not uncommon for a single cannon ball to account for two, three or even more lives. James, the gallant Duke of York, had had an extraordinary escape on board the *Royal*

Charles at Lowestoft when a cannon ball killed three men standing around him – including the Earl of Falmouth – but left him untouched. Pepys described in gory detail how their 'blood and brains' splattered the face of the Duke who, it was said by some, was knocked off his feet by a flying, decapitated head. Whether or not that part was true, the King was alarmed enough by the report to order that his brother, who was heir presumptive to the throne, would not take any further part in the war.

On the day after the Battle of Bergen, 3 August, Rochester charged with both pride and relief, wrote to his mother. It is the only one of his letters to her which has survived and the most immediately striking thing about it is its extraordinary innocence and naivety. Should anyone doubt that it was his initial sense of high romance and great expectancy of life which led him, via reality, to such bitter and chronic cynicism, the evidence of this letter is final. He writes the word 'Madam' in the top left-hand corner with an enormous, majestic sweep of his pen and in the opposite corner gives his address, almost comically, as 'the coast of Norway amongst the rocks aboard the Revenge'. He is watching himself amidst his surroundings; looking down on himself among his peers. In doing so he is excited to see that he is playing a dangerous part in such an heroic event. For Rochester is obviously blinded to the fact that this battle has been a diabolical shambles for the English fleet. Instead, he writes of it in tones suggestive of a victory on the scale of Trafalgar:

> From the coast of
> Norway amongst the rocks
> aboard the Revenge, August the 3.

Madam

I hope it will not be hard for your Ladyship to believe that it hath been want of opportunity and no neglect in me the not writing to your Ladyship all the while. I know nobody hath more reason to express their duty to you than I have, and certainly Savile [would] never be so imprudent as to omit the occasions of doing it. There have been many things past since I wrote last to your Ladyship. We had many reports of De

Ruyter [the great Dutch admiral] and the East Indies Fleet but none true, till, towards the 26 of the last month, we had certain intelligence then of 30 sail in Bergen in Norway, a haven belonging to the King of Denmark. But the port was found to be so little that it was impossible for the great ships to get in, so that my Lord Sandwich ordered 20 sail of fourth and fifth rate frigate to go in and take them. They were commanded by Sir Thomas Teddiman, one of the Vice-Admirals. It was not fit for me to see any occasion of service to the King without offering myself, so I desired and obtained leave of my Lord Sandwich to go with them, and accordingly the thirtieth of this month we set sail at six a clock at night, and the next day we made the haven Cruchfort (on this side of the town fifteen leagues) not without much hazard of shipwreck, for (besides the danger of rock which according to the seamen's judgement was greater than ever was seen by any of them) we found the harbour where twenty ships were to anchor not big enough for seven, so that in a moment we were all together one upon another and ready to dash in pieces, having nothing but bare rocks to save ourselves in case we had been lost. But it was God's great mercy we got clear and only that we had no human probability of safety; there we lay all night and by twelve a clock next day got off and sailed to Bergen full of hopes and expectation, having already shared amongst us the rich lading of the East India merchants, some for diamond[s], some for spices, others for rich silks and I for shirts and gold, which I had most need of; but reckoning without our host we were fain to reckon twice. However, we came bravely into the harbour in the midst of the town and castles and then anchored close by the Dutchmen. We had immediately a message from the Governor full of civility and offers of service, which was returned to us, Mr Montagu being the messenger; that night we had 7 or ten more, which signified nothing but mere empty delays. It grew dark and we were fain to lie still until morning. All the night the Dutch carried above 200 pieces of cannon into the Danish castles and forts and we were by morn drawn into a very fair half moon ready for both town and ships. We received several messages from break of day until four of clock much like those of the over night, intending nothing but delay that they might fortify themselves the more; which being perceived we delayed no more but just upon the stroke of five we let fly our fighting colours and immediately fired upon the ships, who answered us immediately and were seconded by the castles and forts of the town, upon which we shot at all and in a short time beat from one of their greatest forts some three or four thousand men [an exaggeration] that were placed with small shot upon us. But the castles were not to be [taken] for besides the strength of their walls they had so many of the Dutch guns (with their own) which played in the hulls and decks of our ships that in 3 hours' time we lost some 200 men and six captains, our cables were cut, and we were driven out by the wind, which was so directly against us that we could not use our fireships, which otherwise had infallibly done our business; so we came off having beat the town all to pieces without losing one ship. We now lie off a little still expecting a wind that we may send in fireships to make an end of the rest. Mr Montagu and Thomas Wyndham's brother were both killed with one shot just by me, but God Almighty was pleased to preserve me from any kind of hurt. Madam, I have been tedious, but beg your Ladyship's pardon who am

> Your most obedient son,
> ROCHESTER

I have been as good a husband as I could, [i.e., he has tried to be financially prudent] but in spite of my teeth have been fain to borrow money.

Note that he mentions neither the premonitions of death nor the bond he entered with Wyndham. His strictly religious mother would have regarded the premonitions as idle superstition and the bond as blasphemous.

The *Revenge*, along with the twenty other frigates, many of them damaged, returned to join Lord Sandwich and the main fleet just off Flamborough Head on 18 August. There, Rochester heard some encouraging news. Sandwich's son, Hinchingbrooke, who had arrived back in England from the continent on 4 August to pay his attentions to Elizabeth Mallet, had fallen ill with smallpox less than a week later. Pepys, who quite apart from being one of Lord Sandwich's employees was also a friend to Lady Sandwich, felt full of sympathy. 'Poor gentleman!' he wrote on 16 August, 'that he should come from France so soon to fall sick, and of that disease too, when he should be gone to see a fine lady, his mistress! I am most heartily sorry for it.' It was a sentiment Rochester can hardly be expected to have shared.

When the Dutch East Indies Fleet sailed out of the Bergen harbour in the first week of September the English pounced again – and this time had much more success. In a first encounter two East India ships were seized ('and very good prizes', added Pepys), while a few days later a convoy of eighteen Dutch ships – four of them men-of-war – were engaged. Most of them were captured, along with some one thousand Dutch sailors. Bergen had been avenged, and on 12 September Sandwich reported the happy news in a letter to the King which he asked Rochester to take back to England.

For any soldier or sailor returning home from the perils and hardship of war, there can be few more dismaying, not to say insulting sights than that of drinking, gambling, dancing and adultery in the Officers' Mess. In a sense, Whitehall's Court was the Officers' Mess, or at least, a centre of operations to which even Sandwich was answerable. The Court was now based at Oxford, since the plague was raging in London. It reached its peak at precisely the time of Rochetser's arrival back in England, killing (officially, but the real total was probably higher) 6,544 people in the third week of September alone. London was being decimated. The sickness eventually accounted, officially, for some 68,000 people, although again this figure is very suspect and the true number was probably closer to 100,000 – about a quarter of the population. To have lived in the capital in that summer of 1665 was to have lived with death. Red crosses marked doors on virtually every street, horse-drawn carts loaded with bodies trundled up and down the roads and the cry of 'Bring out your dead!' echoed throughout the day and evening.

It is difficult to imagine how good humour could exist in such frightening circumstances. People are fond of saying 'life was cheap in those days', but it was not cheap enough to prevent thousands from fleeing into the countryside, thereby spreading the plague beyond London. Daniel Defoe tells one particularly amusing story in his *A Journal of the Plague Year* which sounds bizarre enough to be true. It concerns a man known simply as 'the piper' who earnt himself a few farthings and was often bought drinks in the ale-houses for playing his pipe around the streets: a seventeenth-century busker. One night he popped into a tavern in Coleman Street for 'just the one' and found the customers in a very generous mood – so generous that having eventually dragged himself away he was compelled to recuperate by lying down in the street near London Wall, not far from Cripplegate. By the time the dead-cart came past he was in such a deep and drink-induced sleep that it was assumed he had died from the plague and had been put out for collection. He was only dumped in the back of the cart by Mr John Hayward, gravedigger and bearer of the dead, and his assistant. Explains Defoe:

> From hence they passed along and took in other bodies, till, as honest John Hayward told me, they almost buried him alive in the cart; yet all this while he slept soundly. At length the cart came to the place where the bodies were to be thrown into the ground, which, as I do remember, was at Mount Mill; and as the cart usually stopped some time before they were ready to shoot out the melancholy load they had in it, as soon as the cart stopped the fellow awakened and struggled a little to get his head out from among the dead bodies, when, raising himself up in the cart, he called out, 'Hey! where am I?' This frightened the fellow that attended about the work; but after some pause John Hayward, recovering himself, said, 'Lord, bless us! There's somebody in the cart not quite dead!' So another called to him and said, 'Who are you?' The fellow answered, 'I am the poor piper. Where am I?' 'Where are you?' says Hayward. 'Why, you are in the dead-cart, and we are going to bury you.' 'But I ain't dead though, am I?' says the piper, which made them laugh a little – though, as John said, they were heartily frighted at first; so they helped the poor fellow down, and he went about his business.

Pepys, who on 15 August met a corpse being carried at night in a narrow alley, gives a sombre account on 14 September of the extent to which the plague threatened every Londoner throughout those dreadful months.

> My meeting dead corpses of the plague, carried to be buried close to me at noonday through the City in Fenchurch Street. To see a person sick of the sores carried close by me by Gracechurch in a hackney-coach. My finding the Angel Tavern, at the lower end of Tower Hill, shut up; and more than that, the alehouse at the Tower Stairs; and more than that, that the person was then dying of the plague when I was last there, a little while ago, at night. To hear that poor Paynel, my waiter, hath buried a child, and is dying himself. To hear that a labourer I sent but the other day to Dagenham, to know how they did there, is dead of the plague; and that one of my own watermen, that carried me daily, fell sick as soon as he had landed me on Friday morning last, when I had been all night upon the water, and I believe he did get his infection that day at Brainford [Brentford], and is now dead of the plague . . . To hear that Mr Lewis hath another daugher sick. And, lastly, that both my servants, W. Hewer and Tom Edwards, have lost their fathers, both in St. Sepulchre's parish, of the plague this week, – do put me into great apprehensions of melancholy, and with good reason.

In these circumstances it would be churlish to accuse the Court of cowardice for retreating to Oxford. It was a practical decision and there was nothing their presence in London could have done to help the situation. Besides, the last thing England needed just five years into the Restoration was a dead monarch. As it was, Charles took a risk by being on the Thames (with Pepys) as late in the summer as 26 July. When the Fire of London broke out the following year, he, his brother James and many of the courtiers proved themselves as ready to help out as anybody, working throughout the day to rescue belongings from burning houses and douse the insatiable flames with pails of water. The Court's only mistake in 1665 – and it was a most undiplomatic one – was to behave in Oxford as though nothing were amiss in the capital. All the usual carefree jollity prevailed, and Rochester came back to find the King more desperate to bed La Belle Stewart than ever, in spite of the fact that Castlemaine was pregnant. When she gave birth to a boy in her lodgings at Merton College on 28 December, somebody posted such a vitriolic message on her door that a £1,000 reward was offered to find the perpetrator – in vain.

Could the mysterious culprit have been Rochester? Certainly, he did not spare his distant cousin's reputation in later years:

> [Castlemaine] I say is much to be admired,
> Although she ne're was satisfied or tired;
> Full forty men a day provided for this whore:
> Yet like a bitch she wags her tail for more.

But on this occasion it is likely that the Earl was innocent. Not only had he yet to acquire a voice of bitterness, but if he was revolted by the public indecencies of this Court in the midst of war and sickness he was hardly alone. The local people of Oxford were disgusted, one of them being Anthony Wood. He noted that although the courtiers were 'neat and gay in their apparel, yet they were very nasty and beastly, leaving at their departure their excrements in every corner, in chimneys, studies, coal-houses, cellars. Rude, rough, whoremongers; vain, empty, careless.'

For eight months after his return, Rochester stayed at the Court – which moved back to London in February 1666, when the plague was almost completely over. Although this period marks one of the 'many steps' by which, according to Burnet, the Earl was brought back to excess, he was certainly still resisting drunkenness and debauchery in general. We can be sure of this on two counts. The first is that he was proud of the distinguished reputation he had won for himself. In Lord Sandwich's letter of 12 September, which Rochester passed on to the King, the naval commander commended him as 'brave, industrious, and of parts fit to be very useful in your Majesty's service'. His half-term report could not have been better. On 31 October Charles rewarded him with a gift of £750 and word quickly spread through the Court that the Earl of Rochester had behaved with great valour at sea. Secondly, and crucially, it is inconceivable that the wealthy heiress Elizabeth Mallet, 'la triste heritiere', as Grammont called her, would have married a man who was not just poor but who had a widespread reputation for drunkenness and profanity. Personal accomplishments were less important for those bachelors who were rich, but if Rochester was to lure Elizabeth he now had to show discretion in his conduct. He had to be able to offer *something*. Moreover, Whitehall was a hotbed of gossip and the Earl would not have been able to commit any gross misdemeanour without her hearing about it. There is no doubt that the man she finally picked as her husband in January 1667 appeared to be, in spite of his lack of an estate, one of Charles's most eligible courtiers.

Years later Rochester mocked himself in a letter to Henry Savile as an 'arrant fumbler' in his dealings with women, but in truth he was very clever indeed at the game of courtship, knowing instinctively just when to give attention and just when to withdraw it. During this spell at Court he was guided in his treatment of Elizabeth by that renowned expert on the wiles and ways of women, King Charles II. Considering that Charles was still inable to fathom how to put Frances Stewart on the hook, and that Buckingham was weighing in with his own irrelevant advice, it is surprising the plan worked at all – but it did. Noting that Elizabeth did not seem exactly overwhelmed by her suitors Hinchingbrooke or Lord John Butler, the Earl simply kept his distance, enquired after her health from time to time and waited for the other contestants to fall over.

Elizabeth was an extremely attractive girl; vivacious, strong-willed and good-humoured. 'She has a great deal of wit,' observed the Duke of Ormonde's agent Nicholls wryly, having been frustrated in his efforts to negotiate marriage for Lord John Butler. When a handful of the country's most eligible bachelors chasing her, she was also thoroughly enjoying herself and soon began testing her suitors in an apparent attempt to sort out the men from the boys. (Rochester may have been rejected but he had already passed this particular test with flying colours.) In February 1666, Elizabeth stunned the honourable and upright Viscount Hinchingbrooke by suggesting that they should elope and marry without anybody's consent. How serious she was being is uncertain (was she yearning for the romantic excitement of her abduction?) but Hinchingbrooke was so appalled that he went and sneaked on her to his father. Pepys reported Sandwich telling him that 'for the match propounded of Mrs Mallet for my Lord

Hinchingbrooke, it hath been lately off, and now her friends bring it on again, and an overture hath been made to him by a servant of hers, to compass the thing without consent of friends, she herself having a respect to my Lord's family; but my Lord will not listen to it but in a way of honour'.

It was difficult for Hinchingbrooke to manage even any civility when, in August, he met Elizabeth in Kent only for her to tell him that she had decided on someone else. If they did not part acrimoniously then neither did they part warm friends. Pepys wrote: 'The business between my Lord Hinchingbrooke and Mrs Mallet is quite broke off; he attending her at Tonbridge, and she declaring her affections to be settled, and he not being fully pleased with the vanity and liberty of her carriage.'

On whom were Elizabeth's affections settled? Almost certainly it was Sir Francis Popham, who, a few months later, Pepys was tipping as the hot favourite. Relations with Lord John Butler had ended when his father, the Duke of Ormonde, decided the financial demands being made by Elizabeth's guardians were too high. This was not before she had astonished Ormonde's agent, Nicholls, by drinking Lord John Butler's health 'in a pretty big glass half-full of claret, which I believe was more than ever she did in her life'.

Elizabeth's audacity and her controversial insistence that she and not her guardians would decide who she married were now rankling with a number of observers, and on 10 September 1666 Sir George Carteret wrote to Lord Sandwich, who was at sea, and took great delight in telling him that: 'The lady of the West is at Court without any suitors, nor is likely to have any.' But Elizabeth could afford to be cocky. She knew perfectly well that her wealth would enable her to pick who she wanted when she wanted – and just for a while it seemed as though the lucky man would be Sir Francis Popham.

Rochester continued to play a waiting game. Elizabeth's sheer nerve made her even more desirable in his eyes, for he always regarded strong women as an irresistible challenge and was not, like many men, frightened of them. Elizabeth Barry was particularly strident and in *The Man of Mode* Dorimant is magnetised by Harriet's self-assurance and boldness. Freudian psychologists might point to the fact that the Earl's mother was such a strong woman. Whatever the reasons, Rochester did admire women who, like Nell Gwyn, could fight their own corner, and he tended to be dismissive of their more winsome, fragile cousins. During his stay at Whitehall he had watched Elizabeth elude and confuse her suitors whilst making a mockery of the negotiations and efforts of not just their guardians but her own, Sir John Warre and Lord Hawley. She was soon proving equally difficult with yet another suitor, Lord Herbert, later sixth Earl of Pembroke.

Rochester left the capital at the end of May and went back to sea. He departed at the end of May in a great hurry (he gave no warning of his intention to anyone – not even his mother) which could suggest he was starting to be tempted by his excesses of old and therefore tore himself away from Whitehall with a sudden resolve. He had enhanced his reputation at the Court and had entertained the Merry Gang with his ready wit without falling prey to his colleagues' dissipation. Anthony Hamilton said that 'every person was eager to obtain the most insignificant trifle that came from the pen of Lord Rochester' – but no lampoon had caused any grave offence. There had been no duels; no banishments from Court. It was drink that gave his tongue a wicked and cutting edge, and he was still not drinking without restraint. When he departed from Whitehall he was not only popular among his peers but respected too.

He boarded Sir Edward Spragge's ship on 31 May and the very next day was plunged into the most terrible battle of the war. At the start of 1666, the French and the Danes had entered the conflict on the side of the Dutch, and during the first four days of June the two sides – fifty-eight English ships against seventy-two of the enemy's – were locked together in the Channel. Once again the crashing and thudding of cannonfire carried all the way to London, where people stood in the streets and listened with dreadful wonderment. The English came off much the worse. They lost 6,000 men – hundreds were burnt to death; hundreds drowned – and seventeen ships (eight sunk; nine captured), while the Dutch lost 2,000 men and seven ships. Much of the enemy's success was due not only to their superior guns but also to the brilliance of the famous and feared Dutch admiral De Ruyter, who had a similar effect on the fighting spirit of his men as Nelson had on English sailors a little more than a century later. On both sides, the number of seriously wounded totalled thousands.

It was in the midst of this unrelenting carnage that Rochester enhanced his reputation for valour and turned it into one for outright heroism. His own ship was in the thick of the action throughout the battle – virtually every volunteer on it was killed – and when Sir Edward Spragge was desperate to pass on a message to a captain in another ship, he had difficulty in finding anyone who would be foolhardy enough to carry it. It was Rochester who volunteered, taking a rowing boat through the hail of gunshot and cannonfire before running the same gauntlet on the return journey. It was, remarked Burnet, 'much commended by all that saw it'.

The defeat had the curious effect of actually lifting the morale of the English. (As the German blitz on London testified this century, it is a very English characteristic to rally under adversity.) Thomas Clifford wrote to Lord Arlington, saying that he wished the King could see such patriotic determination. 'Even the commen men cry out: If we do not beat them now, we shall never do it,' Clifford stated. Rochester took part in further engagements during July which went some way towards rectifying the balance between the two sides, but the emerging situation was clearly one of stalemate.

The Earl landed back on English soil during the autumn of 1666 – probably in October – and can only have been stunned by the sight awaiting him in London.

An area of the capital about one-and-a-half miles long and half-a-mile wide was a smouldering, rubble-strewn wasteland. Cheapside, Cripplegate and the parish of St Bride's had disappeared. St Paul's, one of London's most historic landmarks even then, was just a smoking heap. Fuelled by a stiff breeze, the Great Fire, which had broken out in Pudding Lane on Sunday night, 2 September, had raged until the following Thursday. Its population already ravaged by the plague, the capital of England now lay in ruins.

Reports of Rochester's conduct during the four-day battle in June were soon being circulated by word of mouth around Whitehall, and even Lord Mulgrave, never a friend of the Earl's and eventually his enemy, conceded that 'at that time no man had a better reputation for courage'. He was now moving among his older and distinguished peers – and not just the Merry Gang – with the confidence of knowing that he had their admiration. On 15 November, Pepys saw him dressed in all his periwigged finery at a ball:

> Anon the house grew full, and the candles light, and the King and Queen and all the ladies set: and it was indeed, a glorious sight to see Mrs Stewart in black and white lace, and her head and shoulders dressed with diamonds [given to her by Charles], and the like a great many great ladies more, only the Queen none; and the Duke of York and all the dancers were, some of cloth of silver, and others of other sorts, exceeding rich. Presently after the King was come in, he took the Queen, and about fourteen more couple there was, and begun the Bransles. As many of the men as I remember presently were, the King, Duke of York, Prince Rupert, Duke of Monmouth, Duke of Buckingham, Lord Douglas, Mr Hamilton, Colonel Russell, Mr Griffiths, Lord Ossory, Lord Rochester; and of the ladies, the Queen, Duchess of York, Mrs Stewart, Duchess of Monmouth, Lady Essex Howard, Mrs Temple, Swede's Ambassadress, Lady Arlington, Lord George Barkeley's daughter, and many others I remember not ... My Lady Castlemaine, without whom all is nothing, being there, very rich, though not dancing.

It would be surprising if Elizabeth Mallet had not been there too. She was still sublimely indifferent to the fact that her guardians had now been attempting to marry her off for almost two years, and her determination not to be used as a financial pawn in their self-serving game of social chess was as resolute as it had ever been. On 25 November a Mr Ashburnham told Pepys of the dismissive manner in which Elizabeth was analysing her suitors: 'that my Lord Herbert would have her; my Lord Hinchingbrooke was indifferent to her; my Lord John Butler might not have her; my Lord Rochester would have forced her; and Sir Francis Popham, who nevertheless is like to have her, would kiss her breech to have her.'

But Sir Francis Popham's hopes were shortlived, for it was now, having spent nearly a year-and-a-half waiting patiently on the sidelines, that the gallant of Bergen and hero of the four-day battle in June made his move. In Pepy's account of how she was summing up her list of suitors it is clear from the phrase 'my Lord Rochester *would have* forced her' that as far as Elizabeth was concerned, his courtship of her belonged to the distant, if not dim, past. When the young Earl, who had once daringly abducted her; who had gone to the Tower for her; who had now returned to Court garlanded with honour, advanced in her direction once again, the element of surprise boosted that flavour of romance Elizabeth had always sought and now found over-whelming.

They married so quickly that everyone – closest friends and relatives alike – was caught unawares. Effectively it was an elopement, for the only person whose permission they sought was the King's, who granted it willingly. When the wedding was held on 29 January, 1667, Elizabeth had finally triumphed over the greedy guardians whose demands for her hand as a bride had been too steep for even a man as wealthy as the Duke of Ormonde to find acceptable. Sir John Warre and Lord Hawley could only stand by helplessly as their raffle prize was carried off by a husband whose financial acumen amounted to a £500 annual pension and a house minus an estate at Adderbury in Oxfordshire. At Ditchley Park, the Countess of Rochester was also in a tizz – though a much happier one – as she summoned her adviser Sir Ralph Verney on the occasion of

> my son Rochester's sudden marriage with Miss Mallet contrary to all her friends' expectation. The King I thank God is very well satisfied with it, and they had his consent when they did it – but now we are in some care how to get the estate. They are come to desire two parties with friends, but I want a knowing friend in business, such a man as Sir Ralph Verney – Master Coole the lawyer and Cary [her agent] I have here, but I want one more of quality to help me.

In February, Pepys saw the newly-weds at the Duke's Theatre watching a performance of *Heraclius*, and was pleased to note that there were no hard feelings shown between the unsuccessful suitor Lord John Butler and the happy bride:

> Here I saw my Lord Rochester and his bride, Mrs Mallet, who hath after all this ado married him; and, as I hear some

say in the pit, it is a great act of charity, for he hath no estate. But it was pleasant to see how every body rose up when my Lord John Butler, the Duke of Ormond's son, came into the pit towards the end of the play, who was a servant to Mrs Mallet, – and now smiled upon her, and she on him.

That they were giddily in love is unquestionable. One of Rochester's earliest poems to her was a light-hearted rhyme addressed to his 'More than Meritorious Wife':

> I am by fate slave to your will
> And I will be obedient still,
> To show my love I will compose ye,
> For your fair fingers' ring a posie,
> In which shall be expressed my duty,
> And how I'll be for ever true t'ye,
> With low made legs and sugared speeches,
> Yielding to your fair bum the breeches,
> And show myself in all I can
> Your very humble servant Jan.

One of his first surviving letters to her, sent from Newmarket races, shows a similar skittish vein of good humour and contentment:

I'll hold you six to four I love you with all my heart. If I would bet with other people I'm sure I could get two to one, but because my passion is not so excessive to reach to everybody, I am not in pain to satisfy many. It will content me if you believe me and love me.

She did, and the first months of their marriage saw them riding on a crest of exuberance. In March, the King elevated Rochester's status in the Court still further by appointing him Gentleman of the Bedchamber – the position once held by the Earl's father – while Elizabeth became Groom of the Stole to the Duchess of York. Still only nineteen, Rochester now had everything he could realistically ever had wanted. He had married the most eligible girl at Whitehall; he was a personal friend of the King and other powerful men like Buckingham; he was revered by all his peers for his courage; he had good health and an apparently strong constitution; he had a shining intelligence, good looks and charm and he had his wife's considerable wealth – a position he never abused. Given that Lord Sandwich was obviously impressed with his flair as a sailor, he could have opted for a glittering career at sea. The King, however, gave him every encouragement to become a statesman by overruling the 21-years' age limit for membership of the House of Lords. On 5 October Rochester and the Earl of Mulgrave duly took their seats, and in spite of further protestation by the members, there they remained. To say his future looked bright would have seemed to everyone a ridiculous understatement.

There was just one snag. He was drinking again. Heavily.

The reasons for Rochester's downfall are manifold but easy to explain. What triggered the collapse of his resolve was, perversely, his marriage. In our own society we frequently watch the dismal sight of young pop-stars and sportsmen self-destructing for the simple reason that they have everything too soon in life, and the fact that, with his marriage, the Earl *did* have everything explains in part his sudden and drastic change of course. But only in part. Rochester, after all, had worked for his respected position at Whitehall and one tends not to throw away that which has been earned through bravery, endeavour and sheer self-discipline.

His repeated, numerous infidelities to Elizabeth racked him with remorse and self-disgust throughout his life. To read many of his letters to her is to listen to a condemned man speaking with head hung in shame and eyes shut tight in a bitter, useless despair. Like most alcoholics, Rochester despised himself. With a romantic's sheer naivety, he had expected love to quell the promiscuous desires which are felt by many people and so often by men. He did not want to be another Buckingham, treating his wife with contempt as he fought a duel over his latest mistress; he did *not* want to follow the King's example of rampant infedility. It was a way of life which revolted him. 'All my life long I had a secret value and reverence for an honest man, and loved morality in others,' he told Gilbert Burnet. He would have had a love of morality in himself too, if only he had been able to practise it instinctively. Instead, Rochester was finally drawn into the pleasures provided by the sating of his sexual and alcoholic appetites: fulfilments which he saw as fundamentally honest to his own nature but which also caused him tremendous self-recrimination. As he observed hopelessly after he had married:

> I hate the thing is called enjoyment
> Besides, it is a dull employment;
> It cuts off all that's life and fire
> From that which may be termed desire,
> Just like the bee whose sting is gone
> Converts its owner to a drone.

The fulfilment of desire, then, never lived up to the expectations it aroused in the first place. Marriage took the excitement out of his love for Elizabeth (albeit a love which never died), and the man who St Evremond said was 'soon cloyed with the enjoyment of any one woman, tho' the fairest in the world, and forsook her', forsook his wife because he was feeling as though he had been converted into a bee 'whose sting is gone'. He was frustrated and contained by what he loathed most of all: boredom. 'A Satire against Marriage' contains these lines:

> Out of mere love and arrant devotion,
> Of marriage I'll give you this galloping notion.
> It's the bane of all business, the end of all pleasure,
> The consumption of wit, youth, virtue, and treasure.
> It's the rack of our thoughts, the nightmare of sleep,
> That sets us to work before the day peep.
> It makes us make brick without stubble or straw,
> And a cunt has no sense of conscience or law.
>   If you needs must have flesh, take the way that is noble:
> In a generous wench there is nothing of trouble.
> You come on, you come off – say, do what you please –
> And the worst you can fear is but a disease,
> And diseases, you know, will admit of a cure,
> But the hell-fire of marriage none can endure . . .

Marriage was exactly the kind of social constraint which Rochester saw as being in direct conflict with out natural instincts. How many animals on the earth remain with the same partner throughout their lives? After mentioning swans and pigeons, most people are stuck. One of the continuous themes in the Earl's poetry is his animal imagery (it was base, animalistic nature that he could see at work beneath those polite bows, coy curtsies and flirtations in St James's Park and the Whitehall ballroom), and when he felt shackled by the dreadful guilt of his own infidelities to Elizabeth, his resentment found furious expression:

> Of all the Bedlams marriage is the worst:
> With endless cords, with endless keepers curst.
> Frantic in love you run and rave about,
> Mad to get in, but hopeless to get out.

He had not yielded to excessive drinking until now, so what enabled him to yield to infidelity? Hobbism. It encouraged him in both pursuits. And the bitter disappointment of marriage was coupled with his experience of war. If Bergen had raised religious doubts then the four days' battle in June 1666 had compounded them. He had seen and heard men screaming as they died by the hundred; he had witnessed mass slaughter and had even helped it. The growing suspicion that all this havoc and pain was for absolutely nothing had loomed even larger when he came home to find Charles's courtiers, the most powerful and affluent men in the land, debauching themselves. Despicable though such behaviour seemed to the Earl, it now made more sense than his memories of a war which the country had not been able to afford to wage, and which, since his marriage, had drifted into a hopeless stalemate anyway. In the summer of 1667 the Dutch had inflicted a huge embarrassment when, in spite of Aphra Behn's intelligence warning of their intentions, they were allowed to steal up the River Medway unchallenged and capture the fort of Sheerness, wreak havoc among the English ships and tow the pride of the fleet, the *Royal Charles*, back out into the Channel. It was a humiliation so great that the Government was left with only one course of action: peace. It was duly negotiated. The efforts of Rochester and thousands like him had indeed been for nothing – or so it seemed.

Meanwhile, with a large chunk of London razed to the ground and a considerable portion of the population dead, there had been further discontent at Court when it was realised that Charles had no intention of returning to the royalists those estates which had been taken away from them by the Cromwellians. His policy of appeasement and forgiveness amounted to shaking the country up as little as possible – but one man who had lost an estate at Adderbury and was now angry about a number of things, did not think this amounted to justice:

> His father's foes he doth reward,
> Preserving those that cut off his head;
> Old Cavalier's the Crown's best guard,
> He lets them starve for want of bread.
> Never was any King endowed
> With so much grace and gratitude.

Small wonder that 1666 had ended with Samuel Pepys fearing for the country's future:

> Our enemies, French and Dutch, great, and grow more by our poverty. The Parliament backward in raising, because jealous of the spending of the money; the City less and less likely to be built again, everybody settling elsewhere, and nobody encouraged to trade. A sad, vicious, negligent Court, and all sober men there fearful of the ruin of the whole kingdom this next year; from which, good God deliver us!

Rochester thought the Court sad, vicious and negligent too, but so long as he had had Elizabeth Mallet's expectations of a suitor to live up to, he had remained aloof from its worst excesses. When he found that even marital love was imperfect and disappointing; that marriage was not a fraction as exciting as the chase; he turned to Hobbism as a creed by which he could excuse and make sense of his desires. For this betrayal of the moral principles which had been instilled in him from birth by his mother, he never forgave himself.

It is most relevant in Rochester's case (as it was in the melancholic Charles's) that the foundation stone of Hobbism was despair. Hobbes stated that the life of man was nasty, brutish and short, which was all the more reason to live realistically and not speculate fancifully about religion. Rochester was to live up to the cynicism of this argument just as much as he was to live life itself – which was his tragedy and English literature's gain. Never was the influence of Hobbism seen more clearly in his work than in the poem 'Since Death On All', translated from a chorus by Seneca:

> Since Death on all lays his impartial hand,
> And all resign at his command,
> The Stoic too, as well as I,
> With all his gravity must die;
> Let's wisely manage this last span,
> The momentary life of man;
> And still in pleasure's circle move,
> Giving our days to friends, and all our nights to love.

As if he needed a role model, he was now regularly sleeping in the King's quarters in his capacity as a Gentleman of the Bedchamber, and was able to observe the full extent of his monarch's nocturnal activities: the returns from Lady Castlemaine's at two and three in the morning; the sounds of muffled moaning from behind the curtains of the great royal bed. Charles's influence on the conduct of courtiers much older than Rochester has already been emphasised. Why should a mere twenty-year-old have been the odd man out? Just in case the King's example was insufficient, both Buckingham and Buckhurst were Gentlemen of the Bedchamber around this time, too.

Rochester was being actively and deliberately encouraged by his peers to drink to excess, since it was obvious to all that the more alcohol he had, the sharper his wit became. Burnet explained:

> . . . the natural heat of his fancy, being inflamed by wine, made him so extravagantly pleasant, that many to be more diverted by that humour, studied to engage him deeper and deeper in intemperance: which at length did so entirely subdue him; that, as he told me, for five years together he was continually drunk; not all the while under the visible effect of it, but his blood was so inflamed, that he was not in all that time cool enough to be perfectly master of himself. This led him to say and do many wild and unaccountable things: By this, he said, he had broke the firm constitution of

his health, that seemed so strong, that nothing was too hard for it; and he had suffered so much in his reputation, that he almost despaired to recover it.

In the summer of 1667 he was drinking without restraint at the 'merry house' being run by Buckhurst and Nell Gwyn in Epsom. All the members of the Merry Gang, or Ballers, paid regular calls, and when Pepys was in the town on 14 July, one other visitor was Rochester's heavy-drinking friend, Sir Charles Sedley:

And to the town, to the King's Head; and hear that my Lord Buckhurst and Nelly are lodged at the next house, and Sir Charles Sedley with them; and keep a merry house. Poor girl! I pity her; but more the loss of her at the King's house. [A reference to her departure from the King's Players, where Nell had proved herself a superb comic actress.]

By the end of that summer, Elizabeth knew she was losing control over her husband and could only ignore the stories about his increasing waywardness which were starting to circulate the Court. While Rochester rarely wrote a love poem expressing complete contentment or anything approaching lasting happiness, his wife expressed the bitter-sweet grief that his growing absences were causing, in verses of her own:

> Nothing aids to love's fond fire
> More than scorn and cold disdain;
> I to cherish your desire
> Kindness used, but 'twas in vain.
> You insulted on your slave,
> To be mine you soon refused;
> Hope not then the power to have
> Which ingloriously you used.
>
> Think not Thersis I will ere
> By my love my empire lose [a reference to her estate?]
> You grow constant through despair;
> Kindness you would soon abuse.
> Though you still possess my heart,

> Scorn and rigour I must fain;
> There remains no other art
> Your love (fond fugitive) to gain.

Similarly, in one of the Earl's earliest poems, 'A Dialogue Between Strephon and Daphne' written in the late 1660s, it is not difficult to believe he was imagining a poetic conversation between his wife and himself. Note the emphasis he places in it on *change*, which, to the Hobbist, was integral to a proper understanding of life. Dorimant's statement that 'We are not masters of our own affections, our inclinations daily alter', reflected not just Rochester's belief but any 'perfect' Hobbist's. Although the final stanza, in which Daphne reveals she has been cheating on Strephon all along, is a nice punchline, mistrust was a very real problem for Rochester as a lover: he observed the double dealings and infidelities of couples at Court with a disgust and a cynicism which affected his own relationship and served to fuel his helplessly jealous nature (in his will he most ungenerously ensured that if Elizabeth married again she would lose custody of their son).

Strephon:	Prithee now, fond fool, give o'er.
	Since my heart is gone before,
	To what purpose should I stay?
	Love commands another way.

Daphne:	Perjured swain, I knew the time
	When dissembling was your crime;
	In pity now employ that art
	Which first betrayed, to ease my heart.

Strephon:	Women can with pleasure feign;
	Men dissemble, still with pain.
	What advantage will it prove
	If I lie, who cannot love?

Daphne:	Tell me, then, the reason why
	Love from hearts in love does fly,
	Why the bird will build a nest
	Where he ne'er intends to rest?

Strephon: Love, like other little boys,
               Cries for hearts, as they for toys
               Which, when gained, in childish play
               Wantonly are thrown away.

Daphne: Still on wing, or on his knees,
               Love does nothing by degrees:
               Basely flying when most prized,
               Meanly fawning when despised,
               Flattering or insulting ever,
               Generous and grateful never.
               All his joys are fleeting dreams,
               All his woes severe extremes.

Strephon: Nymph, unjustly you inveigh.
               Love, like us, must fate obey.
               Since 'tis nature's law to change,
               Constancy alone is strange.
               See the heavens in lightnings break,
               Next in storms of thunder speak,
               Till a kind rain from above
               Makes a calm – so 'tis in love.
               Flames begin our first address;
               Like meeting thunder we embrace;
               Then, you know, the showers that fall
               Quench the fire and quiet all.

Daphne: How should I these showers forget?
               'Twas so pleasant to be wet!
               They killed love, I knew it well:
               I died all the while they fell.
               Say, at least, what nymph it is
               Robs my breast of so much bliss!
               If she's fair, I shall be eased;
               Through my ruin you'll be pleased.

Strephon: Daphne never was so fair,
               Strephon scarcely so sincere;
               Gentle, innocent, and free,

Ever pleased with only me.
Many charms my heart enthrall,
But there's one above them all:
With aversion she does fly
Tedious, trading constancy.

Daphne: Cruel shepherd, I submit:
Do what love and you think fit.
Change is fate, and not design;
Say you would have still been mine.

Strephon: Nymph, I cannot; 'tis too true,
Change has greater charms than you.
Be by my example wise:
Faith to pleasure sacrifice.

Daphne: Silly swain, I'll have you know
'Twas my practice long ago.
Whilst you vainly thought me true,
I was false in scorn of you.
By my tears, my heart's disguise,
I thy love and thee despise.
Womankind more joy discovers
Making fools, than keeping lovers.

In 1667 Rochester simply gave up trying to conduct his life according to all the standards and principles he believed were proper. He realised that his hankering for a world of ideal morality; his yearning for a state of perfect love; were simply the stuff of which dreams are made:

How blest was the created state
Of man and woman, ere they fell,
Compared to our unhappy fate:
We need not fear another hell.

Naked beneath cool shades they lay;
Enjoyment waited on desire;
Each member did their wills obey,
Nor could a wish set pleasure higher.

But we, poor slaves to hope and fear,
Are never of our joys secure;
They lessen still as they draw near,
And none but dull delights endure.

Then, Chloris, while I duly pay
The nobler tribute of my heart,
Be not you so severe to say
You love me for the frailer part.

He could explain why it was practical to throw morality and decency to the wind in less lyrical terms too, for now he felt, like the King, that the world was governed by self-interest:

And honesty's against all common sense:
Men must be knaves, 'tis in their own defence.
Mankind's dishonest; if you think it fair
Amongst known cheats to play on the square,
You'll be undone.
Nor can weak truth your reputation save:
The knaves will all agree to call you knave.
Wronged shall he live, insulted o'er, oppressed,
Who dares be less a villain than the rest.
Thus, sir, you see what human nature craves:
Most men are cowards, all men should be knaves.
The difference lies, as far as I can see,
Not in the thing itself, but the degree,
And all the subject matter of debate
Is only: Who's a knave of the first rate?

Rochester was pulled into Hobbism by the encouragement and influence of others, and he eventually succumbed willingly because it helped to dismiss his despair. He despaired of the Court and its behaviour, of the war and its cruelty, of the horror of man's inhumanity to man, of the apparent non-existence of God and salvation, of the laxity and indifference of his King, and of his own inability to be content with marriage. In his own mind, the plague and fire-ravaged streets of the city seemed to symbolise the disaster of this new, amoral age. The only viable alternative to his sense of desolation and his hurt was Hobbism and the pursuit of pleasure. Within those bounds, nothing helped him now as much as drink. Alcohol banished his sadness, allowed him to forget his guilt over his extra-marital promiscuity, and, more than anything, it gave him a feeling he had once known in Oxford: happiness.

But beneath all the laughter, the japes and the new devil-may-care approach to life, there lurked a lethal and dark resentment which would find its voice in unforgiving satire.

> Chaste, pious, prudent Charles the Second,
> The miracle of thy restoration
> May like to that of quails be reckoned,
> Rained on the Israelitish nation:
> The wished-for blessing from Heaven sent
> Became their curse and punishment.

5

THE HAPPY MINUTE

Now piercèd is her virgin zone;
She feels the foe within it.
She hears a broken amorous groan,
Just in the happy minute.

Rochester, in his 'Song' beginning
'Fair Chloris in a pigsty lay' . . .

The sexual references in Rochester's poetry to 'the happy minute', 'the lucky minute' and even 'this livelong minute' not only reflects his belief that happiness is, by nature, elusive and transient; they mirror the alarmingly short period of real joy in his life as a whole. To say that the Earl was laughing until the end of 1669 and was grim-faced thereafter would be far too black and white, but as the 1660s ticked by, his alcoholism ensured that the once steady stream of euphoria which drink had brought him evaporated into shorter, darker, costlier bursts, finally culminating in suicidal thoughts.

When Rochester began to drink heavily again, the obsession with alcohol which he had experienced earlier at Oxford returned. He appointed drink as one of his two new Gods, or saints, and made 'love' (but in reality, sex), the other. This was a substitution of Hobbism's cynical certainty for the pure faith of Christ, and the Earl even had the gall to announce it to the world:

Cupid and Bacchus my saints are;
May drink and love still reign:

With wine I wash away my cares,
And then to love again.

At first, wine did much more than merely wash away his cares: it pushed the pendulum back to the opposite extreme and made him feel that life was fantastical. For approximately two years (1667 to 1669) he lived on a crest of careless euphoria. Metaphorically speaking, he wrote his poem, 'Upon Drinking in a Bowl', with a joyful grin on his face:

Vulcan contrive me such a cup
As Nestor us'd of old;
Shew all thy skill to trim it up;
Damask it round with gold.

Make it so large that, filled with sack
Up to the swelling brim,
Vast toasts, on the delicious lake,
Like ships at sea may swim.

Engrave not battle on his cheek;
With war I've nought to do:
I'm none of those that took Mastrick,
Nor Yarmouth leaguer knew.

Let it no name of planets tell,
Fixed stars or constellations:
For I am no Sir Sindrophel,
Nor none of his relations.

But carve thereon a spreading vine;
Then add two lovely boys:
Their limbs in amorous folds entwine,
The type of future joys. . . .

For as long as drink made him this exuberant, and so long as he had his health, it was impossible for Rochester to understand the damage drink was doing him. To the alcoholic, drink has the calculating manner of a boxer biding his time on the ropes before launching a sudden and devastating assault. It stores all its punishment up – and Rochester's remark to Gilbert Burnet, that his constitution once seemed so strong that nothing was too hard for it, was made with the memory of an enormous capacity, in the 1660s, for holding drink without losing control. Yet while alcohol in those days was making him more charming, more seductive and so happy, it was also secretly undermining his most natural defences against it. The Earl's short-term elixir was a long-term poison, and his physiology only encouraged him to persist. For example, the alcoholic very rarely suffers from hangovers, which for the normal drinker act as a deterrent. While the stinking headache experienced by most people after a night of too much wine persuades them not to touch another drop that day, the alcoholic's flu-like withdrawal symptoms make the hair of the dog which did the biting a necessity. The Chinese have proverbs for most of life's problems, and this is their verdict on alcoholism:

> First the man takes a drink,
> Then the drink takes a drink,
> Then the drink takes the man.

Such was the case with Rochester, who, because of his predisposition to the disease, was incapable, unlike normal drinkers, of preventing the drink from taking another drink. This compulsion, effectively a ruination of life itself, is hard to explain, but smokers might be one group who can find it less difficult to understand. Given the choice between not smoking at all for a whole day, or being allowed just a couple of puffs, the majority would opt for the former. It would be much easier to go entirely without, than to tantalise the system with just a tiny dose of what it is craving. Rochester was not one of those drinkers who find it impossible to go for even short stretches without alcohol; towards the end of his life he had to be sober for periods in order to continue living – and in the 1660s he could stop intermittently with relative ease. What he could not do was *moderate* his drinking nor sustain abstinence. The former, in particular, was already as impossible as it had been at Oxford. This time, there was no Sir Andrew Balfour to take him away and mend him either.

Alcoholics are amazing self-deceivers: when they insist that 'tomorrow will be different' it is not you who they are trying to convince, but themselves. It is clear from Rochester's correspondence with Elizabeth Barry that he promised her he would change his ways, and yet at the same time he could take the line that he was only a Falstaffian Heavy Drinker and not a compulsive addict at all. This is a very common confusion in the alcoholic, who often finds it difficult to believe that he or she is different from the majority of other people. Such a confession is painful; it is easier to draw a parallel with a man who once declared: 'If sack and sugar be a sin, God help the wicked.' This, said Rochester in a letter to Savile, was the saying

of a merry fat gentleman, who lived in days of yore, would be merry with a friend, and sometimes had an unlucky fancy of a wench.

Although Sir John Falstaff is a fictional creation of Shakespeare's, he does represent a character and a type of drinker most people have met before, and however much this might have doctors and therapists shaking their heads, his personality is not alcoholic. Drink to Sir John is just a means of enhancing his huge enjoyment of life that little bit further. He is a greedy drinker (which the alcoholic is not) because he does not actually need the stuff. It is a luxury; not a necessity. Rochester very badly did need drink, and the charm and wit of his following letter to Savile disguises a serious, urgent and direct request:

Mr Savile,

Do a charity becoming one of your pious principles, in preserving your humble servant Rochester from the imminent peril of sobriety; which, for want of good wine more than company (for I can think like a hermit betwixt God and my own conscience) is very like to befall me. Remember what pains I have formerly taken to wean you from your pernicious resolutions of discretion and wisdom! And, if you have a grateful heart (which is a miracle amongst you statesmen), show it, by directing the bearer to the best wine in town: and pray let not this highest point of sacred friendship be perform'd lightly, but go about it with all due deliberation and care, as holy priests to sacrifice, or as discreet thieves to the wary performance of burglary and shop-lifting. Let your well-discerning palate (the best judge about you) travel from cellar to cellar, and then from piece to piece, till it has lighted on wine fit for its noble choice and my approbation. To engage you the more in this matter, know, I have laid a plot may very probably betray you to the drinking of it. . . .

Dear Savile! as ever thou dost hope to outdo Machiavel, or equal me, send some good wine! So may thy wearied soul at last find rest, no longer hov'ring twixt th' unequal choice of politics and lewdness! Mayst thou be admir'd and lov'd for thy domestic wit, belov'd and cherish'd for thy foreign interest and intelligence.

Rochester.

Note the use of the words 'God' and 'soul', which might be thought self-betraying. Hobbes had effectively said that the human soul does not exist.

Rochester's beguiling, seductive manner of dressing up his imperfections and making traditionally immoral habits seem alluring was such a strong characteristic that in 1680 it received attention in the sermon given at his funeral by the family chaplain, Robert Parsons. Calling the Earl 'one of the greatest of sinners', Parsons went on to say:

He seem'd to affect something singular and paradoxical in his impieties, as well as in his writings, above the reach and thought of other men; taking as much pains to draw others in, and to pervert the right ways of virtue, as the apostles and primitive saints, to save their own souls, and them that heard them. For this was the heightning and amazing circumstances of his sins, that he was so diligent and industrious to recommend and propagate them . . . framing arguments for sin, making proselytes to the great enemy of God, and casting down coronets and crowns before his throne.

So why did Rochester become so keen to 'draw others in'? As ever in his case, there is more than one answer, but perhaps the most obvious is that he was *only doing to others what he felt had been done to him*. He had been corrupted by the Court, and just as the abused child often becomes an abusing parent, so the Earl corrupted others with a sense of self-justification. He had also inherited a great zeal from his mother, and once he found he could not practise his brand of ideal morality at Whitehall, it was natural for him to parody the debauchery he saw there with a kind of religious fever. In sin, he was as devout as the most pious churchman. Thirdly, and to quote Robert Wolseley's preface to the Earl's version of Fletcher's *Valentinian*, staged in 1684, Rochester had 'a natural love to justice *and truth*' (my italics). This quest for truth led him to rummage in Nature's dustbin and come up with the absolute certainties of desire, lust and appetite. He knew that anybody who denies having ever felt one of those three things was a liar, and by persuading others to join him in exercising what might be called mankind's lowest common denominators, he could prove his increasing cynicism about human nature to be right. It was a self-justifying process.

There is a fourth reason as to why he tried to wean friends like Savile from their 'pernicious resolutions of discretion and wisdom': alocoholics cannot abide drinking in the company of light drinkers or teetotallers, as it makes them feel awkward and abnormal. They therefore tend to be notably persistent in shoving drink onto others.

The astonishing reach of Rochester's poetry, from gentle lyricism to some of the most brutal satire ever written, was helped and so some extent accounted for by his alcoholism. The implications of the condition go so much further than many people would think. Most experts – the scientists, doctors and therapists – are agreed that while acoholics have personalities as varying as those of normal drinkers, they also tend to share a number of characteristics *quite apart from drunkenness*. Alcoholics are a breed apart, and the organisation Alcoholics Annonymous was formed on the basis that they, at least, understand each other. Chief among the most common characteristics is anger, which courses through Rochester's poetry as fiercely as the wine did through his veins.

Alcoholism marks the Earl's poetry just as distinctly as the Hobbism which not only excused his drinking but encouraged it. 'A Ramble in St James's Park', written in the 1670s, which veers rapidly from wry, almost passive amusement to demonic anger, was written by a man whose aggressive mood swings were symptomatic of the illness, and the ingenious 'Upon Nothing' is a veritable anthem for the drinker who stares through the bottom of a glass darkly and morosely declares that life just 'isn't worth it'. Apart from the havoc it played with his daily existence in general, Rochester's massive consumption of wine certainly limited the actual output of his work and was probably to blame for the sometimes unpolished style of his poetry as well. However, he did work harder at his writing than has often been suggested, and drink paradoxically fuelled his poetic range and lent a menacing edge to his satire. This is not to say that he wrote poetry when he was drunk (not even Dylan Thomas did that), but it does take approximately six months for the alcoholic to completely dry out. On that basis, the Earl was forever 'in drink', and its residues seeped through his brain and body even when he believed he was thinking objectively.

Drinking alcoholics (as opposed to non-drinking ones) are notoriously prone to say exactly what they feel like saying, and for Rochester, who told his confessor that he once went five years without being sober, this was to result in poetry which astonishes for its spontaneity of feeling and freedom of language. There has been some pretty ripe pseudo-intellectual nonsense talked by academics about his supposedly deliberate manner of removing Reichian layers of artificiality, when it would have been rather more relevant to consider the cataclysmic and destructive way in which drink unlocks the mind of the alcoholic, creating what might be called a distoted form of openness. Such pretentious scholarly analysis would have earnt a slapped wrist from Rochester himself:

> And we have modern cloistered coxcombs who
> Retire to think, 'cause they have nought to do.

The only classic symptom of alcoholism which Rochester never exhibited was deceit about his drinking. He revelled in his perceived immorality, waving the bottle under the noses of contemporaries for whom, by and large, he had no respect whatsoever. The tragedy is that even if he were alive today, the tabloid newspapers would simply categorise him as a 'hell-raiser' and a 'boozer'. While the general public has been rightly quick to recognise the eating disorders of anorexia and bulimia as illnesses, moral high ground prevents us from seeing the drinking disorder of alcoholism – for which there is no cure – in the same light. (Abstinence remains the alcoholic's only realistic option, but it is a form of control and *not* a cure.) To this day, many people – particularly the young – view Rochester as a swashbuckling, happy-go-lucky and live-and-let-die cavalier, largely because they associate drinking purely with having fun and are therefore blind to the living hell of 'active' alcoholism. It is not easy for people to understand an addiction to something which the majority can take or leave. Alcohol is not, after all, an intrinsically addictive drug. If it were, then the vast majority of the world's population would be alcoholic. Nevertheless, the following passage, taken from 'The First Special Report to the U.S. Congress on Alcohol and Health' in 1973, describes a condition which has been known by millions down the centuries; a helpless and ghastly path which the Earl of Rochester, without knowing it, was now approaching:

> The pain the alcoholic person feels is the pain of self-loathing and humiliation . . . from loss of respect of his family and friends . . . from growing isolation and loneliness . . from the awareness that he is throwing away much of his unique and creative self and gradually destroying his body and soul. He doesn't usually mean to get drunk, really drunk – he just wants to take the value from alcohol. Getting drunk really drunk as only an alcoholic becomes, is a nightmare of lost memories, retching, vertigo, the shakes, and a profound melancholy of regret. Sometimes it becomes a living nightmare of terrifying visions, screaming accusatory voices, and convulsions.
>
> Who would seek such experiences knowingly? . . .

(Of course, alcoholism afflicts women too and the use of the word 'he' is not the author's discrimination but the language of the 1970s.)

The business of actually identifying an alcoholic seems to cause people a curious amount of difficulty, and this in turn adds to the drinker's overwhelming sense of isolation. Everyone has heard of the condition, and yet unless they spot somebody lying prone and stupified in the gutter, they prefer to use that wonderfully coy phrase, 'a drink problem'. There is no such thing as a drink problem. The phrase is as mythical as it is coy. If anyone with a supposed drink problem evern learns to drink moderately again, then alcohol was being used as a prop and was never the problem in itself. If the problem really is drink, then the person is an alcoholic and will never learn, no matter how hard they try, to drink normally. To omit an explanation of these basic medical laws would be to miss the axis of the Earl's life, the core of his personality. There is no corner of an alcoholic's life which drink will not eventually massacre, and when Rochester was helped into the deathbed at High Lodge he had nowhere left to hide.

Even the medical profession is still struggling to understand this condition, although for the most part doctors have at least come to terms with the fact that it is a definitive illness. The problem lies in comprehending the machinations of the alcoholic's brain, and when Max Glatt, one of the world's leading authorities on alcoholism, told the journalist Jeffrey Bernard that 'if you want to understand alcoholism, ask an alcoholic', he was hardly the first expert to sound a trifle bemused. No wonder that in her brilliant biography of Charles II, Antonia Fraser calls Rochester a 'virtual' alcoholic. Virtual? If a man who, by the age of thirty-three, had drunk himself into impotence, physical collapse, a possible nervous breakdown and finally death was not a *chronic* alcoholic, then: who is?

But what made the Earl so archetypally alcoholic was his substition of drink for God. Alcoholism can be a peculiarly religious condition, and the organisation Alcoholics Anonymous puts such an emphasis on God, or 'a Power greater than ourselves' that many people are put off by the almost evangelical atmosphere of meetings. These even end with a quasi-religious 'prayer' about changing the things in life which can be changed, accepting the things which cannot, and possessing the wisdom to know the difference. Most of the AA's twelve steps to recovery mention God; Step Three, for example, is the affirmation of the alcoholic's decision 'to turn our will and lives over to the care of God as we understand him'. (The actor Sir Anthony Hopkins has told the story of how, when he decided to stop drinking in the 1970s, he went to a self-help group and was advised to 'trust in God'.) This does not necessarily mean the Christian God; it is a substitution of one certainty for a less damaging one, and the meaning of God is open for each recovering alcoholic to interpret in his or her own way – just as it is for all other people. In 1667, Rochester dismissed spirituality as fanciful and turned to the happy oblivion of the bottle instead.

❧ ❧ ❧

As regards Rochester's attitude to women, his twinning of Cupid with Bacchus as his 'saints' does not mean that he put the 'fairer sex' on pedestals and treated them in a romantically naïve way. His treatment of them is much more complicated, and, by the standards of some of his drinking partners at Whitehall, surprisingly full of respect. In the 1660s any woman who married a man of Rochester's standing immediately surrendered all of her rights. In the eyes of the law, married women were not even recognised as independent. So when Elizabeth Mallet walked from the altar she made her money his money, her body his body, and became his goods and chattels. Rochester, however, never abused what he clearly believed was hers and not his. His letters to his wife frequently mention his stewardship of her fortune, and when he spent some of it without her permission he acknowledged that he had done so, in terms of remorse. This is something which was uncharacteristic of most men at the time. At Court, Rochester was surrounded by friends whose treatment of their wives was dismissive at best, contemptuous at worst. The King himself, capable of groping a mistress in any public gallery, hardly behaved towards his own wife with respect, and this became a characteristic which helped him to diminish him in the eyes of the Earl.

Rochester's treatment of his wife and mother was steeped in respect, but his relationship with women in general was tied up in his own dangerous extremities. As we all know, the more passionate love becomes, the greater the risk of hatred stealing in and destroying all that is gentle. Rochester's problem with women was summed up by Catullus:

Odi et amo: quare id faciam, fortasse requiris.
Nescio, sed fieri sentio et excrucior.

(I hate and I love: why I do so you may well ask. I do not know,
but I feel it happen and am in agony.)

The 'Low Life' journalist Jeffrey Bernard, who has much
more self-awareness than Rochester had and enjoys friendships
with many of his former lovers and wives, once described sex
as a means of 'defusing' women. In a spirit of greater aggression,
Rochester took a similar tack nonetheless. One of the lines in
The Man of Mode which gave Dorimant away as being a
representation of the Earl is the triumphant declaration: 'Next
to the coming to a good understanding with a new mistress, I
love a quarrel with an old one.' For Rochester, women were a
glorious enemy, and he could interpret sex in even his most
lyrical poetry as a way of destroying feminine power. This was a
game that could end in tones of defeat for the woman and
victory for the man:

> As Chloris full of harmless thought
> Beneath the willows lay,
> Kind love a comely shepherd brought
> To pass the time away.
>
> She blushed to be encountered so
> And chid the amorous swain,
> But as she strove to rise and go,
> He pulled her back again.
>
> A sudden passion seized her heart
> In spite of her disdain;
> She found a pulse in every part
> And love in every vein.
>
> 'Ah, youth!' quoth she. 'What charms are these
> That conquer and surprise?
> Ah, let me – for unless you please,
> I have no power to rise.'

She faintly spoke, and trembling lay,
For fear he should comply,
But virgins' eyes their hearts betray
And give their tongues the lie.

Thus she, who princes had denied
With all their pompous train,
Was in the lucky minute tried
And yielded to the swain.

No doubt the modern day feminist can smell insinuations of rape in those verses, but Rochester's flippant treatment of such a serious subject should be put into the context of his own age and society. The playwrights of the 1660s and '70s – even the female author of *The Rover*, Aphra Behn – were liberal in their treatment of women. These were not refined, delicate little creatures wafting around the stage in the manner of Shakespeare's Juliet or Ophelia; their sexual appetites were made clear to the audiences while they embarked on a game of mutual flirtation and deception with their male protagonists. Besides, the poem quoted above is about persuasion and not force.

Rochester was now married to the woman who in the spring of 1665 had told him she wanted nothing to do with him, and persuasion to the Earl was fundamental to the art of loving. Seduction, for him, lay at the core of sexuality. The trick was in getting a woman to recognise and give vent to her desires, preferably including him in the performance of them. This has nothing to do with rape, which, as most people understand, is motivated more by a cruel sense of power and abuse than it is by sex itself. However, Rochester went one risky step further in his poetry, provoking the understandable wrath of many female English students today, by cracking an ironic and flippant joke about rape in the following verses:

Fair Chloris in a pigsty lay;
Her tender herd lay by her.
She slept; in murmering gruntlings they,
Complaining of the scorching day,
Her slumbers thus inspire.

She dreamt whilst she with careful pains
Her snowy arms employed
In ivory pails to fill out grains,
One of her love-convicted swains
Thus hasting to her cried:

'Fly, nymph! Oh, fly ere 'tis too late
A dear, loved life to save;
Rescue your bosom pig from fate
Who now expires, hung in the gate
That leads to Flora's cave.

'Myself had tried to set him free
Rather than brought the news,
But I am so abhorred by thee
That ev'n thy darling's life from me
I know thou wouldst refuse.'

Struck with the news, as quick she flies
As blushes to her face;
Not the bright lightning from the skies,
Nor love, shot from her brighter eyes,
Move half so swift a pace.

This plot, it seems the lustful slave
Had laid against her honour,
Which not one god took care to save,
For he pursues her to the cave
And throws himself upon her.

Now piercèd is her virgin zone;
She feels the foe within it.
She hears a broken amorous groan,
The panting lover's fainting moan,
Just in the happy minute.

Frightened she wakes, and waking frigs.
Nature thus kindly eased
In dreams raised by her murmuring pigs
And her own thumb between her legs,
She's innocent and pleased.

Again, allowances should be made for the age in which the Earl was writing. Restoration poets and playwrights were no more politically correct than their audiences, and there were very few subjects which were sacreligious. If life was not exactly cheap in the seventeenth century, it was certainly not treated preciously. In *The Man of Mode*, for example, Rochester's alter-ego, Dorimant, declares: 'Take notice henceforward, who's wanting in his duty; the next clap he gets, he shall rot for an example.' That was a laugh-line – and yet clap, or pox, was a ghastly, often fatal infection which plagued Restoration society. If AIDS had afflicted the age, playwrights like Etherege would certainly have included similar jokes about it and the audiences would still have laughed. Neither do comical references to serious topics on-stage or in poetry necessarily express the view held of them by the author in reality. For Rochester to have made a poetic joke about rape does not mean he laughed about the subject in conversation, and besides, the above poem concerns the *fantasy* of being raped and not rape itself. The verses are as harmless as they are tasteless, and we must be careful of fusing reality with fiction.

Did the Earl actually *like* women? The question is bound to be posed by some readers, but it is largely irrelevant for two reasons. First, the words 'like' and 'dislike' were not really part of this passionate and extreme man's life. He thought no more moderately than he acted. Yet he certainly had female friends, among them Nell Gwyn and Jane Roberts, another of Charles's mistresses. Second, Rochester was a misanthropist and not a misogynist. If he ranted against women it was no more than he did against men, and in fact it was rarely done as contemptuously. In his poetry he generally shows a higher esteem for women than he does for men, and he definitely has higher expectations of them. Men are frequently dismissed *on sight* (in 'Tunbridge Wells' and 'A Ramble in St James's Park', for instance) as idiots. The fact that Rochester does treat the genders so differently opens him up to the charge of being sexist, which is an accusation no seventeenth-century courtier would possibly have understood. It is hardly even fair to level it, when the Earl lived in such a blatantly sexist society. Like all of us, Rochester was a product of his environment.

As a lover, Rochester, like many intrinsic romantics, expected too much. As Daphne's punchline to Strephon indicates ('Whilst you vainly thought me true/I was false in scorn of you'), he fell into a self-protecting and cynical mistrust of women. When his most famous mistress, Elizabeth Barry, finally proved unfaithful to him he gave vent to his fury and despair in tones reeking horribly of self-justification: 'I can see every woman in you, and from yourself am convinced I have never been in the wrong in my opinion of women'. To form such a sweeping generalism about women in general from an opinion about one woman in particular is to lash out in the kind of directionless and impotent rage which may also have accounted for the following lines. Their authorship is uncertain, but an angry and despairing Rochester is a very probable culprit. Certainly, they contain an underlying respect for women (which prevents the poet from being dismissive) which is so characteristic of the Earl:

> Trust not that thing called woman: she is worse
> Than all ingredients crammed into a curse.
> Were she but ugly, peevish, proud, a whore,
> Poxed, painted, perjured, so she were no more,
> I could forgive her, and connive at this,
> Alleging still she but a woman is.
> But she is worse: in time she will forestall
> The devil, and be the damning of us all.

In both his poetry and his life, Rochester could look upon women as having an intrinsic, natural power over man, and this perceived dangerousness absolutely captivated him. In his eyes, it took on a kind of majesty – and for a fleeting moment in 'A Ramble in St James's Park' his fascination for the coldly dismissive Corinna borders on masochism. The poet's former lover stares at him with such contempt that he is moved to murmur in sheer wonderment:

> But mark what creatures women are:
> How infinitely vile, when fair!

The impotence eventually caused by his alcoholism, combined with the bitter taste left by the collapse of his affair with Elizabeth Barry at the start of 1678, resulted in an indifference towards women during his final two years of life. Yet during 'the happy minute' of his early adulthood, Rochester followed the poetic tradition of equating love of women with love of God by adapting some verses by the early Stuart religious poet, Francis Quarles. Taking a poem from Quarles's 'The Divine Emblems', Cupid's young worshipper substituted references to 'Lord' with 'Love':

> Why do'st thou shade thy lovely face? O why
> Does that eclipsing hand of thine deny
> The sunshine of the sun's enlivening eye?
>
> Without any light, what light remains in me?
> Thou are my life; my way, my light's in thee;
> I live, I move, and by thy beams I see.
>
> Thou art my life – if thou but turn away,
> My life's a thousand deaths, thou art my way –
> Without thee (love) I travel not but stray . . .

According to Anthony Hamilton, author of *The Memoirs of Count Grammont*, it was not long before Rochester was stalking the royal maids of honour. When a Miss Goditha Price, Maid of Honour to the Duchess of York, spread gossip about one of the Earl's young mistresses, he responded with a flood of vitriolic satire about her. Miss Price, who, as Hamilton observes, had drawn upon herself the most dangerous enemy in the world, was soon a laughing stock throughout the palace. The Earl also used all his cunning in an attempt to seduce the gullible Miss Anne Temple, another maid of honour to the Duchess of York, and who Pepys had recorded seeing at the ball to celebrate the Queen's birthday on 15 November 1666. Rochester, writes Hamilton,

> began to mislead her by reading to her all his compositions as if she alone had been a proper judge of them. He never throught proper to flatter her upon her personal accomplishments, but told her that if heaven had made him susceptible of the impressions of beauty, it would not have been possible for him to have escaped her chains; but not being, thank God, affected with anything but wit, he had the

happiness of enjoying the most agreeable conversation in the world without running any risk. After so sincere a confession, he either presented her a copy of verses, or a new song, in which, whoever dared to come in competition in any respect with Miss Temple, was laid prostrate before her charms, most humbly to solicit pardon: such flattering insinuations so completely turned her head, that it was a pity to see her.

Hamilton explains how the Duchess of York, in an attempt to ward the Earl off, put Miss Temple under the care of an older woman, Miss Hobart. Since it transpired that Miss Hobart was lesbian, the unfortunate Anne Temple now found herself under seige from two directions. Hamilton, who could tell a story brilliantly, describes a wonderful scene in which the unsuspecting Miss Temple, having been out riding, asked Miss Hobart for permission to get undressed and changed. This request was granted with some enthusiasm by Miss Hobart, who embraced the poor girl and declared: 'You cannot imagine, my dear Temple, how much you oblige me by this free, unceremonious conduct, but, above all, I am enchanted with your particular attention to cleanliness.' She then proceeded to undress Miss Temple, saying it was with the greatest pleasure that she showed her such a small mark of civility, and added: 'Let us retire to the bathing closet, where we may enjoy a little conversation secure from any impertinent visit.' It gets better. Miss Hobart began to impart some advice. 'You are too young, my dear Temple, to know the baseness of men in general and too short a time acquainted with the Court to know the character of its inhabitants.' This led her onto a character assassination of one John Wilmot:

Lord Rochester is, without contradiction, the most witty man in all England; but then he is like-wise the most unprincipled, and devoid even of the least tincture of honour: he is dangerous to our sex alone, and that to such a degree, that there is not a woman who gives ear to him three times but she irretrievably loses her reputation. No woman can escape him, for he has her in his writings, though his other attacks be ineffectual . . . he applauds your taste, submits to your sentiments, and at the very instant that he himself does not believe a single word of what he is saying, he makes you believe it all. I dare lay a wager, that from the conversation you have had with him, you thought him one of the most honourable and sincerest men living . . . what horrid malice possesses him, to the ruin and confusion of innocence. A wretch!

Miss Hobart then produced some of the verses in which Rochester had lampooned Miss Price. She had, however, cunningly replaced Miss Price's name with that of Miss Temple, who, naturally enough, burst into tears. The upshot of the story, which read like something out of *Les Liaisons Dangereuses*, was that Rochester got to hear of Miss Hobart's little game and, with the help of friend and drinking-partner Harry Killigrew, took his revenge, in the end seriously damaging his rival's reputation. Miss Temple, however, appears to have escaped the Earl's clutches, since Hamilton says he was banished from Court soon after and retired to the country. During Rochester's absence, Miss Temple was approached by Sir Charles Lyttelton, the former Governor of Jamaica, and the couple duly married. She spent most of the rest of her life in the country and gave birth to no less than thirteen children.

According to Hamilton, Rochester had much better luck when Miss Hobart fixed her attentions on another girl in her care, 'the governess's niece', Sarah. The 'governess', or mother of the maids, voiced her concern about this relationship to Rochester, who agreed that the girl should definitely be taken out of Miss Hobart's hands and 'contrived matters so well, that she fell into his own'. Both aunt and niece were then dismissed for associating with him, and he took them into the country. Hamilton claims the Earl found Sarah a place the following winter in the King's Players, whereupon the public 'was obliged to him for the prettiest, but, at the same time, the worst actress in the Kingdom'. It has been suggested that this Sarah was the famous Restoration actress Sarah Cook, who created more than a dozen leading roles and spoke two of the three different prologues during the opening nights of Rochester's adaptation of *Valentinian* in 1684. Although the Earl certainly displayed a penchant for nurturing the careers of actresses (as he proved with Elizabeth Barry), the dates do not, in this case, add up. Hamilton's story refers to the mid or late 1660s;

Sarah Cook's first recorded performance was in 1677. Neither does Hamilton's description of 'the worst actress in the Kingdom' apply to the excellent Sarah Cook. While it is tempting to think that Rochester created two great acting careers, it looks much likelier to have been just the one.

Easily the best way of understanding how Rochester moved through life at this time is to look, briefly, at the character of Dorimant in Etherege's *The Man of Mode*. The play was first staged in March 1676, by which time Rochester was a sick man who, beneath the surface, had little in common with the jovial character drawn by his playwright friend. Dorimant has much more in common with the 1660s version of Rochester for, as the 1670s progressed, the Earl presented a public face which was in complete contrast to his increasing private unhappiness. Dorimant is a charming, witty, funny handsome and very civilised rogue. His consumate style and light-hearted spirit disguise his outrageous selfishness. He delights in upsetting women – particularly the temperamental Mrs Loveit – and is ruthless in his pursuit of them. He is also, in a jocular manner, insulting and abusive towards his servants – and this was a particularly strong characteristic of Rochester's. The Earl's friend, Robert Wolseley, said of him:

Never was his talk thought too much or his visit too long; enjoyment did but increase appetite, and the more men had of his company, the less willing they were to part with it. He had a wit that cou'd make even his spleen and his ill-humour pleasant to his friends, and the public chiding of his servants, which wou'd have been ill-breeding and intolerable in any other man, became not only civil and inoffensive, but agreeable and entertaining in him.

Somehow, then, Rochester's charm, like Dorimant's, lifted him clear of censure. When the audiences came to see *The Man of Mode* it was just one or two people who realised that Dorimant represented the Earl – everybody did. The critic John Dennis declared:

. . . upon the first acting this comedy it was generally believed to be an agreeable representation of the persons of condition of both sexes, both in Court and Town; and that all the world was charmed with Dorimont [sic]; and that it was unanimously agreed that he had in him several of the qualities of Wilmot, Earl of Rochester, as, his wit, his spirit, his amorous temper, the charms that he had for the fair sex, his falsehood and his inconstancy; the agreeable manner of his chiding his servants, which the late Bishop of Salisbury [Burnet] takes notice of in his life; and lastly, the repeating, on every occasion, the verses of Waller, for whom that noble lord had a very particular esteem; witness his Imitation of the Tenth Satire of the First Book of Horace:

> Waller, by Nature for the Bays designed,
> With spirit, force, and fancy unconfined,
> In Panegyric is above mankind.

St Evremond agreed too, saying that 'Sir George Etherege wrote Dorimant in *Sir Fopling* [the play's alternative title], in complement to him [Rochester], as drawing his Lordship's character and burnishing all the foibles of it, to make them shine like perfections'. Realising that he was immortalising his friend's character, Etherege was careful to overlook the matter of drink: Dorimant is wayward, but sober. His pace, energy and sheer *joie de vivre* are established from the moment the lights go up:

ACT ONE, SCENE ONE

A dressing-room, a table covered with a toilet, clothes laid ready.

Enter Dorimant in his gown and slippers, with a note in his hand made up, repeating verses.

Dorimant: Now for some ages had the pride of Spain,
             Made the sun shine on half the world in vain.

Then looking on the note.

             For Mrs Loveit. What a dull insipid thing is a billet
             doux written in cold blood, after the heat of the

business is over! It is a tax upon good nature which I have here been labouring to pay, and have done it, but with as much regret as ever fanatic paid the Royal Aid or Church Duties. 'Twill have the same fate, I know, that all my notes to her have had of late; 'twill not be thought kind enough. Faith, women are i' the right when they jealously examine our letters, for in them we always first discover our decay of passion. – Hey! – Who waits!

Enter Handy.

Handy: Sir?

Dorimant: Call a footman.

Handy: None of 'em are come yet.

Dorimant: Dogs! Will they ever lie snoring a-bed till noon?

Handy: 'Tis all one, sir, if they're up, you indulge 'em so, they're ever poaching after whores all the morning.

Dorimant: Take notice henceforward, who's wanting in his duty; the next clap he gets, he shall rot for an example. What vermin are those chattering without?

Handy: Foggy Nan the orange-woman, and swearing Tom the shoemaker.

Dorimant: Go, call in that overgrown jade with the flasket of guts before her; fruit is refreshing in a morning.

It is not that I love you less
Than when before your feet I lay.

Exit Handy.

Enter Orange-Woman.

	How now double tripe, what news do you bring?
Orange-Woman:	News! Here's the best fruit has come to town t'year. Gad, I was up before four o'clock this morning, and bought all the choice i' the market.
Dorimant:	The nasty refuse of your shop.
Orange-Woman:	You need not make mouths at it, I assure you 'tis all culled ware.
Dorimant:	The citizens buy better on a holiday in their walk to Tottenham.
Orange-Woman:	Good or bad, 'tis all one; I never know you commend anything. Lord, would the ladies had heard you talk of 'em as I have done! Here, bid your man give me an angel.

Sets down the fruit.

Dorimant:	Give the bawd her fruit again.
Orange-Woman:	Well, on my conscience, there never was the like of you. God's my life, I had almost forgot to tell you; there is a young gentlewoman come to town with her mother, that is so taken with you.
Dorimant:	Is she handsome?
Orange-Woman:	Nay, gad, there are few finer women, I tell you but so, and a hugeous fortune they say. Here, eat this peach, it comes from the stone, 'tis better than any Newington y'have tasted.

Dorimant: [*taking the peach*]; This fine woman, I'll lay my life, is some awkward ill-fashioned country toad, who, not having above four dozen of black hairs on her head, has adorned her baldness with a large white fruz, that she may look sparkishly in the forefront of the King's box at an old play.

Orange-Woman: Gad, you'd change your note quickly if you did but see her.

And, of course, he does. Harriet is a tough and witty woman who draws Dorimant in and seems likely, at the end of the play, to prove his nemesis.

※ ※ ※

Thomas Hearne's remark that Rochester was 'very barbarous to his own lady, tho' so very fine a woman' is relative, since no other woman ever received such consistent tenderness (fuelled by remorse) from the Earl. His crimes as a husband were twofold: absence and fidelity. She had said herself that nothing aided love's fond fire more than 'scorn and cold disdain', and Rochester was keenly aware of the peculiar way in which many people seem to become hooked on shoddy treatment. However, in the case of Lady Rochester his neglect was never calculated and always regretted. The affection of his letters home was already being matched by the guilt he expressed in them:

I kiss my dear wife a thousand times, as much as imagination and wish will give me leave. Think upon me as long as it is pleasant and convenient to do so and afterwards forget me; for though I would fain make you the author and foundation of my happiness, yet would I not be the cause of your constraint and disturbance, for I love not myself as much as I do you; neither do I value my own satisfaction equally as I do yours. Farewell.

His appreciation of his 'more than meritorious wife' caused him to speak of himself as a 'straying fool', and yet the poem most obviously written with her in mind also implies that self-torment is all he is worth. In these verses Rochester portrays himself with the lack of self-respect so typical of the alcoholic, and we are reminded of Robert Parson's comment at the Earl's funeral that 'so confirmed was he in sin, that he lived, and oftentimes almost died, a martyr for it':

> Absent from thee; I languish still;
> Then ask me not, when I return?
> The straying fool 'twill plainly kill
> To wish all day, all night to mourn.
>
> Dear! from thine arms then let me fly,
> That my fantastic mind may prove
> The torments it deserves to try
> That tear my fixed heart from my love.
>
> When, wearied with a world of woe,
> To thy safe bosom I retire
> Where love and peace and truth does flow,
> May I contented there expire,
>
> Lest, once more wandering from that heaven,
> I fall on some base heart unblest,
> Faithless to thee, false, unforgiven,
> And lose my everlasting rest.

It is as though Rochester saw himself, from the very start of his 'fall', as having a kind of duty to perform in showing his society the error of its ways. He writes like someone who is going out on a very costly solo adventure in order to hurl his indignation.

> At the pretending part of the proud world,
> Who, swollen with selfish vanity, devise
> False freedoms, holy cheats, and formal lies
> Over their fellow slaves to tyrannize.

'If he did not take so much care of himself as he ought,' wrote his friend Robert Wolseley, 'he had the humanity, however, to wish well to others, and I think I may truly affirm, he did the world as much good by the right application of satire as he hurt himself by a wrong pursuit of pleasure.'

And he was not taking care of himself at all. Burnet said:

There were two principles in his natural temper, that being heightened by that heat carried him to great excesses: a violent love of pleasure and a disposition to extravagant mirth. The one involved him in great sensuality; the other led him to many odd adventures and frolics, in which he was oft in hazard of his life. The one being the same irregular appetite in his mind that the other was in his body, which made him think nothing diverting that was not extravagant. And though in cold blood he was a generous and good natured man, yet he would go far in his heats after anything that might turn to a jest or matter of diversion.

Only one story shows him having a self-restraint of sorts: he and his fellow 'Ballers' were at the Bear listening to a fiddler known as 'His Honour' play, when his companions all agreed on leaping into the Thames. Rochester was to have been the last to jump, but, suddenly going off the idea, he shoved the fiddler in and shouted: 'I can't come myself gentlemen, so I've sent my honour.'

The Earl's declaration to Burnet that he had never improved his position at Court by doing a premeditated mischief to other people was an astonishing piece of self-deception. As Burnet observed: 'Yet he laid out his wit very freely in libels and satires, in which he had a peculiar talent of mixing his wit with his malice, and fitting both with such apt words, that men were tempted to be pleased with them.' Not the men (and women) who were the targets of the attacks, however. One of his favoured methods of gleaning information about fornicating or adulterating couples was to use a spy. 'He found out a footman that knew all the Court, and he furnished him with a red coat and a musket as a sentinel, and kept him all the winter long, every night, at the doors of such ladies as he believed might be in intrigues,' said Burnet, who explained that this did not arouse suspicion, for sentinels were usually believed to be guarding a doorway in order to prevent a duel from taking place. 'By this means Lord Rochester made many discoveries, and when he was thus furnished with materials, he used to retire into the country for a month or two to write libels.' Rochester also acquired information by dressing in disguise and moving about the city undetected. 'He took pleasure to disguise himself as a porter or as a beggar,' wrote Burnet, 'sometimes to follow some mean amours, which for the variety of them, he affected; at other times merely for diversion, he would go about in odd shapes, in which he acted his part so naturally that even those who were [in] on the secret and saw him in these shapes could perceive nothing by which he might be discovered.' These shapes included his most famous impersonation, that of Dr Alexander Bendo.

More than any other kind of creature, Rochester was an actor – and he had the actor's classic ego. In one letter to Elizabeth Barry he seems rather pleased to be able to call himself, with perfect accuracy, 'the wildest and most fantastical odd man alive'. He was a sublime eccentric and relished the fact that he was both feared and widely talked about. His apparent, brilliance at dressing in disguise is at the centre of another story told by Anthony Hamilton. According to the author of the *Memoirs of Count Grammont*, Rochester spent a while living in the city among the merchants:

For this purpose he changed his name and dress, so as to gain admission to their entertainments and partake of their pleasures, and, as soon as an opportunity arose, those of their fair spouses. As he was able to adapt himself to every mentality, it was remarkable how soon he insinuated himself into the good graces of the coarse but wealthy merchants and those of their more delicate, magnificent and tender helpmates. He [Rochester] soon gained admittance to all their parties and junketings.

In conversation, he would rail against the disgusting behaviour of the King's courtiers and denounce the royal mistresses. He also said that he could not understand for the life of him why fire had not descended from heaven onto Whitehall for the toleration of wretches such as that disgraceful man the Earl of Rochester.

As far as the wits were concerned, the failure of the Dutch war provided Charles with the perfect opportunity to get rid of the detested Edward Hyde, Earl of Clarendon, who continued to disapprove in the strongest terms of the Court's dissoluteness. Once again, pressure was being put on the King by popular demand and, a month after taking his seat in the House of Lords, Rochester was one of those who followed Buckingham's example and signed a protest in favour of the Lord Chancellor's impeachment. Charles, as weary of Clarendon's chiding manner as anybody, persuaded him to go into exile, and the man who had towered over the politics of the reign since its beginning duly fled to France. His departure only granted the wits even more licence to misbehave and it gave rise to a new wave of politicians led by the dreaded Buckingham. Clarendon's undoubted pomposity was not the only thing about him which Rochester despised; he was bound to have known that the Chancellor had disapproved of his father. That would explain why his epitaph for Clarendon, which included the lines

> This shrub of gentry, married to the Crown
> His daughter to the heir, is tumbled down;
> The grand despiser of the nobles lies
> Grovelling in dust, as a just sacrifice;

was so vicious. On another occasion, when the King and the wits were struggling to find a word which would rhyme with Lisbon, Rochester is said to have called out:

> A health to Kate!
> Our sovereign's mate,
> Of the royal house of Lisbon;
> But the devil take Hyde
> And the bishop beside
> Who made her bone his bone.

In February 1668, at about the time he was made Keeper of the King's game in Oxford, the Earl was promoting John Dryden's poetic credentials at Court. In April, Dryden was appointed Poet Laureate, and Rochester continued to act as his patron until 1675, when the two men fell out. It is unlikely that they were ever close friends – apart from being writers they had very little in common –

but for seven years Rochester was the recipient of some typically theatrical hyperbole from Dryden, who was nonetheless grateful for the part the Earl seems to have played in his appointment as Poet Laureate. Once, when Rochester was staying in the country, he received a letter from Dryden which stated, somewhat preposterously:

> You are that Rerum Natura of your own Lucretius, Ipsa suis pollens opibus, nihil indiga nostri: You are above any incense I can give you . . . Your friends in town are ready to envy the leisure you have given yourself in the country: though they know you are only their steward and that you treasure up but so much health as you intend to spend on them in winter.

This was foolhardy language, since one of Rochester's two pet hates was affectation. (The other was hypocrisy). Self-importance or pretensiousness drew the very worst out of him, for although Hobbism was the philosophy which encouraged him to give vent to baseness, he practised it with a Christian's conviction that everyone was a miserable sinner and had no right whatsoever to be self-admiring. The only question left was who was a knave – or sinner – of the first rate. Thus, there was always something deliberately degrading, punitive and menacing about Rochester's insistence that others should follow his example in the sating of appetite and the pleasures of the flesh; he tended to write about sex, for example, with a relish which was mingled with a puritan's (his mother's) sense of disgust. Half of the Earl's fascination with sex was due to the fact that in his eyes it was dirty; it was original sin and therefore immoral. Meanwhile, the inheritance of the first Earl's traits accounted for Burnet's explanation that the 'licentiousness of his temper, with the briskness of his wit, disposed him to love the conversation of those who divided their time between lewd actions and irregular mirth. And so he came to bend his wit and direct his studies and endeavours to support and strengthen these ill principles both in himself and others.'

In May 1668, Samuel Pepys was appalled to learn that the Ballers had enjoyed an orgy:

> And so to supper in an arbour; but Lord! their mad talk did make my heart ache! And here I first understood by their talk

the meaning of the company that lately were called Ballers; Harris telling how it was by a meeting of some young blades, where he was among them, and my Lady Bennet and her ladies; and their dancing naked, and all the roguish things in the world. But, Lord! what loose company was this, that I was in to-night, though full of wit; and worth a man's being in for once, to know the nature of it, and their manner of talk, and lives.

This reference to Madam Bennet and her girls is not the only reason for believing that Rochester used prostitutes; in his outrageous poem 'The Debauchee' he calls for 'my whore', and Dorimant cruelly mocks the illiteracy of a prostitute he knows called Molly, who sends him an almost indecipherable letter. Granger, in his *A Biographical History of England from Egbert the Great to the Revolution*, says Rochester was 'ever engaged in some amour or other, and frequently with women of the lowest order, and the vilest prostitutes of the town'. In 1669, the Earl was, not surprisingly, being treated for pox. It was around this time that he probably wrote one of his most libertine lyrical poems:

> How perfect Chloris, and how free,
> Would these enjoyments prove,
> But you with formal jealousy
> Are still tormenting love.
>
> Let us, (since wit instructs us how)
> Raise pleasure to the top;
> If rival bottle you'll allow,
> I'll suffer rival fop.
>
> There's not a brisk insipid spark
> That flutters in the town,
> But with your wanton eyes you mark
> Him out to be your own.
>
> Nor ever think it worth your care
> How empty or how dull
> The heads of your admirers are,
> So that their purse be full.

All this you freely may confess
Yet we'll not disagree,
For did you love your pleasures less
You were not fit for me.

While I my passion to pursue
Am whole nights taking in
The lusty juice of grapes, take you
The juice of lusty men –

Upbraid me not that I design
Tricks to delude your charms,
When running after mirth and wine
I leave your longing arms.

For wine (whose power alone can raise
Our thoughts, so far above),
Affords ideas fit to praise
What we think fit to love.

It was in a similar vein that he wrote his poem 'Against Constancy':

Tell me no more of constancy,
The frivalous pretence
Of cold age, narrow jealousy,
Disease, and want of sense.

Let duller fools, on whom kind chance
Some easy heart has thrown,
Despairing higher to advance,
Be kind to one alone.

Old men and weak, whose idle flame
Their own defects discovers,
Since changing can but spread their shame,
Ought to be constant lovers.

But we, whose hearts to justly swell
With no vainglorious pride,

Who know how we in love excel,
Long to be often tried.

Then bring my bath, and strew my bed,
As each kind night returns;
I'll change a mistress till I'm dead -
And fate change me to worms.

Dullness and boredom genuinely frightened Rochester, and he spent all his short life trying to escape them. It is remarkable how often dullness is referred to in his poetry. Apart from the 'duller fools' mentioned in the second stanza of the above poem, there was his realisation that 'none but dull delights endure' in 'The Fall', while in 'The Platonic Lady' he says he hates enjoyment because 'it is a dull employment'. He returned to the subject of tedium in the following snippet too:

Your conquering eyes so partial are,
Or mankind is so dull,
That while I languish in despair,
Many proud, senseless hearts declare
They find you not so killing fair
To wish you merciful.

And again, in another 'Song':

At last you'll force me to confess
You need no arts to vanquish:
Such charms from nature you possess,
'Twere dullness not to languish.
Yet spare a heart you may surprise,
And give my tongue the glory
To scorn, while my unfaithful eyes
Betray a kinder story.

One last example, from 'The Mistress':

When'er those wounding eyes, so full
Of sweetness, you did see,

Had you not been profoundly dull,
You had gone mad like me.

   The philosophy of change so fundamental to Hobbism embraced promiscuity, and Rochester encouraged all his lovers to be as unfaithful as he was. It is easy, however, to be indifferent to infidelity within a casual relationship. Would he still feel the same about someone with whom he was in love? Or would his Hobbism let him down and give way to a jealous, helpless rage? Time would tell.

6

COWARD!

Look to the bottom of his vast design
Wherein man's wisdom, power, and glory join:
The good he acts, the ill he does endure,
'Tis all from fear, to make himself secure.
Merely for safety, after fame we thirst,
For all men would be cowards if they durst.
Rochester, 'A Satire against Reason and Mankind'.

S o long as the Earl of Rochester's reputation for bravery remained intact, he could commend a respect even from those who did not like him. Whereas it is not remarkable in our own times to hear a young man casually confess to being a coward, such a declaration in the Court of King Charles II would have caused a stunned silence resulting in a unanimous contempt. The honour accorded to any man depended upon his readiness and ability to defend that honour. Take, for example, Samuel Pepys's disapproval of Mr Edward Montagu's conduct in a duel with Mr Hugh Cholmeley, first gentleman-usher to the Queen. Cholmeley had 'received many affronts' from Montagu and, when the pair fought, he

proved too hard for Montagu, and drove him so far backward that he fell into a ditch, and dropped his sword, but with honour would take no advantage over him; but did give him his life: and the world says Mr Montagu did carry himself

131

very poorly in the business, and hath lost his honour for ever with all people . . . of which I am very glad, in hopes that it will humble him.

In the space of a few disastrous minutes, then, Montagu wrecked his reputation. At the end of 1669, in peculiar circumstances which are shrouded in mystery, Rochester did precisely the same thing.

All round, 1669 was a bad year for him. On 17 February, Pepys recorded:

The King dining yesterday at the Dutch Ambassador's, after dinner they drank, and were pretty merry; and, among the rest of the King's company, there was that worthy fellow my Lord of Rochester, and Tom Killigrew, whose mirth and raillery offended the former so much, that he did give Tom Killigrew a box on the ear in the King's presence, which do give much offence to the people here at Court, to see how cheap the King makes himself, and the more, for that the King hath not only passed by the thing, and pardoned it to Rochester already, but this very morning the King did publicly walk up and down, and Rochester I saw with him as free as ever, to the King's everlasting shame, to have so idle a rogue his companion. How Tom Killigrew takes it, I do not hear . . .

This incident is the first indication we have that the nature of the Earl's alcoholism was changing and becoming acute. In *The Disease Concept of Alcoholism*, the book which in 1960 took the world of research into alcoholism by storm, Dr E.M. Jellinek warned that both alpha and beta alcoholics could eventually become gamma alcoholics – which is physically and psychologically the most damaging category. Until now, Rochester had been a typical alpha alcoholic, drinking to relieve emotional pain, or, in his own words, 'to wash away my cares'. His eccentricity had certainly violated accepted rules of behaviour, which is one defining factor, and he had not previously lost control to the extent of violence, which is another. (For interest's sake, beta alcoholism involves physical ailments such as nerve disorders and gastritis, but does not mean the drinker is either physically or psychologically hooked. Withdrawal symptoms do not occur, and it is probably the easiest form of alcoholism to beat.) A letter from Lady Sunderland, in which she said that Rochester 'was in a case not to know what he did', confirms that he was drunk at the time.

Gamma alcoholism involves a shift from psychological to physical dependence. (This means Rochester now suffered withdrawal symptoms every time he stopped drinking, even if only for a day.) Most importantly – and this is what signifies the change – it causes extreme behavioural swings, which are all part of the disease syndrome. A 'generous and good-natured man' when sober, Rochester could now be irrational, unpredictable and thoroughly dangerous when drunk. Henceforward, violence would be part of his life.

Jellinek states that gamma alcoholism is a specific disease because it concerns the disturbance of cell metabolism, besides an increase in tissue tolerance to drink, a loss of control and/or the inability to abstain. Both mentally and physically, Rochester was now a sick man. In effect, he was living with a terminal illness, and when one considers that alcoholism weakens all the body's defences against disease and sickness, it is remarkable that the Earl survived until he was thirty-three years old during such a disease-ridden era.

In *Alcohol and the Addictive Brain*, which was recently described by one of the world's leading experts on addictive diseases as a medical classic, and which is dedicated to all people who have died prematurely from alcoholism (which includes Rochester), co-authors De Kenneth Blum and James Payne describe the effects of the worsening alcoholic process.

Other psychological symptoms now begin to appear, and become more apparent as the disease progresses. Memory, reasoning, and judgement become increasingly faulty. Impulsiveness, irritability, and arrogance, even megalomania, may alternate with a growing need for sympathy and understanding. There may be a loss of inhibitions, leading to bizarre behaviour and violations of personal ethics; reality may become hazy, giving way to a rich fantasy life sometimes accompanied by aggressive sexual behaviour. Heavy drinking bouts may be followed by blackouts that leave no memory of events, or a distorted memory that ignores unpleasant happenings . . . the alcoholic is likely to experience a developing sense of panic, interspersed with irritability, quick outbursts of rage, or periods of deep depression.

Gilbert Burnet drew attention to Rochester's bouts of deep depression. 'These exercises in the course of his life were not always equally pleasant to him; he had often sad intervals and severe reflections on them.'

A 'box on the ear' is, of course, a friendly way of saying that Rochester smacked Killigrew in the face. (He later apologised profusely to his friend Harry Killigrew for hitting his father. The apology was accepted.) Although Rochester was banned from Court, the fact that he was strolling along with the King the following day indicates that Charles was merely going through the motions of punishing him and was personally indifferent to the entire episode. If it had not been necessary for him to be *seen* to take some sort of action, one suspects he would have let the matter pass. Pepys was surely right to be appalled to see Charles walking with the Earl, for news of the incident went abroad and cannot have done the Court's reputation any good at all. To hit someone in front of the King was, after all, a grave insult to the authority of monarchy.

So what accounted for the King's amazing tolerance of Rochester, not just with regard to this episode but in general? After all, no other courtier during the reign enjoyed such a licence to misbehave. The answer is twofold. First, Charles's cynicism about human nature was *black*. Burnet reckoned that the King thought nobody was sincere or honest out of principle, that he did not believe anyone served him out of love, 'and therefore he endeavoured to be quits with the world by loving others as little as he thought they loved him'. Rochester's absurdist and satirical view of life suited Charles perfectly. He regarded the Earl, who invariably said exactly what he thought, as much more honest than the courtiers who bowed and scraped before him muttering insincere praises. The two men were very different emotionally – the King was placid and wholly unromantic, while Rochester was fired with passion and he idealised love – but, intellectually, they were close in their cynicism. In particular, the Earl's intellectual doubts about religion shadowed those of Charles, who if anything was even more sceptical than Rochester. He would certainly not have disagreed with the scorning of the clergy in 'A Satire against Reason and Mankind'. Typically, this passage focuses on hypocrisy:

> Is there a churchman who on God relies;
> Whose life, his faith and doctrine justifies?
> Not one blown up with vain prelatic pride,
> Who, for reproof of sins, does man deride;
> Whose envious heart makes preaching a pretence,
> With his obstreperous, saucy eloquence,
> To chide at kings, and rail at men of sense;
> None of that sensual tribe whose talents lie
> In avarice, pride, sloth, and gluttony;
> Who hunt good livings, but abhor good lives;
> Whose lust exalted to that height arrives
> They act adultery with their own wives,
> And ere a score of years completed be,
> Can from the lofty pulpit see
> Half a large parish their own progeny . . .

Rochester then sets out his ideal. What he wants, he says, is

> . . . a meek, humble man of honest sense,
> Who, preaching peace, does practice continence;
> Whose pious life's a proof he does believe
> Mysterious truths, which no man can conceive.
> If upon earth there dwell such God-like men,
> I'll here recant my paradox to them,
> Adore those shrines of virtue, homage pay,
> And, with the rabble world, their laws obey.

But the cynicism takes over for the final couplet:

> If such there be, yet grant me this at least:
> Man differs more from man, than man from beast.

The second reason for Charles's extraordinary toleration of Rochester is quite simply that he thought him terribly funny. Whenever he banished the Earl from Court, he only found himself missing him. In his *History of His Own Time*, Bishop Gilbert Burnet indicates that Charles used Rochester as a means of escaping his own intrinsic melancholy. 'The King loved his [Rochester's] company for the diversion it afforded, better than his person: and there was no love lost between them. He [Rochester] took his revenge in many libels.' Just a couple of months before the Killigrew incident, a disapproving Samuel Pepys had listened to Charles chuckling over Rochester's latest misdemeanour having

> . . . heard the silly discourse of the King, with his people about him, telling a story of my Lord Rochester's having of his clothes stole, while he was with a wench; and his gold all gone, but his clothes found afterwards, stuffed in a feather bed by the wench that stole them.

From an account of a conversation between the King and the Earl, it seems that Rochester knew how Charles used him and that he resented it. The exchange, full of wit, was printed in Edmund Waller's *Letters to M. St. Evremond*, and although the authorship is in doubt it does seem to be a genuine attempt by somebody to record a real conversation. One would have expected a more dramatic dialogue – an argument, perhaps – if the account had been fictional.

Waller explains that he was dining at Rochester's with a 'select party' and that the Earl was being comparatively reserved (in other words, he was reasonably sober): 'On such occasions he is not ambitious of shining . . . you find something in that restraint, which is more agreeable than the utmost exertions of talent in others.' Unexpectedly, towards the end of the evening the King turned up. Rochester turned to his guests and murmured: 'Something has vexed him. He never does me this honour but when he is in an ill-humour.' He was right: Charles was in a bad mood. The most striking aspect of the ensuing dialogue is the way Rochester raises himself and, like a performing monkey or a fool to a Shakespearian monarch, switches on his wit as though it is his duty.

King:	How the devil have I got here? The knaves have sold every cloak in the wardrobe.

Rochester: Those knaves are fools. That is a part of dress, which, for their own sakes, your Majesty ought never to be without.

King: Pshaw! I'm vexed.

Rochester: I hate still-life – I'm glad of it. Your Majesty is never so entertaining as when –

King: Ridiculous! I believe the English are the most intractable people upon earth.

Rochester: I most humbly beg your Majesty's pardon if I presume in that respect . . .

King: You would find them so were you in my place and obliged to govern.

Rochester: Were I in your Majesty's place I would not govern at all.

King: How then?

Rochester: I would send for my good Lord Rochester and command him go govern.

King: But the singular modesty of that nobleman!

Rochester: He would certainly conform himself to your Majesty's bright example! How gloriously would the two grand social virtues flourish under his auspices!

King: O, prisca fides! What can these be?!

Rochester: The love of wine and women!

King: God bless your Majesty!

Rochester:	These attachments keep the world in good humour, and therefore I say they are social virtue. Let the Bishop of Salisbury deny it if he can –
King:	He died last night; have you a mind to succeed him?
Rochester:	On condition that I shall neither be called upon to preach on the thirtieth of January, nor on the twenty-ninth of May [respectively, the dates of Charles I's execution and the Restoration of the monarchy].
King:	These conditions are curious . . . You object to the first, I suppose because it would be a melancholy subject, but the other –
Rochester:	Would be a melancholy subject too.
King:	That is too much –
Rochester:	Nay, I only mean that the business would be a little too grave for the day. Nothing but the indulgence of the two grand social virtues could be a proper testimony of my joy upon that occasion.
King:	Thou art the happiest fellow in my dominions! Let me perish if I do not envy thee thy impudence!

Similarly, Rochester could not help enjoying the King's company. Their mutual love of horse racing accounted for days with each other at Newmarket and they 'made merry' together on many evenings. What angered the Earl about Charles was not only his moral shortcomings as Head of the Church of England but in particular his amazing *passivity*; his sheer *easiness*. Some of Rochester's satire almost seems designed to goad Charles into a response. He succeeded a number of times, and was said by Burnet to have been banned from Court on one occasion because, while drunk, he accidentally took the wrong poem out of his pocket and handed it to Charles. Perhaps the story refers to the Earl's most famous verses about the King, 'A Satire on Charles II':

> I'th' isle of Britain, long since famous grown
> For breeding the best cunts in Christendom,
> There reigns, and oh! long may he reign and thrive,
> The easiest King and best-bred man alive.
> Him no ambition moves to get renown
> Like the French fool, that wanders up and down
> Starving his people, hazarding his crown.
> Peace is his aim, his gentleness is such,
> And love he loves, for he loves fucking much.
> Nor are his high desires above his strength:
> His sceptre and his prick are of a length;
> And she may sway the one who plays with th'other,
> And make him little wiser than his brother.

(His observation in the penultimate line is untrue. As has been noted, the only women who ever really held sway over Charles was his sister, 'Minette'.)

> Poor Prince! thy prick, like thy buffoons at Court,
> Will govern thee because it makes thee sport.
> 'Tis sure the sauciest prick that e'er did swive,
> The proudest, peremptoriest prick alive.
> Though safety, law, religion, life lay on't,
> 'Twould break through all to make its way to cunt.
> Restless he rolls about from whore to whore,
> A merry monarch, scandalous and poor.
> To Carwell, the most dear of all his dears,
> The best relief of his declining years,
> Oft he bewails his fortune, and her fate:
> To love so well, and be beloved so late.
> For though in her he settles well his tarse,
> Yet his dull, graceless ballocks hang an arse.
> This you'd believe, had I but time to tell ye
> The pains it costs to poor, laborious Nelly,

Whilst she employs hands, fingers, mouth and thighs,
Ere she can raise the member she enjoys.
All monarchs I hate, and the thrones they sit on,
From the hector of France to the cully of Britain.

Rochester's poetic language became increasingly aggressive and
lewd as his alcoholism worsened, and this satire was certainly
written after 1670, for it was in 1669 that 'poor, laborious Nelly' –
who was quite bawdy enough to take such a reference to her in
good part – established herself as a royal mistress. She was
pregnant by 1670, the same year that 'Carwell' – Louise de
Kéroualle – came to Court and raised Charles's temperature by
resolutely (at first) clinging on to her virginity. Lady Castlemaine,
Rochester's cousin, was at last falling from favour. Not only had
her sexual avarice become embarrassing but she was now nearly
thirty. As Dorimant informs us with a quite stupendous arrogance,
a woman is in her prime at twenty, decayed at four-and-twenty
and insupportable at thirty. In 1669, Charles was evidently on the
rampage, for besides Nell (who became the most enduring of all
his mistresses) he was enjoying a dalliance with another actress,
Moll Davis. Moll – who bore the King one child compared with
Nell's two – apparently inspired the theatre-going Charles with her
rendering, in *The Rival Ladies*, of a song called 'My Lodging is on
the Cold Ground'. It was John Downes who wrily observed that
this performance raised her from her bed on the cold ground to
the bed royal.

For a biographer of Rochester it is frustrating to note that the
King, wrapped-up in his own intrigues, never seriously attempted
to discipline the Earl or halt his decline. By 1669 it was already
too late, since it is a complete waste of time ever to try and stop a
fully fledged alcoholic from drinking. If he or she wishes to carry
on (and most do) then they will. The only true key to stopping
drinking is to *want* to stop, and very badly at that. Rochester did
not want to until 1678, by which time he had all but drunk himself
to death. Charles could surely, however, have tried to arrest the
dissipation which started to take place under his nose in the
middle of 1667. He could have remembered how a spell in the
Tower had once calmed the heated young Earl down, for a second
dosage might well have had a similarly galvanising effect. But

Charles did absolutely nothing, because his cynicism about other people always prevented him, ultimately from reaching out. Banishments from Court were no more than slaps on the wrist which enabled Rochester to go into the country, spend a while with his wife, and write.

Instead of imprisoning Rochester for the assault on Killigrew, Charles, having strolled with the Earl the following day, suggested in the friendliest terms that he should lie low in France for a while. Before departing, the Earl almost landed himself in further trouble by agreeing to act as a second in a duel between the Duke of Richmond and Mr James Hamilton, which was prevented at the last minute. The King could not abide duelling – he had just put Rochester's friend Henry Savile in the Tower for carrying a challenge from the Duke of Buckingham to Sir William Coventry – and was anxious to stamp it out. It was an insurmountable task given the hot-headedness of the courtiers and their interpretation of honour; the second Earl of Chesterfield, for example, a former lover of Castlemaine's and a veritable lunatic with a sword, had been put in the Tower in 1658 for killing one man in a duel. He then promptly killed another in 1660.

Rochester left for France via a trip to Newmarket races with the King, who gave him a letter to take to his sister 'Minette', Duchess of Orléans. It stated that the Earl had a mind to 'take a little journey to Paris, and would not kiss your hands without a letter from me; pray use him as one I have a very good opinion of. You will find him not to want wit, and did behave himself, in all the Dutch war, as well as any body, as a volunteer.'

The visit got off to an ominous start when Louis XIV chose to ignore the fact that Charles had forgiven Rochester for assaulting Tom Killigrew in the royal presence, and refused to receive him. As much of an insult to Charles himself as it was to the Earl, this was a worrying sign that Rochester really had damaged the credibility of the English Court abroad and had offended even foreign monarchs with such insulting behaviour in the presence of royalty. And even when he was not looking for trouble, it now seemed that trouble was coming in search of him. A few weeks after arriving in France, following a 'ceremony of great guns' in a field, he was robbed of about twenty pistols and a periwig whilst crossing Pont Rouge in Paris in a sedan chair. Not suprisingly, his letter home to Elizabeth, sent three days later, sounds distinctly unamused. Lady Rochester was expecting their first child in the summer, which is why he said he would be 'infinitely pleased' with news of her health. So far, he said, he had not been so 'fortunate to hear any of you but assure yourself my wishes are of your side as much as is possible and pray only that they may be effectual, and you will not want for happiness'.

Through no fault of his own Rochester was in trouble again in July, when a gang of about half a dozen Frenchmen set on a group of Englishmen, including the Earl and Lord Cavendish, during an opera in Paris. The result was mayhem. Rochester's own part in the ensuing fight is unclear, but the French came off the worst. Cavendish was reported to have killed two of them, receiving serious injuries himself, and Louis XIV was so enraged with the Frenchmen that he threatened to hang the survivors. This became unnecessary when Rochester and Cavendish very nobly won them a pardon, saying they had quite forgiven them.

These events – the robbery and the fight in the playhouse – were particularly unfair on the Earl, since he clearly made every effort to conduct himself properly throughout his four months in France. Anxious to be home in time for the baptism of his new-born child, on 15 July he applied for permission to return to England and the English ambassador, Montagu, supported his request in a letter of recommendation to Secretary of State, Lord Arlington. He said there was nothing Rochester wanted more 'than your Lordship's favour and countenance; and if hereafter he continues to live as discreetly as he has done ever since he was here, he has other good qualities enough to deserve it, and to make himself acceptable wherever he comes'. The Earl was duly allowed back into the fold, and on 30 August his daughter Anne was baptised in Oxfordshire. She would become noted for her beauty ('a tall, handsome body', said Thomas Hearne), would write poetry and would marry twice, first to Henry Baynton, of Wiltshire, and then to Francis Greville, son of Lord Brooke.

Less than two months after the baptism, the ill health which would plague Rochester for the rest of his life reared its head and he took himself off to Madam Fourcard's bathing establishment in Leather Lane, Hatton Garden, to be treated for pox. He had probably contracted the infection in France, and the following letter, sent on 17 October, is further evidence of the extraordinarily frank relationship the Earl had with his wife:

> Wife, our gut has already been griped, and we are now in bed so that we are not in a condition of writing either according to thy merit or our desert; we therefore do command thy benign acceptance of these our letters in what way so ever by us inscribed or directed, willing thee therewithall to assure our sole daughter and heir issue female, the Lady Anne, part of our best respects; this with your care and diligence, in the erection of our furnaces is at present the utmost of our will and pleasure . . .

A few weeks later the reputation for valour which Rochester had fought so hard to acquire during the Dutch War lay in tatters. The celebrated but frustrated duel with John Sheffield, Earl of Mulgrave, referred to at the start of this chapter, is clouded with confusion to this day – but two things, at least, are clear: it was a significant turning-point in Rochester's life, and he displayed a complete lack of judgement which was symptomatic of his alcoholism.

Before Mulgrave's side of the story is examined, it is worth emphasising that judgement and ambition are two of alcoholism's earliest casualties. As the alcoholic begins to lose touch with reality (and Rochester's love of disguising himself was symptomatic of that), he or she will find it harder and harder to evaluate situations correctly or see the consequences of their actions. Eventually they find themselves making incorrect and even irrational decisions. Along with this comes a dying of ambition and an inability to hold on to things which were once held dear – such as pride and self-respect. (The most famous example of this in recent times concerns the career of that wonderful actor Richard Burton. In the 1950s he was widely regarded as the heir apparent to Olivier's crown. By the end of the 1960s he had not just lost the ability to judge the difference between a good film script and a bad one, but his sense of ambition had disintegrated.) Because the alcoholic is aware that this process is taking place, anger and bitterness begin to assert themselves even more strongly. There may be sporadic attempts at recovering the self-respect, drive and reputation of old, but without the abstinence from drink these will be unsustainable.

Lord Mulgrave, fractionally younger than Rochester, was unpopular among the wits even though he was one of them. He reckoned himself to be an outstanding poet, lover and soldier, and it was Rochester who later lampooned him as 'Monster All-Pride'. In his *Memoirs*, Mulgrave explained: 'I was informed that the Earl of Rochester had said something of me which, according to his custom, was very malicious: I therefore sent Colonel Aston, a very mettled friend of mine, to call him to account for it. He denied the words, and indeed I was soon convinced that he had never said them; but the mere report, though I found it to be false, obliged me (as I then foolishly thought) to go on with the quarrel.' That in itself all sounds contradictory. On the one hand he says it was Rochester's custom to be malicious; on the other hand he says he believed the Earl's word. Then he goes ahead with the fight anyway. A duel did not have to be undertaken once it was established that there was no cause to disagree, and surely Mulgrave knew that. Why should he have gone ahead with a fight against an opponent who was famed for his bravery, if he believed him innocent? Mulgrave is trying to make himself sound decent and understanding, and, at the same time, courageous enough to go ahead with the duel. He attempts to put himself in the best possible light from every perspective. He continues:

. . . the next day was appointed for us to fight on horseback, a way in England a little unusual, but it was his part to choose. Accordingly, I and my second lay the night before at Knightsbridge privately, to avoid the being secured at London upon any suspicion; which yet we found ourselves more in danger of there, because we had all the appearance of highwaymen that had a mind to lie skulking in an odd inn for one night; but this, I suppose, the people of that house were used to, and so took no notice of us, but liked us the better.

The following morning they met Rochester as arranged, but found that instead of having brought a Mr James Porter as his second, as he had said he would do, he had come with 'an errant lifeguardman whom nobody knew'.

to this Mr Aston took exception, upon the account of his being no suitable adversary; especially considering how extremely well he was mounted, whereas we had only a couple of pads: Upon which we all agreed to fight on foot.

Then, according to Mulgrave, Rochester had second thoughts.

. . . as my Lord Rochester and I were riding into the next field in order to it, he told me that he had at first chosen to fight on horseback because he was so weak with a certain distemper, that he found himself unfit to fight at all any way, much less afoot. I was extremely surprised, because at that time no man had a better reputation for courage; and (my anger against him being quite over, because I was satisfied that he never spoke those words I resented) I took the liberty of representing what a ridiculous story it would make if we returned without fighting, and therefore advised him for both our sakes – especially for his own – to consider better of it, since I must be obliged in my own defence to lay the fault on him by telling the truth of the matter. His answer was, that he submitted to it and hoped that I would not desire the advantage of having to do with any man in so weak a condition. I replied that by such an argument he had sufficiently tied my hands, upon condition I might call our seconds to be witnesses of the whole business; which he consented to, and so we parted. When we returned to London, we found it full of quarrel, upon our being absent so long; and therefore Mr Aston thought himself obliged to write down every word and circumstance of the whole matter, in order to spread everywhere the true reason of our returning without having fought, which, being never in the least either contradicted or resented by the Lord Rochester, entirely ruined his reputation as to courage (of which I was really sorry to be the occasion) though nobody had still a greater as to wit; which supported him pretty well in the world notwithstanding some more accidents of the same kind, that never fail to succeed one another when once people know a man's weakness.

This account swings from the merely unconvincing to the ridiculous. Mulgrave is talking in riddles. Instead of laying 'the fault' of not fighting on Rochester, who had explained why he could not duel on foot, why did Mulgrave – who refused to fight on horseback as they had arranged – not suggest a future date? What cleverly increases the suspicion of Rochester's cowardice is Mulgrave's claim that Rochester momentarily agreed to fight on foot when they met, but then backed down again. In fact, it is obvious that he really did have something wrong with him, since he had asked well in advance for the duel to be fought on horseback, which, as Mulgrave observed, was an unusual way of proceeding. By stating that it was Mr Aston who 'thought himself obliged' to spread the story around the Court, Mulgrave attempts to portray himself as an innocent party to all the gossip which followed, and his claim that he was 'really sorry' to have been the cause of Rochester's loss of reputation for valour is absurd.

House of Lords records show that when the King realised a duel was going to be fought he sent an officer of his guards, on the morning of the fight on 22 November, to try and stop both men from proceeding. Mulgrave was at this point in Knightsbridge, but Rochester was found at his lodgings. He assured the officer that he would not try to escape, but then found an excuse to go into a back room and promptly ran out of the door. The House of Lords then ruled that both men should be arrested and brought before the members. Mulgrave was caught on 24 November and was held in custody in Suffolk Street. He was then brought before the Lords and told to issue no further challenges to Rochester. If he received any then he was to inform the House.

On 25 November Black Rod delivered the news that Rochester too was now in custody. The following day he was brought to the House and given the same message as Mulgrave. Somehow he was able to keep a straight face as he informed the House that he had never been angry with the Earl of Mulgrave and had no reason to believe Mulgrave had ever been angry with him. 'His Lordship hath always carried himself so gently and civilly towards me that I am confident there will be no occasion of any difference between us,' he declared.

Rochester's readiness to take part in duels in later years shows a desperation on his part to recover his reputation. He never succeeded, largely because he had, in truth, lost much of his hunger for pride. This was not the same man who risked his life in the Dutch war for the sake of having a good name. The distemper from which he claimed he was sufferig could have been tied up with his recent treatment for pox, but it is likelier to have been connected to his drinking. Like most alcoholics he did not eat properly – he was noted for his thinness – and weakness, nausea and aching legs are all regular, daily symptoms of chronic drinking. As *delerium tremens* testifies, the nervous system becomes shattered, and while the Earl was never *intrinsically* a coward, neither would he ever again have the stomach for a fight whilst sober. Panic attacks would have been as common to him as they are to all alcoholics.

Having decided to fight the duel on horseback, Rochester displayed extraordinary lack of judgement and an inability to take the whole matter seriously. Duelling, like most other conventions in his society, seemed as ridiculous to him as it seems to us now. He was finding it increasingly hard to take either the customs of his age or life in general, seriously. By bringing along a brawny second, whom no one knew, on a larger than average horse, he was effectively winding Mulgrave up. He seems not to have realised that his opponent would naturally object (a second was *always* named in advance) and ask for the fight to be on foot. Neither does he seem to have realised what the consequences would be of not fighting at all. He made no attempt to arrange for a fight on a later date and, according to Mulgrave, simply said he hoped his Lordship would taken no advantage of the situation, since he was in so weak a condition. He just could not see what was going to happen.

What did happen, of course, is that Mr Aston told everyone in the Court that Lord Rochester was a yellow-bellied coward. At last, all those who disliked the Earl for his cheerful arrogance had something to taunt him with – and not just that, but the most insulting taunt of all. The tragedy is that without the drink, Rochester had been, as he had proved, an extremely courageous man. Now, he was in no condition, mentally or physically, to show it. Superficially he was no longer particularly brave at all, and his alcoholism was to drive him to a possible nervous breakdown at the end of the 1670s.

He still had one weapon left to him which he *could* use though: his pen. When the first broadside of 'A Satire against Reason and Mankind' appeared in 1675 it contained one line in particular – arguably the greatest single line he ever wrote – which was designed to outrage his growing number of enemies:

> For all men would be cowards if they durst.

The implication that he was braver than anyone else for daring to be a coward fuelled the indignation of his principal foes at Whitehall. It was a dangerous flippancy though, and he duly paid the penalty for it when, in 1676, another incident gave his enemies just the excuse they needed to resurrect the charge of cowardice with even more malevolence.

The Mulgrave affair and the talk of cowardice which followed it increased Rochester's hatred for himself and his society. It was his sense of alienation which inspired the great satires of the 1670s. From now on he would laugh at what he saw as the idiocy of his contemporaries, the crassness of mankind in general and the absurdity of life. He would go down fighting with an anger as wonderful as it was frightening:

> Oh, but the world will take offence hereby!
> Why then the world shall suffer for't, not I.
> Did e're the saucy world and I agree
> To let it have its beastly will on me?

7

WHAT THING IS MAN?

> Bless me! thought I, what thing is man, that thus
> In all his shapes, he is ridiculous?
> Ourselves with noise of reason we do please
> In vain: humanity's our worst disease.
>
> *Rochester, from 'Tunbridge Wells'*

In the summer of 1670 and for at least several years afterwards, Rochester lived in Portugal Row, Lincoln's Inn Fields, in 'the house next to the Duke's Playhouse'. He was already lodging there when, on 30 June, Charles's beloved sister 'Minette' died of suspected poisoning in Paris and became, according to the Earl, the most lamented person in France and England 'since which time dying has been the fashion'. That apparently flippant remark disguises the kindness he showed at the time to Charles, who collapsed at the news and shut himself inside his bedroom for days on end. In a letter home, Rochester hinted to his wife at the support he was giving to the King:

> Pray do not take it ill that I have writ to you so seldom since my coming to town, my being in wanting upon the sad accident of Madam's death (for which the King endures the highest affliction imaginable) would not allow me time, or power to write letters . . .

The services of the Court Jester, then, were badly required. Beneath the cynicism, the satirical outlook on life and the anger,

149

Rochester was a good-natured man whose guilt-racked letters home go to prove it. It is usually said that the mistress knows more about the husband than the wife does but, in Rochester's case the opposite was true. His letters to his most famous mistress, Elizabeth Barry, show him very consciously playing the role of the romantic lover. There is a kind of subconscious artifice about their style which is entirely missing from the stream of letters he sent to Adderbury in Oxfordshire throughout his thirteen-year marriage.

He appears to have spent at least part of each summer with his wife, either at Addersbury or at her estate in Somerset. Lady Rochester visited London in March 1671 and attended the theatre, but otherwise seems to have been fully occupied in bringing up their children (four, eventually) in the country. Her husband's view of country life was strikingly different to that of most other courtiers, who thought it a desperate place full of unsophisticated, backward people. In Restoration plays the countryman is often depicted as an idiot who can easily be cuckolded by the witty, suave gentleman-about-town and, at the end of *The Man of Mode* audiences laughed approvingly of the way in which Harriet scorns Dorimant's protestations of love, with her observation that:

> This is more dismal than the country! Emilia, pity me, who am going to that sad place. Methinks I hear the hateful noise of rooks already – kaw, kaw, kaw – there's music in the worst cry in London!

For Rochester, the worst cries of London were, on occasions, too much to bear. In a letter to Henry Savile he said the country was the only place in which a man could think – 'for you at Court think not at all, or, at least, as if you were shut up in a drum. You can think of nothing but the noise that is made about you.' He idealised rural life through poetic eyes but was in practice easily bored by it. London magnetised him. Life there was chaotic – he made sure of that – and at least it kept 'still-life' at bay. The Earl's visits home were recuperative and he tried hard to bring his best behaviour home with him. This means he did his best to restrain his drinking. It cannot have been an entire success, but it was enough for John Aubrey to record that Rochester was 'wont to say that when he came to Brentford the Devil entered into him and never left him till he came into the country again'.

His wife, that once elusive Somerset heiress, was never far from his thoughts, no matter who the latest mistress was in London, be it the actress Mrs Boutel, the part-time royal mistress Jane Roberts or even his own dramatic protégée Elizabeth Barry. Besides remorse for his infidelity, his letters home show great tenderness even when relations between husband and wife became increasingly strained during the 1670s. 'I am sorry, Madam, to hear that you are not well and as much troubled that you should believe I have not writ to you all this while,' he wrote once. 'I, who am not used to flatter, do assure you that if two letters from me came not to your hands this last week and that before, they have miscarried . . .' There is no doubt that this was the truth. To his wife, he did not lie.

This was a love which refused to die, in spite of the anguish his atrocious behaviour caused him and the sadness it gave to her. Perhaps the long periods of absence actually helped. In the early days of the marriage he could be in the mood to tease her with a touching affection, just as he did when she sent him some self-portraits:

I received your three pictures and am in a great fright lest they should be like you. By the bigness of the head I should apprehend you far gone in the rickets; by the severity of the countenance, somewhat inclined to prayer and prophecy; yet there is an alacrity in your plump cheeks that seems to signify sack and sugar, and your sharp-sighted nose has borrowed quickness from the sweet-smelling eye. I never saw a chin smile before, a mouth frown, or a forehead mump. Truly the artist has done his part (God keep him humble) and a fine man he is if his excellence don't puff him up like his pictures. The next impertinence I have to tell you is that I am coming into the country. I have got horses but want a coach: when that defect is supplied, you shall quickly have the trouble of Your humble servant, Rochester.

As we might expect, Rochester was a superb letter-writer who felt obliged to 'perform' with his wit in his correspondence with others. It is a common paradox, however, that the more complicated a relationship is, the more direct and less delicate the letters become. Rochester rarely had time for frivolity in his messages home. 'Since my coming to town,' he wrote, 'my head has been perpetually turned round, but I do not find it makes me giddy. This is all the wit you shall receive in my first letter; hereafter you may expect more, God willing . . .' But the sentiments of his letters to her tended to be too sincere to allow room for even those little flippancies. At least once, he expressed the wish that she would write to him more often:

> You know not how much I am pleased when I hear from you; if you did you would be so obliging to write oftener to me. I do seriously with all my heart wish myself with you and am endeavouring every day to get away from this place, which I am so weary of, that I may be said rather to languish than live in it . . .

It puts one in mind of the poem beginning 'Absent from thee I languish still', in which he fears falling on some 'base heart unblest'. The theme of restlessness; of never being in a place in which he really wants to be, is often repeated and it is reminiscent of the father who, as Clarendon observed, was 'incapable of being contented'.

Rochester was not afraid to admit his misbehaviour to his wife. Long silences were usually followed by some kind of explanation, expressed as honestly as it was sensitively:

> If you hear not from me it is not that I either want time or will to write to you. I am sufficiently at leisure and think very often of you, but you would expect an account of what has befallen me, which is not yet fit for you to know. Only thus much I will tell you; it was a vindication of you. I am now at Battersea and have been this week here; wonder not if you receive few letters from me, and be satisfied with this: that I think continually of you, and am
>
> your
> Rochester.

(Was this an affair which he was too guilty about to confess while it still lasted?)

Unlike so many of his friends, he did not forget his duties as a husband – which included stewarding the money from her estate. 'I shall be with you shortly,' he wrote once, 'and if my mother pleases I will take the trouble of you and yours upon me and think myself a very happy man . . . money you shall have as soon as ever I come to you.' He seems never to have overlooked that the mney was hers and not his – although this did not prevent him from guiltily spending it:

> It is now some weeks since I writ you word that there was money returned out of Somersetshire for your use, which I desired you to send for by what sums yourself pleased. By this time I believe I have spent it half. However, you must be supplied if you think fit to order it; shortly I intend to give you the trouble of a visit. 'Tis all I have to beg your pardon for at present, unless you take it for a fault that I still pretend to be
>
> Your humble servant,
> Roch.
> I do not know if my mother be at Ditchley or Adderbury; if at home present my duty to her.

Always regretfully aware of his failings, he sought ways of improving himself as a husband:

> I am very glad to hear news from you and I think it very good when I hear you are well. Pray be pleased to send me word what you are apt to be pleased with, that I may show you how good a husband I can be; I would not have you so formal as to judge of the kindness of a letter by the length of it but believe of everything that it is as you would have it . . .

Once, at least, he was more inclined to think that he was not such a dreadful husband after all. This gave him the confidence to address his wife in slightly self-righteous tones, and if they are tinged with anger then perhaps that emotion was reserved for himself:

> I know not who has persuaded you that you want five pounds to pay a servant's wages, but next week Blancourt is going

into the West, at whose return you may expect an account of your entire revenue, which I will be bound to say has hitherto, and shall (as long as I can get bread without it) be wholly employed for the use of yourself and those who depend on you. If I prove an ill steward, at least you never had a better, which is some kind of satisfaction to

Your humble servant.

Not many of Lady Rochester's letters have survived, but it is clear from her husband's own that she corresponded just as regularly as he did:

You are very kind to wish me in the country. Perhaps that is best for me, and I wish I had rather been in this town a month ago than at this time, and certainly when I am in my tolerable health I shall wait upon you.

Rochester's health began to nose-dive from about 1671 onwards, when he was still only twenty-four. That was the year in which he first revealed that his eyes could not tolerate either wine or water. Rheumatism, gout, kidney trouble and growing blindness, all attributable to his drinking, began to plague him. The eye trouble points to Wernicke's syndrome, which is very common in alcoholics and is caused by vitamin B1 deficiency. It is more often than not accompanied by Korsakoff's psychosis, which is a form of amnesia that destroys the powers of short-term memory. The Earl's recollection of heavy drinking sessions was now often hazy and incomplete. Later, it would sometimes be non-existent.

During the winter of 1670, the couple's only son, Charles, was born. It is reasonable to believe that if Rochester had disliked the King as a man – as opposed to merely disapproving of him as a monarch – he would hardly have given his son the same name. All of Rochester's children were good-looking, but Charles was exceptionally so. Thomas Hearne thought him one of the handsomest children in England and an old woman from Woodstock told him the child was 'the finest boy she had ever beheld'. He was to die only a year after his father, thus bringing the Wilmot line to an end. The baptism took place on 2 January 1671, with both Sir Charles Sedley and Lord Buckhurst present as godfathers. Rochester must have been living at home regularly during this period, for when Henry Savile wrote, on 26 January, to apologise for having missed the ceremony, he said he hoped to be at the next one and explained: 'Your lordship staying much with your lady will, I presume, once a year furnish us with such solemnities.'

Savile then went on to give Rochester the shocking news that a consignment of imported dildoes had been burnt by 'the farmers' – customs officers – in spite of two attempts made by himself and Sedley to save them. According to Savile, Rochester had taken one of these instruments into the country with him. If it was not to give to his wife, one wonders who it can have been for.

> . . . your lordship has been extremely wanting here to make friends at the custom house, where has been lately unfortunately seized a box of those leather instruments your lordship carried down one of, but these barbarian farmers, prompted by the villainous instigation of their wives, voted them prohibited goods so that they were burnt without mercy notwithstanding that Sedley and I made two journeys into the City in their defence. By this, my Lord, you see what things are done in your absence, and then pray consider whether it is fit for you to be blowing of coals in the country when there is a revenge due to the ashes of these martyrs! Your lordship is chosen general in this war betwixt the Ballers and the farmers, nor shall peace by my consent ever be made till they grant us our wine and our dildoes custom free . . .

It was precisely this kind of anarchic, wonderful silliness which would draw Rochester back to London. He did not have the willpower to resist the jollity of his healthier friends, and always sensed, while he was in the country, that he was missing out on fun and games in the capital. He knew that to spend time with the likes of his friends Sedley and Buckhurst rather than with his wife was against his better judgement, and in a letter to the solitary Elizabeth he once dismissively referred to his drinking companions as 'rakehells'. Perhaps he was trying to comfort her.

His satirical poem 'Signior Dildo' was written after James, Duke of York, had married Mary of Modena towards the end of 1673.

Following a proxy marriage in July she came to England, where the couple repeated the ceremony. Rochester's attention to the subject of dildoes was surely prompted, though, by the burning of this consignment by the 'farmers'. All he needed was an event which would lend some verses topicality. Typically, the poem hits at the hypocrisy of a society whose leading members are, in the Earl's eyes, sexually voracious, but which is too coy to tolerate a perfectly practical instrument of pleasure.

> You ladies all of merry England
> Who have been to kiss the Duchess's hand,
> Pray, did you lately observe in the show
> A noble Italian called Signior Dildo?
>
> This signior was one of Her Highness's train
> And helped to conduct her over the main;
> But now she cries out, 'To the Duke I will go!
> I have no more need for Signior Dildo.'
>
> At the Sign of the Cross in St James's Street,
> When next you go thither to make yourselves sweet
> By buying of powder, gloves, essence, or so,
> You may chance t'get a sight of Signior Dildo.
>
> You'll take him at first for no person of note
> Because he appears in a plain leather coat;
> But when you his virtuous abilities know,
> You'll fall down and worship Signior Dildo. . . .
>
> Our dainty fine duchesses have got a trick
> To dote on a fool for the sake of his prick:
> The fops were undone, did Their Graces but know
> The discretion and vigour of Signior Dildo.
>
> That pattern of virtue Her Grace of Cleveland
> Has swallowed more pricks than the ocean has sand;
> But by rubbing and scrubbing so large it does grow,
> It is fit for just nothing but Signior Dildo. . . .

Doll Howard no longer with his Highness must range
And therefore is proffered this civil exchange:
Her teeth being rotten, she smells best below,
And needs must be fitted for Signior Dildo. . . .

This signior is sound, safe, ready, and dumb
As ever was candle, carrot, or thumb;
Then away with these nasty devices and show
How you rate the just merits of Signior Dildo. . . .

In all there are more than twenty verses, and they combine to show the three most common components of Rochester's expressed view of sex: intellectual libertinism, emotional, underlying disgust and a schoolboy's sense of delightful naughtiness. The same conflicting feelings are at work in the following ditty, even though there is a question-mark over its authorship:

By all love's soft yet mighty powers,
It is a thing unfit
That men should fuck in time of flowers,
Or when the smock's beshit.

Fair nasty nymph, be clean and kind
And all my joys restore,
By using paper still behind
And spunges for before.

My spotless flames can ne'er decay
If after every close,
My smoking prick escape the fray
Without a bloody nose.

If thou wouldst have me true, be wise
And take to cleanly sinning;
None but fresh lovers' pricks can rise
At Phyllis in foul linen.

The Earl's obsession with dildoes apparently returned in a short lampoon on Cary Frazier, whose father was the King's physician and whose mother was a maid of honour to the Queen:

> Her father gave her dildoes six,
> Her mother made 'em up a score,
> But she loves nought but living pricks
> And swears by God she'll frig no more.

As the 1670s progressed, Rochester's poetry became more sexually explicit and aggressive, and this, as ever, was tied up with his alcoholism. It is a common myth that the active alcoholic must be sexually incapable, for more often than not precisely the opposite is true. To the alcoholic, drink (and particularly withdrawal from drink *the morning after*) is something of an aphrodisiac. To a partner, the alcoholic can become nothing more than a 'sexual pest'. Impotence can occur in the long term, and sustained abstinence commonly results in a total loss of sexual interest for possibly as much as six months. However, because the alcoholic usually has a comparatively enormous capacity for drink and can function with amounts inside him which would render most other people unconscious, he has to be pretty helplessly drunk before he suffers from what is colloquially known as 'brewer's droop'.

Yet the 1670s did not just see Rochester writing bawdy rhymes; for it was in this decade that he established himself as a master satirist with the great works 'A Satire against Reason and Mankind', 'A Ramble in St James's Park', 'The Imperfect Enjoyment', 'Tunbridge Wells', 'A Letter from Artemisia in the Town to Chloe in the Country' and 'Timon'. No less a person than Andrew Marvell (according to John Aubrey) thought Rochester was 'the best English satirist and had the right vein'. Whatever had become of his credentials as a man of honour, there was never any doubt at Court about his poetic genius and he wielded considerable power as a patron to other writers.

Clarendon had noted that the first Earl was fickle in his friendships, and so Rochester also proved in his relationships with London's leading playwrights. Boredom and the need for change largely accounted for this. For three years, the only writer under his wing was Dryden, whose greatest work was yet to come. Then, in 1671, Rochester wrote one of two prologues for Elkanah Settle's *The Empress of Morocco*, which, thanks to the Earl of Norwich's influence, was performed at Court that year in preference to anything by Dryden. Lord Mulgrave, with whom Rochester was in constant competition throughout the 1670s (Mulgrave took his place as Dryden's patron), wrote the other prologue. Rochester's address, given by Lady Elizabeth Howard, was aimed at Charles and boosted further his already sated ego as a lover:

> To you (great Sir) my message hither tends,
> From youth and beauty, your allies and friends.
> See my credentials written in my face;
> They challenge your protection in this place,
> As may give check ev'n to your prosperous arms.
> Millions of cupids hovering in the rear,
> Like eagles following fatal troops appear,
> All waiting for the slaughter which draws nigh,
> Of those bold gazers who this night must die.
> Nor can you 'scape our soft captivity
> From which old age alone must set you free . . .

Although Rochester had not been directly responsible for the performance of this play at Court, he had, by dint of writing the prologue, helped with it. Neither had he stood in the way of its being favoured by the King. Then, in 1672, John Crowne dedicated his play *Charles VIII of France* to Rochester. The Earl's involvement with not one but two other dramatists seems to have annoyed Dryden, who in his otherwise warm dedication to Rochester in *Marriage à la Mode* – first performed in 1672 and published the year after – made the very telling remark: 'Your lordship has but one step to make, and from the patron of wit, you may become its tyrant.' The implication is that the Earl was not far from beginning to abuse his position at Whitehall. Elsewhere in the dedication, Dryden is full of flattery, publicly acknowledging that Rochester, who has 'not only been careful of my reputation, but of my fortune', has made amendments to the play in order for it to be 'fit to be presented'. The extent of the Earl's help with *Marriage à la Mode* is unclear, but from several of Dryden's comments ('you have not forgot either the ties of friendship or the practice of generosity') it is obvious that he appreciates the assistance he has received since his appointment – which was probably due to Rochester's influence – as Poet Laureate.

Commentators on the age have often tried to identify a single and specific reason for the breakdown in relations between the two men, but it was evidently a gradual process of mutual disenchantment which was well-advanced by the end of 1674, completed in 1675 and which finally exploded at the beginning of 1676 when Rochester struck home with his devastating satire, 'An Allusion to Horace'. As early as 1672 the Earl had made a disapproving mental note of Dryden's 'Essay on the Dramatic Poetry of the Last Age'. The Poet Laureate bewailed the fact that on every page of Shakespeare and Fletcher it was possible to find 'some solecism of speech' or 'some notorious flaw in sense', but that while those two authors were revered in spite of such mistakes, the present generation of writers 'are not forgiven' for them. Rochester thought Dryden the best writer of the age ('Nor dare I from his sacred temples tear/ That laurel which he best deserves to wear') but he also had the foresight to reaslise, at a time when Shakespeare was not particularly popular, that the Bard of Stratford was a genius in a sphere of his own. If Dryden thought he could attack Shakespeare, then would it not be reasonable for Rochester to attack Dryden? For now, though, the Earl kept quiet.

Several other factors then contributed to the Rochester-Dryden showdown. In 1673, Settle printed his *Empress of Morocco* with a criticism of Dryden, to which the latter replied in 1674 with the help of Crowne and Shadwell. Rochester's connection with the play and with Settle himself was hardly helping relations with the Poet Laureate, but what really wrecked them was Dryden's growing friendliness with Lord Mulgrave. The rift with Rochester became unavoidable when, in December 1674, Mulgrave was involved in a second frustrated duel, this time with Henry Savile. Savile, not surprisingly, named his friend Rochester as his second. Even though the fight never took place, Rochester and Mulgrave were once again, metaphorically speaking, outstaring each other. Dryden was going to have to choose between the two Earls as patron, and his natural choice was Rochester's arch-enemy, Lord Mulgrave. Quite apart from anything else – and this was a very practical consideration – Rochester was frequently ill throughout the 1670s and did not seem likely to live very long. The mid-1670s were embraced by the five years of continual drunkenness mentioned by Burnet, and Rochester was simply not a sound investment. Dryden, though, must be seen as equally responsible for the distance which now lay between himself and Rochester, and when, in 1675, the Earl ensured John Crowne's *The Masque of Calisto* was preferred over Dryden's work at Court, it should not have surprised the Poet Laureate, who was now rubbing shoulders with Mulgrave. Perhaps it did though, since, in 1721, John Dennis recalled that Rochester had opted for Crowne in order to 'mortify' Dryden. It was only a matter of time before the Earl went one step furhter and satirised the Poet Laureate, or, for that matter, before the Poet Laureate's new patron satirised him . . .

❧ ❧ ❧

The outbreak of war with the Dutch again in March 1672 provided Rochester with a perfect opportunity to restore his good name, but he was too sick to take it and too cynical to even be interested. The duels in which he was ready and willing to take part in the 1670s were all cancelled or prevented, which, if not his fault, was somehow still reflective of his half-hearted approach to the whole question of honour. Like Falstaff, he now thought of honour as nothing more than 'a word', and it was fatuousness and artifice which became the prime targets of much of his satirical work. 'That a man's excellency should lie in neatly tying of a ribbon or a cravat!' exclaims Dorimant, 'How careful's nature in furnishing the world with necessary coxcombs!'

The Earl's friend Henry Bulkeley, who became Master of the King's Household, knew that the letter he sent Rochester in the spring of 1672 would have him smiling in approval. In it he complained that

> . . . the fop is the only fine gentleman of the times and a committee of those able statesmen assemble daily to talk of nothing but fighting and fucking at Lockett's and will never be reconciled to men who speak sense and reason at the Bear or Covent Garden. It is they who are the hopeful sprigs of the

161

nation; whose knowledge lies in their light periwigs and trimmed shoes; who herd with one another not because they love themselves but understand nobody else; whose honour, honesty and friendship is like the consent of hounds, who know not why they run together but that they hunt the same scent; fellows that would make the world believe that they are not afraid of dying and yet are out of heart if the wind disorders their hair or ruffles their cravats . . .

In his extraordinary satire 'Tunbridge Wells', Rochester describes himself visiting that town in order to observe the human beings at play, as though he is on a nature trip to study an inexplicably stupid and bizarre breed of animal. The poem lashes foppery and affectation, and what is today known as 'posing'. One strongly suspects that the Earl based the satire, however loosely, on a real visit to Tunbridge Wells, and the fantastical view of the people he describes in it is enhanced by the alcoholic's loss of touch with reality. Hilariously, the very first thing he does in the poem, having arrived in the town, is to vomit at the sight of an approaching human being:

> My squeamish stomach I with wine had bribed
> To undertake the dose that was prescribed;
> But, turning head, a sudden cursèd view
> That innocent provision overthrew;
> And, without drinking, made me purge and spew.
> From coach and six a thing unwieldy rolled,
> Whose lumber, cart more decently would hold.
> As wise as calf it looked, as big as bully,
> But handled, proves a mere Sir Nicholas Cully:
> A bawling fop, a natural Nokes, and yet
> He dares to censure as if he had wit.
> To make him more ridiculous, in spite,
> Nature contrived the fool should be a knight.

Endeavouring to escape from such an 'irksome sight', Rochester slinks off to a place called the Lower Walk. He has no better luck there,

For here it was my cursèd luck to find
As great a fop, though of another kind:
A tall stiff fool that walked in Spanish guise;
The buckram puppet never stirred its eyes,
But grave as owl it looked; as woodcock wise.
He scorns the empty talking of this mad age
And speaks all proverbs, sentences, and adage;
Can with as much solemnity buy eggs
As a cabal can talk of their intrigues;
Master o'th Ceremonies, yet can dispense
With the formality of talking sense.

The Earl moves on again:

From hence unto the upper end I ran,
Where a new scene of foppery began;
A tribe of curates, priests, canonical elves,
Fit company for none besides themselves,
Were got together. Each his distemper told,
Scurvy; stone; strangury; some were so bold
To charge the spleen to be their misery
And on that wise disease brought infamy . . .

The comical nature of this satire lies in its steadfast objectivity, for Rochester really does describe each motley collection of people with a wide-eyed incredulity, mingled with horror. He might never have seen a human being before:

Next after these, a fulsome Irish crew
Of silly Macs were offered to my view.
The things did talk, but th' hearing what they said
I did myself the kindness to evade.
Nature has placed these wretches beneath scorn;
They can't be called so vile as they are born.

He is soon overhearing the embarrassing advances being made by a 'would-be wit' to a young damsel. It is, he observes, 'dismal stuff':

. . . 'Madam, methinks the weather
Is grown much more serene since you came hither.
You influence the heavens, but should the sun
Withdraw himself to see his rays outdone
By your bright eyes, they would supply the morn
And make a day before the day be born.'
With mouth screwed up, conceited winking eyes,
And breasts thrust forward, 'Lord, sir!' she replies.
'It is your goodness and not my deserts,
Which makes you show this learning, wit and parts.'
He, puzzled, bites his nail – both to display
The sparkling ring and think what next to say –
And thus breaks forth afresh: 'Madam, egad!
Your luck at cards last night was very bad!
At cribbage fifty-nine, and the next show
To make the game, and yet to want those two.
God damn me, madam, I'm the son of a whore
If in my life I saw the like before!'
To peddler's stall he drags her, and her breast
With hearts and such-like foolish toys he dressed
And then, more smartly to expound the riddle
Of all his prattle, gives her a Scotch fiddle.

The Earl flees only to be confronted by further scenes of
monotony and absurdity. There is no escape. The final verses hint
at a theme which is more fully developed in 'A Satire against
Reason and Mankind':

Bless me! thought I, what thing is man, that thus
In all his shapes, he is ridiculous?
Ourselves with noise of reason we do please
In vain: humanity's our worst disease.
Thrice happy beasts are, who, because they be
Of reason void, are so of foppery.
Faith, I was so ashamed that with remorse,
I used the insolence to mount my horse;
For he, doing only things fit for his nature,
Did seem to me by much the wiser creature.

It is characteristic of Rochester that in 'Tunbridge Wells' he spends most of his time laughing at men and not at women. The young damsel's statement that the would-be wit has learning, wit and parts, only emphasises his lack of all three qualities, and in both 'The Imperfect Enjoyment' and 'A Ramble in St James's Park' women are used to show up men's stupidity. In the latter satire Rochester is infuriated by Corinna's poor judgement over men and accuses her of turning herself into a 'passive pot for fools to spend in'. One thing the Earl could not abide was the sight of an attractive woman doting on a man he regarded as a fool. He thought women had an odd tendency to give themselves away to patently unworthy men and wondered out loud, in this case in a woman's voice, just why they did it:

> What vain, unnecessary things are men!
> How well we do without 'em! Tell me, then,
> Whence comes that mean submissiveness we find
> This ill-bred age has wrought on womankind?
> Fall'n from the rights their sex and beauties gave
> To make men wish, despair, and humbly crave,
> Now 'twill suffice if they vouchsafe to *have* . . .

Of Dorimant, the Orange-Woman says: 'I never knew you commend anything,' and Rochester did not always believe men of wit were worth a woman doting on either. One wonders if, during the mid-1670s, he believed in anything. For in 'A Letter from Artemisia in the Town to Chloe in the Country', he shows he is aware of the pain and damage his inconstancy has caused certain women. Artemisia relates the downfall of Corinna thus:

> That wretched thing Corinna, who had run
> Though all the several ways of being undone,
> Cozened at first by love and living then
> By turning the too dear-bought trick on men;
> Gay were the hours, and winged with joys they flew,
> When first the town her early beauties knew;
> Courted, admired, and loved, with presents fed,
> Youth in her looks and pleasure in her bed;
> Till fate, or her ill angel, thought it fit

To make her dote upon a man of wit
Who found 'twas dull to love above a day;
Made his ill-natured jest and went away.
Now scorned by all, forsaken and oppressed,
She's a *memento mori* to the rest;
Diseased; decayed; to take up half a crown
Must mortgage her long scarf and manteau gown . . .

Earlier in the satire, Artemisia highlights Rochester's own belief that women were above fops, and were right to make them look like the fools they really were:

But the kind easy fool, apt to admire
Himself, trusts us; his follies all conspire
To flatter his, and favour our desire.
Vain of his proper merit he with ease
Believes we love him best who best can please.
On him our gross, dull, common flatteries pass,
Ever most joyful when most made an ass.
Heavy to apprehend, though all mankind
Perceive us false, the fop concerned is blind,
Who, doting on himself,
Thinks everyone that sees him of his mind.
These are true women's men.

Rochester distinguished strongly between love and sex, and one of his funniest poems, 'The Imperfect Enjoyment', suggests that he thought the two rarely met. Never does he ridicule the self-deceiving sexuality of the male more than in this poem, and once again a woman is the foil. Given that women are fond of saying that men 'are only after one thing', the poem is rather ironic. Its hero – if that is not too strong a word – believes he is full of the most romantic intent in the world. It is Rochester who makes him pay the penalty for that. The opening, deliberately highly flown, comprises the words of a foolish young man who believes he is so in love that he mentally elevates sex with his mistress, Corinna, into something ethereal:

Naked she lay, clasped in my longing arms,
I filled with love, and she all over charms;
Both equally inspired with eager fire,
Melting through kindness, flaming in desire.
With arms, legs, lips close clinging to embrace,
She clips me to her breast and sucks me to her face.
Her nimble tongue, Love's lesser lightning, played
Within my mouth and to my thoughts conveyed
Swift orders that I should prepare to throw
The all-dissolving thunderbolt below.

Such hyperbolic excitement is only going to end in disaster, but he goes on underterred:

My fluttering soul, sprung with the pointed kiss,
Hangs hovering o'er her balmy brinks of bliss,
But whilst her busy hand would guide that part
Which should convey my soul up to her heart,
In liquid raptures I dissolve all o'er,
Melt into sperm and spend at every pore.

The way Rochester changes the man's tone is quite brilliant:

A touch from any part of her had done 't:
Her hand, her foot, her very look's a cunt.

The message of the poem is now delivered by the woman, who, as the poet implies, is far less agitated by this premature mishap than the man.

Smiling, she chides in a kind murmuring noise
And from her body wipes the clammy joys,
When, with a thousand kisses wandering o'er
My panting bosom, 'Is there then no more?'
She cries. 'All this to love and rapture's due;
Must we not pay a debt to pleasure too?'

He attempts to pay that debt, but 'succeeding shame does more success prevent', and 'rage at last confirms me impotent'. His vanity shattered, the man, having begun the poem declaring such rapturous love, now conveniently forgets about Corinna (who is not even named until the final line) and goes on to deliver a self-obsessed, egotistical and pathetic diatribe against his disobedient member:

> Thou, treacherous, base deserted of my flame,
> False to my passion, fatal to my fame;
> Through what mistaken magic dost thou prove
> So true to lewdness, so untrue to love?
> What oyster-cinder-beggar-common whore
> Didst thou e'er fail in all thy life before?
> When vice, disease and scandal lead the way,
> With what officious haste dost thou obey!
> Like a rude, roaring hector in the streets
> Who scuffles, cuffs and jostles all he meets,
> But if his King or country claim his aid,
> The rakehell villain shrinks and hides his head;
> Ev'n so thy brutal valour is displayed,
> Breaks every stew, does each small whore invade,
> But when great Love the onset does command,
> Base recreant to thy prince, thou dar'st not stand.
> Worst part of me and henceforth hated most,
> Through all the town a common fucking post
> On whom each whore relieves her tingling cunt
> As hogs on gates do rub themselves and grunt,
> Mayst thou to ravenous chancres be a prey,
> Or in consuming weepings waste away;
> May strangury and stone thy days attend;
> May'st thou ne'er piss, who didst refuse to spend
> When all my joys did on false thee depend.
> And may ten thousand abler pricks agree
> To do the wronged Corinna right for thee.

Rochester despised conceit in men more than he seems to have done in women, and in 1675 he satirised Mulgrave's arrogance with a fictional letter from the Earl, explaining his infidelity to a mistress, 'A Very Heroical Epistle in Answer to Ephelia' begins:

Madam,
If you're deceived it is not by my cheat,
For all disguises are below the great.
What man or woman upon earth can say
I ever used 'em well above a day?
How is it, then, that I inconstant am?
He changes not who always is the same.
In my dear self I centre everything:
My servants, friends, my mistress, and my King.
Nay, heaven and earth to that one point I bring.
Well mannered; honest; generous and stout
(Names by dull foools to plague mankind found out)
Should I regard, I must myself constrain,
And 'tis my maxim to avoid all pain.
You fondly look for what none e'er could find,
Deceive yourself and then call me unkind,
And by false reasons would my falsehood prove:
For 'tis as natural to change, as love . . .

That last line echoes a sentiment which Rochester had repeatedly expressed in his earlier lyrical poetry, and although he had never throught himself 'great', there are other Rochesterian values in the satire (''tis my maxim to avoid all pain', for example) which hint at a certain degree of self-castigation.

Unquestionably, Rochester's own sexuality embraced young men, literally, as well as young women. To call him bisexual would perhaps be over-stressing the point, since he was essentially a fierce heterosexual whose love affairs were all with women. He was also, however, an aesthete who appreciated beauty of every kind. In 'Upon Drinking in a Bowl' he demands that his cup should be engraved with 'two lovely boys' and in 'The Platonic Lady' he declares:

I love a youth will give me leave
His body in my arms to wreathe;
To press him gently and to kiss,
To sigh and look with eyes that wish
For what, if I could once obtain,
I would neglect with flat disdain.

> I'd give him liberty to toy
> And play with me and count it joy.
> Our freedom should be full complete,
> And nothing wanting but the feat . . .

But in reality the feat was not always wanting, and what committed him was his increasingly self-punitive desire to sink himself into perceived debauchery. To a man with Rochester's puritannical upbringing, homosexuality would have been morally 'out of bounds', which became all the more reason to practise it. In 'The Maimed Debauchee' he writes:

> Nor shall our love-fits, Chloris, be forgot,
> When each the well-looked linkboy strove t'enjoy,
> And the best kiss was the deciding lot
> Whether the boy fucked you, or I the boy.

In the last years of his life Rochester had a French servant called Baptiste whom he invariably christened Mr Baptist. On several occasions Mr Baptist delivered letters from the Earl, and in one, sent at the end of 1679 to Henry Savile, Rochester describes the bearer as 'this pretty fool' and says members of both sexes in the Court have 'tasted his beauties'. In his will the Earl bequeathed Mr Baptist some clothes and linen. Boys, or youths, appear to have sometimes acted as substitutes for women. When the Earl's whore disappeares in his poem 'The Debauchee' he says that 'missing my lass, I fall on my page'. And in one of his songs he says he intends to have nothing more to do with women and that if he does have any sexual urges, 'There's a sweet, soft page of mine/Does the trick worth forty wenches.' Was Mr Baptist sometimes such a consolation prize?

From about 1672 to 1675, Rochester's debauchery hit a peak. He was not yet constrained by his affair with Elizabeth Barry; in between bouts of illness he still had the strength, inclination and potency to be sexually very active, and the period also coincided with the five years of continual drunkenness reported by his confessor, Gilbert Burnet. There has been some conjecture about when these five years were. Perhaps the most basic law of alcoholism is that the inability to control drinking only ever worsens and never improves. It would have been physiologically impossible, for instance, for the Earl to have been drunk between 1667 and 1672 and only nicely tipsy thereafter. The truth is the reverse. From a letter to Henry Savile in the spring of 1677 it is clear that illness had finally induced him into an attempt at abstinence, and he duly began attending the House of Lords. The new resolution was shortlived though: the five years of constant inebriation ran from 1673 to 1678, taking in the famous affray at Epsom as well as his celebrated performance on Tower Hill as the mythical Dr Alexander Bendo. It must be remembered that when the alcoholic stops drinking, he or she invariably falls into a very studied, serious and insular frame of mind. Rochester could *never* have performed as Bendo without drink. A jape of that nature would have seemed boring and unfunny if he had been abstaining at the time. In drink, it became hilarious fun.

Throughout the mid-1670s he lived, when health permitted, at a ferocious pace and wrote with a passionate abandonment. Quite apart from the great satires already mentioned, it was during this period that he wrote 'The History of Insipids' too. In particular he remembered the disastrous Dutch war of 1665 to 1667 with bitterness:

> Charles in the first Dutch war stood fair
> To have been the sovereign of the deep;
> When Opdam blew up in the air,
> Had not his Highness gone to sleep.
> Our fleet slacked sails, fearing his waking,
> The Dutch had else been in sad taking . . .
>
> Mists, storms, short victuals, adverse winds,
> And once the Navy's wise division
> Defeated Charles his best designs
> Till he became his foes' derision.
> And he had swinged the Dutch at Chatham,
> Had he had ships but to come at 'um . . .
>
> But Charles, what could thy policy be
> To run so many sad disasters;
> To join the fleet with false d'Etrees;

To make the French of Holland masters;
Was't Carwell, brother James, of Teague
That made thee break the Triple League? . . .

New upstarts, pimps, bastards, whores,
That locust like devour the land
By shutting up the exchequer doors
When thither our money was trapan'd,
Have rend'red Charles his Restoration
But a small blessing to the nation . . .

As the mention of 'Carwell' suggests, Louise de Kéroualle, brought to England in 1670 by Charles's obliging sister 'Minette', was now a regular at Whitehall. She frustrated the King terribly. Like Frances Stewart, her determination to keep her virginity drove him to distraction – until he finally managed to remove it in the autumn of 1671. By February 1673 she had become, to Rochester's customary disgust, the Duchess of Portsmouth. When an old Parisian flame of Charles's years in exile, Hortense Mancini, Duchesse de Mazarin, arrived at the Court in 1675 and made a bee-line for the royal bedroom, Rochester felt obliged to sum up the state of England's monarchy with the following dialogue:

Nell:
When to the King I bid good morrow
With tongue in mouth and hand on tarse [penis],
Portsmouth may rend her cunt for sorrow
And Mazarin may kiss mine arse.

Portsmouth:
When England's monarch's on my belly
With a prick in cunt, though double crammed,
Fart of mine arse for small whore Nelly
And great whore Mazarin be damned.

King:
When on Portsmouth's lap I lay my head
And Knight does sing her bawdy song,
I envy not George Porter's bed
Nor the delights of Madam Long.

The People: Now heavens preserve our faith's defender
From Paris plots and Roman cunt;
From Mazarin, that new pretender,
And from that politique, Grammont.

Unimaginable though it may seem, these were not the most scandalous terms in which the Earl satirised the Court. The idealism so fundamental to his thinking made him more aware than anybody of the sexually charged atmosphere at Whitehall, and this developed into an obsession which he found revolting and fascinating by turns. During the 1670s he wrote a pornographic drama called *Sodom*, which depicted the gross debauchery of a royal Court in the form of an Adults Only cartoon. As pornography goes, it at least has the virtue of being terribly funny. A number of coy academics have decided either to overlook this work or deny Rochester's authorship of it. A poor innocent called Fishbourne has even been blamed by, among others, the antiquary Anthony Wood. Some people seem unable to grasp that – to borrow from Sir George Etherege's phrase – Rochester could write like an angel or like a devil, whichever pleased him. This work shows the devil in him, and an impish one at that. It has been suggested, by John Adlard, that the Earl wrote the drama in the last years of his life while he was revising Fletcher's *Valentinian*, which also features a debauched Emperor and his lascivious courtiers. But Rochester's frame of mine from 1678 onwards was surely far too dark for such frivolity. This work was written earlier than that and it seems to have been written in drink. Perhaps the wittiest exchange is between Prince Prickett and Princess Swivea:

Swivea: Twelve months will pass 'ere that thou canst arrive
To be a perfect man – that is, to swive
As Pockanello,
Your years to fifteen does not now incline.

Prickett: You know I would have stocked my prick at nine.

Swivea: I ne'er saw it since: let's see how much 'tis grown.
By heavens, a neat one! Now we're all alone
I'll shut the door and you shall see my thing.

Prickett: Strange how it looks; methinks it smells like ling.
It has a beard so sad. The mouth's all raw;
The strangest creature that I ever saw –
Are these the beasts that keep men in such awe?

(That question is *typical* of Rochester.)

Swivea: By such a thing philosophers have taught
That all mankind into the world was brought.
'Twas such a thing our sire the King bestrid,
Out of whose loins we came –

Prickett: The devil we did!

Swivea: It is the workhouse of the world's great trade;
On this soft anvil all mankind was made.
Come; 'tis a harmless thing. Draw near and try.
You will desire no other death to die.

Prickett: Is't death then?

Swivea: Ah, but with such pleasant pain
That straight it tickles you to life again.

Prickett: I feel my spirits are in agony!

Swivea: These are the symptoms of young lechery.
Does not your prick stand and your pulse beat fast?
Don't you desire some unknown bliss to taste?

Prickett: My heart invites me to some new desire.
My blood boils o'er –

Swivea: I can allay that fire.
Come, my dear rogue, and on my belly lie.
A little lower yet – now, dearest, try.

Prickett: I am a stranger to these unknown parts
And never versed in love's obliging arts.
Pray guide me. I never was this way before.

Swivea: Then enter now, since you have found the door.

Prickett: I'm in! I vow it is as soft as wool!

Swivea: Then thrust and move it up and down, you fool.

❧ ❧ ❧

Rochester's most famous work 'A Satire Against Reason and Mankind', is of huge significance to a biographer, for in it he hints heavily, for the first time, at self-doubt. The first version of the poem was written in the mid-1670s – possibly as early as 1674. At first sight it seems to be an unmitigated mockery of the man of reason by the man of instinct and appetite. Indeed, one of its greatest qualities is the passion with which the poet argues his case. Inspired by the satire of Boileau – as was 'Timon' – it begins where 'Tunbridge Wells' leaves off, expressing more respect for the beast than for the human being:

> Were I (who to my cost already am
> One of those strange, prodigious creatures, man)
> A spirit free to choose for my own share
> What case of flesh and blood I pleased to wear,
> I'd be a dog, a monkey or a bear,
> Or anything but that vain animal
> Who is so proud of being rational.

He explains why:

> The senses are too gross and he'll contrive
> A sixth to contradict the other five,
> And before certain instinct will prefer
> Reason, which fifty times for one does err.

The most obvious paradox about this work is that it took a tremendous amount of reason to write it, and Rochester, acutely aware that as an intellectual Hobbist he was also, by definition, a man of reason, begins to write in terms which can clearly be applied to the hedonistic Earl who became, at the end of his life, a Christian convert:

Reason, an ignis fatuus in the mind
Which, leaving light of nature, sense, behind,
Pathless and dangerous wandering ways it takes
Through error's fenny bogs and thorny brakes,
Whilst the misguided follower climbs with pain
Mountains of whimseys heaped in his own brain;
Stumbling from thought to thought, falls headlong down
Into doubt's boundless sea, where, like to drown,
Books bear him up awhile and make him try
To swim with bladders of philosophy;
In hopes still to o'ertake the escaping light,
The vapour dances in his dazzling sight
Till, spent, it leaves him to eternal night.

He now, in effect, writes his own epitaph:

Then old age and experience, hand in hand,
Lead him to death and make him understand
After a search so painful and so long,
That all his life he has been in the wrong.
Huddled in dirt the reasoning engine lies,
Who was so proud, so witty and so wise.
Pride drew him in, as cheats their bubbles catch
And made him venture to be made a wretch.
His wisdom did his happiness destroy,
Aiming to know that world he should enjoy.
And wit was his vain, frivolous pretence
Of pleasing others at his own expense.
For wits are treated just like common whores:
First they're enjoyed and then kicked out of doors.
Women and men of wit are dangerous tools
And ever fatal to admiring fools.
Pleasure allures, and when the fops escape,
'Tis not that they're beloved but fortunate,
And therefore what they fear at heart, they hate . . .

He breaks off suddenly, as though he has distracted himself from
the intended task, which is to play the part of the committed
Hobbist versus the man of reason. The latter then launches his

attack on Hobbism by upholding the very beliefs which the Earl had held upon first coming to Court in 1664 and which still represented his stifled idealism:

> What rage ferments in your degenerate mind
> To make you rail at reason and mankind?
> Blest, glorious man! to whom alone kind heaven
> An everlasting soul has freely given;
> Whom his great Maker took such care to make
> That from himself he did the image take,
> And this fair frame in shining reason dressed
> To dignify his nature above beast;
> Reason, by whose aspiring influence
> We take a flight beyond material sense,
> Dive into mysteries, then, soaring, pierce
> The flaming limits of the universe,
> Search heaven and hell, find out what's acted there,
> And give the world true grounds of hope and fear.

Rochester was really arguing with himself in this satire, and he now adopts the Hobbist's argument to destroy the one he has just put forward. He sounds convinced by it, but only because he knew it backwards. In truth, he was believing in his own propaganda with less and less conviction:

> Our sphere or action in life's happiness,
> And he who thinks beyond thinks like an ass.
> Thus, whilst against false reasoning I inveigh,
> I own right reason, which I would obey:
> That reason which distinguishes by sense
> And gives us rules of good and ill from thence;
> That bounds desires with a reforming will
> To keep 'em more in vigour; not to kill.
> Your reason hinders; mine helps to enjoy,
> Renewing appetites yours would destroy.
> My reason is my friend; yours is a cheat;
> Hunger calls out, my reason bids me eat;
> Perversely, yours your appetite does mock:
> This asks for food, that answers, 'What's o'clock?'

This plain distinction, sir, your doubt secures.
'Tis not true reason I despise, but yours . . .

He then goes back to the theme of beasts and explains why they
are cleverer than men:

'Tis evident beasts are, in their degree,
As wise at least and better far then he,
Those creatures are the wisest who attain,
By surest means, the ends at which they aim.
If therefore Jowler finds and kills his hares
Better than Meres supplies committee chairs,
Though one's a statesman, the other but a hound,
Jowler, in justice, would be wiser found . . .

This brings him on to mankind's cruelty:

Which is the basest creature, man or beast?
Birds feed on birds, beasts on each other prey
But savage man alone does not betray
Pressed by necessity they kill for food;
Man undoes man to do himself no good.
With teeth and claws by nature armed they hunt
Nature's allowance, to supply their want.
But man, with smiles; embraces; friendship; praise;
Inhumanly his fellow's life betrays;
With voluntary pains works his distress,
Not through necessity but wantonness.
For hunger or for love they fight and tear,
Whilst wretched man is still in arms for fear.
For fear he arms and is of arms afraid,
By fear to fear successively betrayed.
Base fear, the source whence his best passions came:
His boasted honour and his dear-bought fame;
That lust or power, to which he's such a slave,
And for the while alone he dares be brave;
To which his various projects are designed,
Which makes him generous, affable and kind;
For which he takes such pains to be thought wise

And screws his actions in a forced disguise,
Leading a tedious life in misery
Under laborious, mean hypocrisy . . .

Those last two lines remind us of Hobbes's ground rule: that the life of man is nasty, brutish and short.

The schizophrenic quality of his satire is indicative of the confusion and uncertainty which alcoholism, sickness and increasing unhappiness were causing Rochester. Still only in his twenties, it was already becoming difficult for him to look into a mirror and understand how Hobbism had benefited him. The superstitious doubt, which had been prompted by the premonitions of Montagu and Wyndham but which the Earl had quashed for a decade with his carefree hedonism, was rearing its head again. To compound his wavering, he witnessed a similar premonition of death during the 1670s which again proved to be prophetic. He talked about this incident on his death-bed too, and Burnet recorded:

He told me of another odd presage that one had of his approaching death in the Lady Warre, his mother-in-law's house. The chaplain had dreamt that such a day he should die, but being by all the family put out of the belief of it he had almost forgot it, till the evening before at supper, there being *thirteen* at table. [my italics] According to a fond conceit that one of these soon die, one of the young ladies pointed to him, that he was to die. He, remembering his dream, fell into some disorder, and the Lady Warre reproving him for his superstition, he said he was confident he was to die before morning; but he being in perfect health, it was not much minded. He went to his chamber and sat up late, as appeared by the burning of his candle, and he had been preparing his notes for his sermon, but was found dead in his bed the next morning . . .

That Rochester could be affected by such superstition shows that although he is often thought of as a man ahead of his times, he belonged very much to the uncertain and credulous era into which he was born. So was there such a thing as the soul after all?

Could life be less transient than he had believed? Questions like these were still only being addressed during his 'sad intervals and severe reflections', but they were starting to surface with a growing insistence none the less. As the possibility of some kind of permanency to life developed, so did the idea that an affair might mean love between two souls and not just a payment of the 'debt to pleasure'. For the first time in his adult life, Rochester was becoming vulnerable to the risk of believing in someone; of clinging to one ideal at least. At the Dorset Gardens Theatre one afternoon in September 1675, his attention was drawn to a vulnerable-looking fifteen-year-old actress called Elizabeth Barry. She needed his help.

8

NEMESIS

Dorimant: I will renounce all the joys I have in friendship
           and in wine, sacrifice to you all the interest I
           have in other women -
Harriet: Hold – though I wish you devout, I would not
           have you turn fanatic.

Rochester became involved with Elizabeth Barry because she was such a dreadful actress. That, at least, is the explanation which has been handed down. Desperate to tread the boards, she approached the Duke's Players and they duly tried her out in a performance. Her first recorded stage appearance was in the tiny role of Draxilla in Thomas Otway's *Alcibiades*, which was produced at the Dorset Gardens Theatre in September 1675 through Rochester's influence as a patron, and it was in this part that she was given her audition. She had a terrible ear for speech though, and the players found it impossible to teach her the cadences which were conventional for all performers to adopt at the time. According to Curll's *History of the English Stage*, Barry was so hopeless that 'several persons of wit and quality being at the play, and observing how she performed, positively gave their opinion she never would be capable of any part of acting'. It was also reckoned that she could 'neither sing, nor dance, no, not even in a country dance'. Her future as an actress seemed non-existent.

It was then that Rochester, having also seen her perform, 'entered into a wager, that by proper instruction, in less than six months he would engage she should be the finest player on the stage'. It is not known with whom Rochester made the bet, but it is sure that he won it. Under his training she became the greatest actress of the age.

Rochester had spotted potential and, as ever, was in the mood for a challenge. It is unlikely that he was drawn to Barry because of her looks, because, although she had a commanding presence, she was no beauty. She was of medium height, had dark hair and was rather plump. Anthony Aston said: 'this fine creature was not handsome, her mouth opening most on the right side, which she strove to draw t'other way, and, at times composing her face, as if sitting to have her picture drawn.' She was very much her own woman, and it was her strength and self-determination which captivated Rochester once he had introduced himself. Elizabeth Barry may have been strong; she was also, reportedly, bad-tempered, demanding and hard-natured. Her mercenary nature eventually gained her a widespread reputation for using any man who could advance her career and prospects. The sudden affections of Rochester, who by 1675 was one of the most powerful patrons in the London theatre, were an unexpected boon for her ambitions. Calling her a 'mercenary prostituting dame', Tom Brown said that 'should you lie with her all night, she would not know you next morning, unless you had another five pounds at her service'; more than twenty years later a wag was declaring that 'slattern Betty Barry' was still 'at thirty-eight a very hopeful whore' and would always choose 'the highest bidder'; and, years after Rochester's death, the poet Robert Gould wrote of her:

> Who counts her sins, may as well count the stars:
> So insolent! it is by all allowed
> There never was so base a thing, so proud:
> Yet covetous, she'll prostitute with any,
> Rather than waive the getting of a penny;
> For the whole harvest of her youthful crimes
> She hoards, to keep herself in future times,
> That by her gains now she may then be fed,
> Which in effect's to damn herself for bread.
> Yet in her morals this is thought the best;
> Imagine, then, the lewdness of the rest.

Curll said that Rochester 'never loved any person so sincerely as he loved Mrs Barry'. That such a dangerous-sounding woman was the object of his greatest passion was peculiarly apt and characteristically self-punitive. For more than two years he fought to contain her, and one suspects that it was this continuous challenge which, as much as anything else, kept him hooked. He had met his match at last, just as Dorimant meets his at the hands of Harriet:

Dorimant [aside]: I love her, and dare not let her know it. I fear sh'as an ascendant o'er me and may revenge the wrongs I have done her sex. [To her] Think of making a party madam; love will engage.

Harriet: You make me start! I did not think to have heard of love from you.

Dorimant: I never knew what 'twas to have a settled ague yet, but now and then have had irregular fits.

Harriet: Take heed, sickness after long health is commonly more violent and dangerous.

Dorimant [aside]: I have took the infection from her, and feel the disease now spreading in me. [To her] Is the name of love so frightful that you dare not stand it?

Harriet: 'Twill do little execution out of your mouth on me, I am sure.

Dorimant: It has been fatal –

Harriet: To some easy women, but we are not all born to one destiny. I was informed you use to laugh at love, and not make it.

Dorimant: The time has been, but now I must speak –

Harriet: If it be on that idle subject, I will put on my

> serious look, turn my head carelessly from you, drop my lip, let my eyelids fall, and hang half o'er my eyes – thus – while you buzz a speech of an hour long in my ear, and I answer never a word. Why do you not begin?

Dorimant: That the company may take notice how passionately I make advances of love, and how disdainfully you receive 'em.

Harriet: When your love's grown strong enough to make you bear being laughed at, I'll give you leave to trouble me with it. Till when, pray forbear, sir.

It seems likely that Barry had invented a glamorous past for herself because, although she had been a lowly servant to a Lady Shelton of Norfolk, she claimed that her father was a wealthy lawyer called Colonel Robert Barry. Rochester is said to have worked on both her speech and gait, turning her 'bad ear' to advantage by making her feel and express the *meaning* of the language she was speaking, instead of worrying about the sound. She was soon 'perfectly changing herself as it were into the person, not merely by the proper stress or sounding of the voice, but feeling really, and being in the humour, the person she represented, was supposed to be in'.

If this account of her training is true – and there is no reason not to believe it – Rochester can be credited with making Barry the first modern actress of the English theatre. Hers is a lineage which stretches down through the centuries to Sarah Bernhardt, Sybil Thorndike, Flora Robson, Edith Evans, Peggy Ashcroft, Maggie Smith, Judi Dench. . . . By breaking through the conventions of acting at the time and going for real emotion rather than concentrating on the way speech sounded, Barry was doing a similar thing to what Laurence Olivier did with Shakespearian verse in the early 1930s. He believed that John Gielgud, who was then the prince of the London stage, 'sang' Shakespeare. Olivier aimed to 'find the truth *through* the verse'. Some thought it brilliant; others favoured Gielgud's method and thought his ambitious rival could not speak verse for toffee.

Rochester's and Barry's method caused less controversy than that and was widely admired by all. Colley Cibber, the playwright and later Poet Laureate, said she developed a presence of 'elevated dignity, her mien and motion superb and gracefully majestic, her voice full, clear and strong, so that no violence of passion could be too much for her: and when distress or tenderness possessed her, she subsided into the most affecting melody and softness'. This last quality was as evident on the stage as it was absent off it. 'In the art of exacting pity,' Cibber added, 'she had a power beyond all the actresses I have yet seen, or what your imagination can conceive.'

The Earl was a hard taskmaster: he is said to have made Barry rehearse a party thirty times on the stage, twelve of them in full costume. Such exhaustive and exhausting work on a role was then unheard of, but Rochester always was a perfectionist. According to Curll, the Earl took 'extraordinary pains with her as not to omit the least look or motion' and her page was instructed to manage the train of her dress 'in such a manner, so as to give each movement, a peculiar grace'.

When Rochester had Barry re-engaged by the Duke's Players she took the audiences by storm. Curll said Rochester brought Charles and the Duke and Duchess of York to see the Earl of Orrery's tragedy *Mustapha*, in which Barry played the Hungarian Queen Isabella, and that 'the whole theatre resounded with applause' at her performance. In her long and glittering career (she died in 1713, aged fifty-five), Barry played more than one hundred leading roles including the heroines of Dryden, Otway, Congreve, Etherege, Vanbrugh and Lee.

The Earl and his young protegee were quickly in the throes of a passionate affair, but Rochester never found her as easy to manage as a lover as he did as an actress. Johannes Prinz, in his 1927 biography of the poet, cast doubt on the authenticity of the surviving letters to Barry which are said to have been from Rochester. Part of his mistrust concerned the fact that they never mention the theatre, or acting. This is an odd objection, since love letters are usually about emotions: happiness, sadness, hopes and fears. They tend not to be about work – an unfit subject for conversation at the best of times. The only letter Prinz thought genuine was the following one, which was published by the highly unreliable Captain Alexander Smith complete with a reply allegedly from Barry:

Since I am out of your presence (which is more intolerable to me than the sweetest death) I cannot live without a sight of you; so I wait your directions how I may once more be happy in the enjoyment of your company, which, if you forbid me, you stick a dagger to my heart, which now bleeds for you.

Her practical and comparatively unromantic reply reads:

Sir,
Tomorrow the Earl of P—ke goes out of town and at ten in the morning I will meet your Lordship in the long Piazza in Covent Garden. Till then, farewell, my dear, my dearest Rochester.
Barry.

How an undoubted expert on Rochester could have been so convinced that the first of these two letters was written by him is a mystery. The exchange is palpably fake. The tired phrases 'I cannot live without a sight of you' and 'you stick a dagger to my heart, which now bleeds for you' – enough to send any woman to sleep – are, if genuine, the only clichés Rochester ever used in his correspondence to anybody. It is the language of the fops who so angered him; the hyperbole of the unfortunate lover in 'The Imperfect Enjoyment'. This, for example, is much more his style, and while the difference may seem negligible it is significant:

There is now no minute of my life that does not afford me some new argument how much I love you. The little joy I take in everything wherein you are not concerned; the pleasing perplexity of endless thought which I fall into wherever you are brought to my remembrance; and lastly, the continual disquiet I am in during your absence, convince me sufficiently that I do you justice in loving you so as woman was never loved before.

No less passionate, but perfectly believable. There is a very self-conscious quality to these letters though. Rochester himself was an outstanding actor and now he was playing the role of the impassioned lover. That does not mean the passion was not real – quite the contrary – but that whatever he did in life, he did with the panache of a polished performer. Whether or not he was as honest about himself in his letters to Barry as he was in the ones he wrote to his wife is quite another matter. . . .

❦ ❦ ❦

As the 1670s progressed, Rochester's relationship with his wife became increasingly strained, mainly due to interference in the marriage by their respective mothers. His reputation was notorious enough for news of his latest misdemeanours, both real and supposed, to reach the ears of his mother-in-law, Lady Warre, down in Somerset. On her annual visits to her daughter at Adderbury she aggravated a delicate situation with gossip and criticism about her son-in-law. Rochester was always as frank as possible with his wife but at the same time tried to protect her sensibilities. This was hopeless when she was receiving every rumoured and gory detail of his life in London from her mother. Following these visits he would invariably have to reply to an unhappy and complaining letter. Once he wrote back angrily of 'your late conversations with those whom I should extremely honour if they would do me the right and you the justice never to come near you when I am really as well with you as I wish and you pretend'. He felt he had no option but to 'exercise my usual talent of patience and submission'.

His wife's friends, too, seem to have done their best to poison her against him, and in a surviving fragment of a letter to her he speaks with a wonderful defiance of the great disproportion between

> our desires and what is ordained to content them. But you will say this is pride and madness, for there are those so entirely satisfied with their shares in this world that their wishes nor their thoughts have not a farther prospect of felicity and glory. I'll tell you, were that man's soul placed in a body fit for it, he were a dog, that could count anything a benefit obtained with flattery, fear and service.

> Is there a man, ye Gods, whom I do hate,
> Dependance and attendance be his fate.
> Let him be busy still and in a crowd,
> And very much a slave and very proud.

I would not have you lose my letter; it is not fit for everybody to find.

Roch.

Your wine was bought last week but neglected to be sent.

(Note the reference to 'man's soul'.)

Far from disowning him, Rochester's mother was always very defensive of her son. Perhaps she chose not to believe too much of what she heard: she was certainly single-minded enough. She compounded the couple's problems, however, by visiting Adderbury regularly in his absence and criticising her daughter-in-law. Rochester's wife would then send him a letter of complaint about this haranguing. He once implored her in his reply 'not to be too much amazed at the thoughts my mother has of you, since being mere imaginations they will as easily vanish as they were groundlessly created'.

It is a classic example of how mothers-in-law, thinking they have some kind of automatic right to poke around in their children's marriage, only ever seem to make matters worse. Small wonder that when Rochester was bitten on the leg by a dog in a London street, he stared at it with contempt and declared: 'I wish that you were married and living in the country.' As Henry Savile had indicated, the turn of the decade saw the Earl staying at Adderbury a good deal, but on one later occasion when he was there with various relatives, the atmosphere became so unbearable that he walked out of the house and took a carriage back to London without saying goodbye to anybody. By the time he reached the capital, remorse had set in and he confessed in a letter that to 'run away like a rascal without taking leave, dear wife', had been

an unpolished way of proceeding which a modest man ought to be ahamed of. I have left you a prey to your own imaginations amongst my relations, the worst of damnations, but there will come an hour of deliverance, till when, may my mother be merciful to you. So I commit you to what shall ensue, woman to woman, wife to mother, in hopes of a future appearance in glory.

(Note the parody of religion.)

The contentment of the summer of 1672, when Rochester stayed with his wife at both Adderbury – where guests enjoyed dancing one evening in both the garden and the forecourt until nearly midnight – and at her estate in Enmore, often seemed a far cry during these troubled altercations. That year, Rochester had increased his standing in the West country with his appointment as deputy-lieutenant of Somerset. (In November 1677 he was elected an alderman of Taunton.) There were also festivities at home every September when the four-mile Woodstock Plate was run, and the Earl was usually in attendance. On 16 September 1679 his grey won the race, but although Rochester was a fine horseman it is unlikely that he was well enough to have been the rider.

He was at home again in July 1674 for the baptism of his second daughter, Elizabeth. She became the most beautiful of his three girls – 'a pretty little body', declared Thomas Hearne – and ironically she married Edward Montagu, the third Earl of Sandwich, son of Rochester's rival to her mother's hand in marriage, the then Viscount Hinchingbrooke. Elizabeth took after her father in many respects. She was formidably intelligent and became widely celebrated for her vivacious wit and infectious sense of fun. She had a happier and much longer life than her father though, dying at the ripe old age of eighty-three.

Rochester's increasingly wayward behaviour during the 1670s did not help to soothe the disturbed waters of his marriage. Alcoholics are remarkable for the way in which they can appear (up to a point) to be sober when deep in drink, and one can only assume that since John Aubrey said the Earl was 'generally civil enough' in the country, he continued to behave reasonably well when he was with his family, even during the five years of continual inebriation.

H.J. Gepp, in his 1924 publication *Adderbury*, related two anecdotes about Rochester's conduct in the area which are very hard to believe. It is said that he once went to Barford, to the south-west of Adderbury, dressed up as a tinker and asked the locals there whether he could mend their pots and pans. He was then put in the village stocks for knocking all the bottoms out.

He then persuaded a man to take a note from him to Lord Rochester at Adderbury, upon which his carriage and four arrived at Barford, the stocks were dug up and he returned home. Shortly afterwards he sent the people new pots and pans.

The second story is no more likely. In this, he disguised himself as a tramp and, upon bumping into another tramp, asked the fellow where he was going.

The latter replied that he was going to Lord Rochester's, not that it was of any use, for he never gave anything. Lord Rochester said he would go with him. The tramp went to the back of the house, while Lord Rochester went to the front and gave the servants instructions to detain him and put him in a barrel of beer. Every time the tramp put his head up the Earl threatened to 'bash him' and he kept him there for some time. On releasing him he gave him a good meal and a new suit of clothes, and told him never again to say there was nothing to be got from Lord Rochester.

These reported incidents would be more believable if they related to London. Rochester simply did not behave like this when he was at home. An explanation of their origins is easy: anyone who lives in a village even today will testify to the amazing degree of myth and rumour which will surround any resident who happens to be an eccentric. Multiply that a few times to allow for the credulity of the countryman in mid seventeenth-century England and we have the villainous Lord Rochester, a terror from that foreign place called London, demolishing people's kitchen equipment and beating up innocent tramps.

His alcoholism ensured that, in London, his behaviour was becoming increasingly violent. In the middle of March 1673, he quarrelled at Court with Robert Constable, Viscount Dunbar, but the opportunity of re-establishing his honour was cut short when a duel which they had arranged was prevented by the King. When his health allowed it, Rochester could still be one of Whitehall's most glittering ornaments, and his public facade accounted for the general belief in 1676 that he was Dorimant to the core. Behind the scenes though and during the worst plunges into alcoholism's abyss, there was the despair, the depression, the decaying eyesight, the night-time sweats, the lethargy, the panic attacks, the wretching, vomiting and stomach trouble. The reader can afford to grin at the following lines, but they were written by a man who at times like this no longer knew how he could help himself:

> I rise at eleven; I dine about two;
> I get drunk before seven and the next thing I do,
> I send for my whore, when for fear of the clap,
> I dally round her and spew in her lap.
> Then we quarrel and scold, till I fall asleep
> When the jilt growing bold, to my pocket does creep.
> Then slyly she leaves me and to revenge the affront,
> At once both my lass and my money I want.
> If by chance then I wake, hot-headed and drunk,
> What a coyl do I make for the loss of my punk!
> I storm and I roar and I fall in a rage,
> And missing my lass, I fall on my page;
> Then crop-sick, all morning I rail at my men,
> And in bed I lie yawning till eleven, again.

It was this level of dissolution which accounted for letters to his wife being as depressing as the following:

I recover so slowly and relapse so continually that I am almost weary of myself. If I had the least strength I would come to Adderbury, but in the condition I am, Kensington and back is a voyage I can hardly support. I hope you excuse my sending you no money, for till I am well enough to fetch it myself they will not give me a farthing, and if I had not pawned my plate I believe I must have starved in my sickness.

In January 1675, the Earl was back in Adderbury for the baptism of his third daughter, Mallet. A little plainer than her sisters and brother, she eventually married John Vaughan, Viscount Lisburne. Rochester returned to London to be told by Charles that he was now to become Master of the King's hawks. Like his monarch, the Earl was a keen and accomplished falconer and knew it had once been a disguise reluctantly adopted by his father. A few months after this latest appointment, on 25 June, Rochester smashed up one of Charles's most highly prized possessions: the rarest sundial in Europe.

If this instrument were still intact today it would be invaluable. It was made of glass spheres and fascinated the King, whose love of science and mechanics included an obsession with watches, clocks and time generally. He had some half-a-dozen clocks in his bedroom alone and he used the sundial to synchronise his watch. The destruction of this rarity was exactly the kind of wanton, boorish behaviour which can make it so hard to sympathise with the plight of the alcoholic. Rochester, whose memory of the incident was probably clouded, later made a profuse apology to Charles, who, with his characteristic cynicism, as though he had never expected anything else, forgave him. There was one mitigating circumstance which is commonly overlooked: Rochester did take the lead in destroying the dial – but he *was* helped by other courtiers.

Following a night-time drinking session with the King, a number of the wits were weaving their way across Whitehall's Privy Garden when Rochester's eyes just about managed to focus on the sundial. When he was drunk, certain innocent objects took on a phallic appearance to him (in 'A Ramble in St James's Park', for instance, he looks at a row of tall plants 'whose lewd tops fucked the very skies') and in the case of the sundial he was affronted by its shape with a certain degree of justice. By all accounts it did look, with its glass balls, slightly suggestive. Rochester went beserk, screamed: 'Dost thou stand here to fuck time?!' and began wrecking it. Both Sir Francis Fane the Elder and John Aubrey, in his life of Franciscus Linus, stated that Lord Buckhurst was one of those who helped him. Aubrey said that the others included Fleetwood Shepherd, while Fane listed Lord Sussex and Henry Savile. Fane also recorded that they were shouting: 'Kings and Kingdoms tumble down and so shall thou!'

Inadvertently, the King gained a kind of revenge by appointing the Earl as ranger and keeper of Woodstock Park. These offices had been given to him on separate occasions earlier in the year, and with the rangership came the remote and imposing High Lodge. This was disastrous for Rochester's health. Until now, his visits to the country had had a relatively rehabilitating effect on his constitution, because the only place to stay had been with his family at Adderbury. High Lodge offered no such constraint. It became not only a refuge from London (and in 1675 he was banished from Whitehall by Charles for writing 'The History of Insipids') but a sanctuary to which he could beat a ten-mile retreat from his unhappy wife and her critical friends at Adderbury. Before long Henry Savile was distinguishing in a letter between the 'sobriety of Adderbury and the debauchery of Woodstock'. Anthony Wood said that the Earl had a number of lascivious pictures drawn at the Lodge and, according to Thomas Hearne he played host to several local girls including 'one Nell Browne of Woodstock'.

It seems that occasionally his wife made the forty-five minute coach ride from Adderbury and stayed with him, but more often it was he who journeyed to the family home. Once, having returned to the Lodge after a spell at Adderbury, he wished that she had come back with him:

> I fear I must see London shortly, and begin to regret that I did not bring you with me; for since these rakehells are not here to disturb us you might have passed your devotions this Holy Season as well in this place as at Adderbury.

But visits from these rakehells – who sometimes included the Duke of Buckingham, Lord Buckhurst, Sir Charles Sedley, Sir George Etherege, Henry Savile *et al.* – meant Rochester did not usually want his wife there at all. His tendency to lie low from her when so close to home often goaded her.

> Though I cannot flatter myself so much as to expect it, yet give me leave to wish that you would dine tomorrow at Cornbury, where necessity forces.

> Your faithful humble wife,
> E. Rochester.

Below, she drives the point home:

> If you sent to command me to Woodstock when I am so near
> as Cornbury I shall not be a little rejoiced.

There is a certain type of woman who makes her unhappiness
known to her partner by sighing very loudly and then, upon being
asked what the matter is, replies: 'nothing'. She then sighs again,
even more loudly. The faithful and humble E. Rochester
understandably did this a great deal, and it sometimes resulted in
her husband's exasperation:

> The difficulties of pleasing your ladyship do increase so fast
> upon me, and are grown so numerous, that to a man less
> resolved than myself never to give it over, it would appear a
> madness ever to attempt more . . . I confess there is nothing
> will so much contribute to my assistance in this as your
> ladyship dealing freely with me, for since you have thought it
> a wise thing to trust me less and have reserves, it has been
> out of my power to make the best of my proceedings . . .
> I intend to be at Adderbury some time next week.

This new licence to misbehave in the country makes one
anecdote, about some silliness just outside Woodstock,
much more credible than H.J. Gepp's two stories. Thomas
Hearne said that one morning 'the wild Earl of Rochester' and
his rakehell companions met with 'a fine young maid' on her way
to market with butter, which, having bought it from her, they
stuck all over the trunk of a tree. Not wanting to see it wasted
and thinking they had all gone, the maid sneaked back and
removed it. But Rochester and his rakehells spotted her doing
this and, riding after her, 'set her upon her head and clapped the
butter upon her breech'.

When he was at the Lodge with no one but his servants,
the Earl was more inclined to read – 'His Lordship read all
manner of books,' said John Aubrey – and work on his satires,
which Gilbert Burnet claimed often employed him for 'some
months'. (This may be an accidental exaggeration by the
otherwise trustworthy Burnet. The lure of London seems likely

to have limited Rochester's stays in the country, at both Adderbury and later at High Lodge, to weeks at a time and not months on end.)

The Earl was easily distracted, and among his friends the most pernicious influence came from a man only marginally less outrageous, the Duke of Buckingham. The 'lord of useless thousands' descended on the Lodge a number of times, once having warned that he intended to bring with him the finest pack of hounds that ever ran upon English ground. As his expertise at falconry suggests, Rochester, when his health was up to it, was very keen on country pursuits and he must have awaited that particular visit with some enthusiasm. The greatest danger Buckingham posed to him at this stage of his life was that the Duke was a Falstaffian Heavy Drinker with a formidable constitution, and not an alcoholic. (He outlived his childhood friend the King by two years, dying at the age of sixty in 1687.) Rochester could not afford to even try and keep up with him. Buckingham, who unlike the Earl was astonishingly insensitive, tended to leave a trail of devastation in his wake. On a weekend visit he was quite capable of draining the wine cellar, ravishing the odd wench and then, leaving his host for dead, departing at dawn on Monday morning to be back in London for a council meeting later that day. Rochester liked his style, and the Duke was one of the very few people he never chose to attack satirically. (Even Lord Buckhurst, whom Rochester called 'the best good man with the worst natured muse', received an affectionate teasing.) Buckingham's shortlived obsessions with new projects, pastimes and subjects have been noted, and as these letters sent to Rochester at High Lodge show, he at one point became fascinated with fish:

My Lord,

I can truly assure your Lordship, as my Lord of Bristol did the Duchess of Richmond, that I have not contaminated my body with any person below my quality since I saw you . . . I am now very busy drinking your Lordship's health and shall very shortly have the honour to receive your and Mrs Nelli's commands. In the meantime I have sent you two of the civillest carp that ever I had do with, and if they could speak they would infallibly . . . assure your Lordship that I am, more than any man living,

> My Lord,
> Your Lordship's
> Most humble
> and faithful
> servant,
> Buckingham.

(This 'Mrs Nelli' is most unlikely to have been Nell Gwyne as has been suggested, and there is no reason to think that the royal mistress ever even visited the Lodge. Presumably, the reference is to the local Woodstock girl, Nell Browne.) But Buckingham had not finished with carp yet. He wrote again to say that he had received from a Mr Pome

> some instructions about the breeding of carp, which I shall acquaint your Lordship with when I have the honour to see you. The circumstances of the matter are something long, but this in short is the sum of it: that you must be sure to cleanse your pond very well, and let no fish in it whatsoever but only two carp, a male, and a female, and then that the next year you must take them out of that pond, and put them into another for fear of their being eaten by pikes. [He does not explain how pike – which would decimate stock in no time – could possibly be in the pond when there are no fish in it except two carp.] This, he says, will make them breed infinitely, and grow very fat, though he has not as yet been pleased to tell me what they are to be fed with . . .

Rochester was playing host to Buckingham at High Lodge when he sent the following letter to his wife, and it is most appropriate that he should include the phrase 'various accidents succeed':

Dear Wife

I have despatched your messenger away tonight to save you the trouble of rising early, hoping you have no concern to communicate to me of your own; the D of B [Duke of Buckingham] came hither tonight and stays two days; I must lend him my coach half way back – therefore, pray send it me. My condition of health alters, I hope, for the better though various accidents succeed. My pains are pretty well over, and my rheumatism begins to turn to an honest gout. My pissing of blood Doctor Witherley [a physician to the King] says is nothing. My eyes are almost out, but that he says will not do me much harm; in short he'll make me eat flesh and drink diet-drink.

R.
God bless you.
My duty to my mother. Thank her for my cordials.

While probably fictional in part, one particular story about Buckingham and Rochester is in essence convincing. It is said that for a while they were landlords of the Green Mare Inn at Six Mile Bottom, a village so named after the distance from the bottom of its hill into Newmarket. This joint enterprise would have been rather like the brides of Dracula running a blood bank – but the two men did often accompany Charles on his horse-racing trips to Newmarket, where the Nell Gwyn stakes are run today, and it is perfectly conceivable that one year they overstayed their welcome while passing through the village. Certainly, Six Mile Bottom was on the London to Newmarket route. Doubt creeps into the story with the allegation that, in order to make a cuckold of an elderly man with a particularly comely young wife, Rochester avoided suspicion by entering their home dressed as a woman. Having duly ravished the young wife behind her husband's back, the Earl is said to have taken her to the Green Mare Inn (naturally, she took all her husband's savings with her), where Buckingham had his turn as well. When the old man realised what had happened he hanged himself. The story ends with the King and the other courtiers arriving at the inn. When the joing landlords told him their story they laughed as merrily as Robin Hood and his band of men.

⚜ ⚜ ⚜

In 1675, Rochester was busy with the theatre. Quite apart from promoting Crowne over Dryden, seeing that Tom Otway's *Alcibiades* was performed and training Elizabeth Barry, he became a patron to Nathaniel Lee, who duly dedicated his play *Nero* to the Earl. He also received lavish thanks from Sir Francis Fane for ensuring that *Love in the Dark* was staged. The insincerity, conceit and hyperbole of 'theatre people' was something Rochester could not tolerate and, even allowing for the elaborate language of the day, Sir Francis Fane's dedicatory epistle to his play was so absurd that it must have damned him in the eyes of his new patron:

All poems in their dedications ought to return to your Lordship, as all rivers to the sea, from whose depth and saltness they are seasoned and supplied: none of them ever coming to your Lordship's hands without receiving some of the rich tinctures of your unerring judgement; and running with much more clearness, having passed so fine a strainer . . . Others, by wearisome steps and regular gradations, climb up to knowledge; your Lordship is flown up to the top of the hill: you are an enthusiast in wit; a poet and philosopher by revelation; and have already, in your tender age, set out such new and glorious lights in poetry, yet those so orthodox and unquestionable that all the heroes of antiquity must submit or Homer and Virgil be judged nonconformists . . . I never return from your Lordship's most charming and instructive conversation but I am inspired with a new genius and improved in all those sciences I ever coveted the knowledte of: I find myself not only a better poet, a better philosopher, but, much more than these , a better Christian: your Lordship's miraculous wit and intellectual powers being the greatest argument that ever I could meet with for the immateriality of the soul; they being the highest exaltation of humane nature; and, under divine authority, much more convincing to suspicious Reason than all the pedantic proofs of the most learned peevish disputants: so that, I hope, I shall be obliged to your Lordship not only for my reputation in this world but my future happiness in the next . . .

Those latter sentiments cannot have pleased Rochester, who was renowned as an atheist and still preferred to keep any private thoughts about religion to the back of his mind. It was an amazing *faux pas* by Fane.

Meanwhile, relations with Dryden were simmering nicely. The Poet Laureate took great pleasure in dedicating his 1675 publication of *Aurengzebe* to Rochester's enemy Mulgrave, praising him effusively and making a subtle jibe at his former patron by writing of 'the character of a courtier without wit'. Such men, he said, crushed with ease 'those who are under them' and thus revealed themselves in their natural antipathy.

Rochester's response was a little more direct. Precisely when he wrote 'An Allusion to Horace' is unclear, but it seems to have been percolating through the hands of his admirers and detractors by the spring of 1676. Taking his lead from the great Roman poet's analysis of contemporary writers, Rochester managed, with one sweep of his pen, to insult both Dryden *and* Mulgrave in the first three lines:

> Well, sir, 'tis granted, I said Dryden's rhymes
> Were stolen, unequal, nay dull many times.
> What foolish patron is there found of his,
> So blindly partial to deny me this?
> But that his plays, embroidered up and down
> With wit and learning, justly pleased the town,
> In the same paper, I as freely own,
> Yet having this allowed, the heavy mass
> That stuffs up his loose volumes must not pass,
> For by that rule I might as well admit
> Crowne's tedious scenes for poetry and wit.

That, of course, is exactly what he had done, and those last two lines were designed to be more of an insult to Dryden than they were to the unfortunate Crowne. For the Poet Laureate to have been passed over for a writer whom Rochester admired would have been one thing, but to have been cast aside for someone who the Earl thought wrote 'tedious scenes' was an even bigger put-down.

In 'An Allusion to Horace' Rochester gave his verdict on a whole range of contemporary writers, but still found time to return to the chief target. In this second wave of attack he at last revealed why the Poet Laureate so offended him:

> Dryden in vain tried this nice way of wit,
> For he to be a tearing blade thought fit.
> But when he would be sharp, he still was blunt:
> To frisk his frolic fancy, he'd cry, 'Cunt!'
> Would give the ladies a dry bawdy bob,
> And thus he got the name of Poet Squab.

To Rochester, Dryden was a fine writer who betrayed himself by wanting to be – to use a modern colloquialism – one of the lads. He lowered himself by showing off in places like Will's Coffee House to a coterie of sycophantic admirers who had not an ounce of his capability. He wanted to be a 'tearing blade'. A 'dry-bob' meant coition without ejaculation, and it suggests that Dryden's attempts to fit in with the earthier side of life were pretentious. Rochester believed that life should be lived with immense style by those who could lift themselves to it and physically wrecked though he was, the Earl never failed in this self-appointed duty. Only two other writers in the English language have *lived* their art to the same degree: Lord Byron and Oscar Wilde. Dryden, then, was a let-down.

However, the Earl did not think anyone else in the age was more talented than Dryden:

> But, to be just, 'twill to his praise be found
> His excellencies more than faults abound;
> Nor dare I from his sacred temples tear
> That laurel which he best deserves to wear.

Now he turned to the Poet Laureate's 'Essay on the Dramatic Poetry of the Last Age', which had been bugging him for so long:

> But does not Dryden find even Jonson dull;
> Fletcher and Beaumont uncorrect, and full
> Of lewd lines, as he calls 'em; Shakespeare's style
> Stiff and affected; to his own the while
> Allowing all the justness that his pride
> So arrogantly had to these denied?

And may not I have leave impartially
To search and censure Dryden's works, and try
If those gross faults his choice pen does commit
Proceed from want of judgement, or of wit;
Or if his lumpish fancy does refuse
Spirit and grace to his loose, slattern muse?
Five hundred verses every morning writ
Proves you no more a poet than a wit.
Such scribbling authors have been seen before;
Mustapha, The English Princess, forty more,
Were things perhaps composed in half an hour.
To write what may securely stand the test
Of being well read over thrice at least,
Compare each phrase, examine every line,
Weigh every word, and every thought refine . . .

Of others, he was kinder. It is amusing to note that his friend Sir George Etherege, who, as Rochester knew, was planning a production in the coming months which would immortalise his character, was loudly applauded for being 'refined' and a 'sheer original'. He was also generous but very discerning in dealing with Thomas Shadwell and William Wycherley:

Of all our modern wits none seems to me
Once to have touched upon true comedy
But hasty Shadwell and slow Wycherley.
Shadwell's unfinished works do yet impart
Great proofs of force by nature, none of Art.
With just bold strokes he dashes here and there,
Showing great mastery with little care,
And scorns to varnish his good touches o'er
To make the fools and women praise 'em more.
But Wycherley earns hard what e're he gains,
He wants no judgement, nor he spares no pains;
He frequently excels, and, at the least,
Makes fewer faults than any of the best.

Two other friends, Buckhurst and Sedley, also received the Earl's approval – but his analysis of them was none the less perfectly accurate:

> For pointed satyrs I would Buckhurst choose:
> The best good man with the worst natured muse.
> For songs and verses mannerly obscene
> That can stir nature up by springs unseen
> And, without forcing blushes, warm the Queen,
> Sedley has that prevailing art
> That can with a resistless charm impart
> The loosest wishes to the chastest heart;
> Raise such a conflict, kindle such a fire
> Betwixt declining virtue and desire,
> Till the poor vanquished maid dissolves away
> In dreams all night; in sighs and tears all day.

In *An Allusion to Horace*, Rochester also pulled his literary sword on the squint-eyed and ugly Sir Carr Scrope, who had had the impertinence to start lampooning the master of satire. Indeed, it may have been Scrope who had the temerity to circulate *On the Author of a Play called Sodom*, castigating the playwright as a 'weak feeble strainer at mere ribaldry'. The Earl now snapped back:

> Should I be troubled when the purblind knight
> Who squints more in his judgement than his sight,
> Picks silly faults and censures what I write;
> Or when the poor-fed poets of the town,
> For scraps and coach room, cry my verses down?

The Earl ends by dismissing, unlike Dryden, the worth of popularity and says he would rather have the approval of those few writers he respects. The word 'rabble' is not a class distinction; it means popular opinion:

> I loathe the rabble; 'tis enough for me
> If Sedley, Shadwell, Shepherd, Wycherley,
> Godolphin, Butler, Buckhurst, Buckingham,
> And some few more whom I omit to name,
> Approve my sense: I count their censure fame.

In 1677, a similar satire on current writers, called 'A Session of the Poets', began to circulate at Court. At the time, even

Rochester's immediate circle, including his best friend Savile, believed the Earl to have been the author. The satire was so admired, wrote Savile to Rochester in the country, that it seemed most likely to have been 'composed at Woodstock'. But Rochester's reply to Savile shows that he was not the author of the piece. He asked his friend to send him a copy, and added, 'He cannot want wit utterly, that has a spleen to those rogues'.

'Those rogues' included, amongst other lampooned writers, the playwright Thomas Otway, who had previously dedicated his *Titus and Berenice* to Rochester. The writer of 'A Session of the Poets' mocks Otway's conceitedness, and comments unkindly that, after the financial success of his play *Don Carlos*, 'Otway's mange was quite cured, and his lice were all killed'. The belief that Rochester penned these lines persisted until sixty years ago, when Professor Roswell Ham convincingly pointed to one of Rochester's protégés, Elkanah Settle, as the culprit. The previous idea that Rochester was the author presumably held credibility for so long because it supported another accusation, compounded by the critic Sir Edmund Gosse, that Rochester viciously persecuted Otway.

It is true that, in his 'An Allusion to Horace', the Earl had not exactly spared Otway, whom he called 'puzzling', but he never singled him out for attack either. The relationship between the two men – which started out as a professional one – hinges on the fact that Otway became obsessed with Elizabeth Barry. 'Since the first day I gazed upon you, now for seven years I have loved your image with all the violence of despair', wrote the playwright to the actress after Rochester's death. Otway's passion for Barry is the reason, Gosse believes, that Rochester hounded him out of the country. It is known that Otway became a soldier and went to Flanders for about a year, but whether, as the story goes, he joined up to flee a seethingly jealous Rochester or to escape the cold dismissiveness of Elizabeth Barry, is open to question. Rochester had never before blamed men for doting on his lovers – he was more likely to criticise the woman's lack of judgement if she accepted their romantic advances – and might he not, who himself was shortly to feel Elizabeth Barry's icy withdrawal, have felt sympathy for Otway?

Certainly, Otway turned against Rochester and later, in 'A Poet's Complaint to His Muse', described Rochester's verse as 'rank'. But this comment, engineered by spite, probably had less to do with the Earl's treatment of him as a rival in love than the playwright's belief that Rochester had made him look absurd in 'A Session of the Poets'. It is, perhaps, some consolation to historians who spend time trying to assign authorship of these anonymous lampoons and satires to various courtiers and professional playwrights, that the people of the time were equally bewildered.

The spring of 1676 saw John Dryden, who had read 'An Allusion to Horace' with particular interest, looking rather angry in Will's Coffee House. Henry Savile wrote a letter to Rochester, which has not survived, informing the Earl that Mr Dryden was not terribly pleased with him. In his reply to Savile, Rochester again pointed to the discrepancy between Dryden's artistic gifts and his personal qualities. This letter, which is very important in the light of what came to pass, was always reckoned to have been written in 1679 until Professor J.H. Wilson proved that it was sent much earlier than that, and almost certainly in the spring of 1676. Since Rochester is widely assumed to have orchestrated the severe beating of Dryden in 1679, the date of the letter is just as important as what the Earl says in it:

> You write me word that I'm out of favour with a certain poet, whom I have ever admired for the disproportion of him and his attributes. He is a rarity which I cannot but be fond of, as one would be of a hog that could fiddle, or a singing owl. If he falls upon me at the blunt, which is his very good weapon in wit, I will forgive him, if you please, and leave the repartee to Black Will, with a cudgel.

❖ ❖ ❖

Rochester watched art imitating life in *The Man of Mode* on the London stage in March 1676 and we can only wonder if he thought Dorimant's and Harriet's sparring was an accurate reflection of his relationship with Elizabeth Barry. The fact that no genuine love-letters from her to him survive may well be indicative of the number she wrote, and the giddy euphoria of his early correspondence soon gave way to an awareness that she was a taker of love and not a giver; that underneath the hardness there was more hardness; that she was impossible to please. Yet in the opening months of the affair he had been able to tell her that the time between his last visit and his next one was 'no part of my life, or at least like a long fit of the falling-sickness, wherein I am dead to all joy and happiness . . . but in the evening I will see you, and be happy in spite of all the fools in the world.'

Initially, his power in the thearre meant a power over her too, and it would have been madness for her to have done anything other than encourage his love. But as her professional independence rose and the applause grew louder, she came nearer and nearer to being on an equal footing with him. Eventually, she could criticise him for his drinking, pick faults in him, shout at him and accuse him of infidelity. 'My visit yesterday was intended to tell you I had not dined with other women,' he wrote imploringly. Perhaps, refusing to listen, she had shut the door on him. Soon he was making his own complaints, commenting sarcastically on her astonishing lack of warmth or romanticism:

> Madam,
> If it were worth anything to be beloved by me you were the richest woman in the world. But since love is of so little value, chide your own eyes for making such poor conquests . . . 'tis not through vanity that I affect the title of your servant, but that I feel warmth in my heart which my mouth rather does confess than boast of . . . when I deserve so ill that you would torment, kill and damn me Madam, you need not hate me.

But no matter how hard he tried to draw her back in, she remained capricious and intrinsically unyielding:

> I know not well who has the worst on't, you, who love but a little, or I, who dote on to an extravagance; sure, to be half kind is as bad as to be half witted, and madness, both in love and reason, bears a better character than a moderate state of either . . .

As Harriet warns Dorimant, 'sickness after long health is commonly more violent and dangerous' – and the probability is that Rochester had not been deeply in love with anybody since asking the King during the winter of 1666 if he could marry

Elizabeth Mallet. His passionate outpourings were only tipping the balance of power in the relationship further in Barry's favour, besides lowering him in her estimation. Of Thomas Otway's similarly helpless overtures to her after the Earl had died, William Oldys shrewdly observed that 'such language of doting madness and despair, however it may succeed with raw girls, is seldom successful with such practitioners in that passion as Mrs Barry, since it only hardens their vanity. For she could get bastards with other men . . .' Barry's rapid ascent on the stage following her re-engagement by the Duke's Players meant that by the end of 1676 she had no professional need for Rochester; but she kept him dangling until some time around the winter of 1677, when, having given birth to his daughter, she found somebody else. Until that happened, Rochester continued to struggle with her in the hopelessly romantic belief that tiffs, arguments and slanging matches were an indication not of a doomed relationship but of true love. In his beautiful and moving poem 'The Mistress' he took the two steps of writing openly about the soul and treating jealousy with a respect. Once upon a time he had laughed at it, but now, with a master poet's metaphysical touch, he turned it into something *holy*:

> An age in her embraces passed
> Would seem a winter's day,
> Where life and light with envious haste
> Are torn and snatched away.
>
> But oh, how slowly minutes roll
> When absent from her eyes,
> Which feed my love, which is my soul:
> It languishes and dies.
>
> For then no more a soul, but shade,
> It mournfully does move
> And haunts my breast, by absence made
> The living tomb of love.
>
> You wiser men, despise me not
> Whose lovesick fancy raves

On shades of souls, and heaven knows what:
Short ages live in graves.

Whene'er those wounding eyes, so full
Of sweetness, you did see,
Had you not been profoundly dull,
You had gone mad like me.

Nor censure us, you who perceive
My best beloved and me
Sigh and lament, complain and grieve:
You think we disagree.

Alas! 'tis sacred jealousy,
Love raised to an extreme:
The only proof 'twixt her and me
We love, and do not dream.

Fantastic fancies fondly move
And in frail joys believe,
Taking false pleasure for true love;
But pain can ne'er deceive

Kind jealous doubts, tormenting fears,
And anxious cares, when past,
Prove our hearts' treasure fixed and dear,
And make us blest at last.

It was typical of Rochester that his discovery that he was a
jealous man resulted not in a sheepish hiding of that emotion but a
public exposé of it. To most people, jealousy is an embarrassing
and unsavoury sentiment which it to be suppressed at all costs. To
Rochester, it now represented another part of human nature and
therefore deserved an airing:

My dear mistress has a heart
Soft as those kind looks she gave me;
When with love's resistless art,
And her eyes, she did enslave me.

But her constancy's so weak,
She's so wild, and apt to wander;
That my jealous heart would break
Should we live one day asunder.

Melting joys about her move,
Killing pleasures, wounding blisses;
She can dress her eyes in love,
And her lips can arm with kisses.
Angels listen when she speaks;
She's my delight, all mankind's wonder;
But my jealous heart would break
Should we live one day asunder.

Was the Earl faithful to Barry, apart from relations with his wife?
There is every reason to think so. For Rochester, this was an affair
with a difference. It is true that, in December 1677, Savile told the
Earl in a letter of a fifteen-year-old girl 'who has more beauty and
sweetness than ever was upon the stage since a friend of ours left it'
and that the Earl would be 'delighted above all things with her', but
this was men's idle tittle-tattle and does not necessarily mean Savile
would have expected Rochester to try and bed the girl.

Barry kept a very watchful eye on Rochester too. Like his wife,
she had certain friends – two in particular, one of whom the Earl
called 'fat' and the other 'lean' – who were doing their utmost to
pull her away from this notorious man. He was aware of their
interference, hated it and wrote bitterly of

'. . . that fat, with the other lean one of yours, whose prodent
advice is daily concerning you how dangerous it is to be kind
to the man upon earth who loves you best. I, who still
persuade myself by all the argument I can bring, that I am
happy, find this none of the best; that you are too unlike
these people every way to agree with 'em in any particular.'

Until the winter of 1677, he carried on trying to persuade
himself. . . .

❖ ❖ ❖

During this period of frenetic theatrical activity, Rochester began writing a comedy, the surviving fragment of which indicates that he may have lost his resolve after just a few hours at his desk:

Scene One

Mr Dainty's chamber. Enter Dainty in his nightgown singing –

Dainty: *J'ai l'amour dans le coeur et la rage dans les os* – I am confident I shall never sleep again, and 't were no great matter if it did not make me look thin, for naturally I hate to be so long absent from myself – as one is in a manner those seven dull hours he snores away – and yet methinks not to sleep till the sun rise is an odd effect of my disease and makes the night tedious without a woman. Reading would relieve me, but books treat of other men's affairs, and to me that's ever tiresome. Beside, I seldom have candle, but I am resolved to write some love-passages of my life. They will make a pretty novel, and when my boy buts a link, it shall burn by me when I go to bed, while I divert myself with reading my own story, which will be pleasant enough. Boy!

[Enter Boy.]

Boy: Sir!

Dainty: Who knocked at door just now? Was it some woman?

Boy: Mrs Mannours' maid, sir, with a posset for you.

Dainty: And you never brought her up, you rascal? How can you be so ill bred and belong to me? See who knocks there. Some other woman.

[Exit Boy.]

This Mrs Mannours' fondness of me is very useful, for besides the good things she always sends me, and

money I borrow of her sometimes, I have a further
prospect. Sir Lionel's daughters, which are in her charge.
Both like me, but the youngest I pitch upon, and because
I can't marry 'em both, my young nobility Mr Squabb
shall have the other sister – but I'll trouble him
afterwards. Thus, I'll raise my fortune, which is all I
want, for I am an agreeable man and everybody likes me.

[Enter Boy.]

Boy: 'Tis Mr Squabb, sir.

Dainty: Call him up, but comb your periwig first. Let me comb
         it. You are the laziest sloven.

If he started the play in the early summer of 1676 then certain
events overtook him and easily explain why he seems to have got
no further with it.

When even the most gentle-natured alcoholic starts regularly
behaving violently when drunk, it is time for friends to stay away.
The tendency is irreversible. Violent drunks *never* turn into pacific
ones and, if anything, their conduct will worsen. One night late in
June, Rochester's drunken aggression caused the death of a friend.

Some of the Merry Gang, or Ballers, had turned up at Epsom –
possibly for the horse-racing there, which, as at Newmarket,
enjoyed the King's patronage and was well-established. Rochester
and his friends, including Sir George Etherege, still high on the
success of his play *The Man of Mode*, became too boisterous. When
some local fiddlers refused to play for them, the Ballers began
tossing them up and down in a blanket. Curious to discover the
cause of the racket, a barber came over and they grabbed hold of
him too. In order to free himself he offered to lead them to the
home of the best-looking woman in Epsom, but instead he
cunningly walked them to the local constable's house. The
constable asked them all what they wanted and they told him it
was a whore. When he refused to let them in they smashed his
door down, hit him around the head and 'beat him very severely'.
Somehow he managed to escape and called his watch, whereupon
Etherege summoned up enough self-composure to assure them

that there would be no further trouble. The constable took his word and dismissed his men. It was then that Rochester drew his sword on the constable. One of his companions, a Mr Downs, flung his arms round the Earl to stop him from making a pass and the constable yelled 'Murder!!' The watch ran back, came up behind Downs and, presuming he was the offender (they may not even have been able to see Rochester) split his head open with a staff. Panic broke out, Rochester and everyone else ran off and Downs, who did not have a sword, snatched a stick and began lashing out. He was run through the side of his body with a half-pike and later died of his wounds.

It is probable that, as Lady Sunderland said of the Earl after he punched Tom Killigrew in front of the King, 'he was in a case not to know what he did'. One wonders how much of the incident, if any of it, he could remember the following morning. He was not the only person to run off and leave Downs – they all did – and that suggests that they did not even realise Downs had been left behind until they had stopped running. There is no indication of what time in the evening all this happened, but if it was after 10 p.m. then the darkness of the unlit street would only have added to everyone's drunken confusion. The tragedy is that, not being armed with a sword himself, Downs can hardly have been looking for trouble.

When the news filtered through Whitehall the day after, Lord Mulgrave and Sir Carr Scrope were among those whose eyes lit up with glee. The man who had ridiculed the contemporary values of honour with his arrogant assertion that all men would be cowards if they dared, had now left his friend to be beaten to death in a street. They were determined: this time they would really humiliate him.

The King was in no mood to forgive either. Orders were given to arrest the Earl, who was to be tried – possibly for murder. Like the Scarlet Pimpernel, he was sought everywhere. But he was not at his lodgings; he was not at Adderbury or High Lodge; he was not in Epsom and he was certainly not at Court. They should have been looking under their noses. On Tower Hill, an extraordinary-looking fellow with a beard as long as his green coat was doing a roaring trade with his amazing astrological predictions and his miraculous potions for London's sick . . .

9

THE LAST HURRAH

And I wish it possible for me by this narrative to procure your
Ladyship that real mirth and continual hearty laughs . . . as this
frequently gave us whilst we plied our peculiar operations in the
laboratory; some stirring an old boiling kettle of soot and urine,
tinged with a little asafetida and all the nasty ingredients that
would render the smell more unsavoury . . .

> *Thomas Alcock, former assistant to Dr Bendo,*
> *writing to Rochester's daughter, Anne,*
> *seven years after her father's death.*

Quite apart from showing unbelievable style whilst under
tremendous pressure, and besides proving that as an actor
he was nothing short of a genius, the Earl of Rochester's
performance as Dr Alexander Bendo paved the way for the satire
of the eighteenth century in general, and the cheeky brilliance of
Jonathan Swift, author of that modest proposal that people should
eat babies, in particular.

This was no little side-show in a back alley: while Rochester was
being hunted by the royal guards, Dr Bendo was the talk of the
town. The Earl even gave his pursuers a couple of clues. In his
long and suspiciously well-written handbill, the good doctor stated
that he had gathered his knowledge during his travels in France
and Italy, where he had gone when he was fifteen. He was now, he
said, aged twenty-eight. Rochester had gone to France and Italy
when he was fourteen and he was now twenty-nine.

Doubt has always surrounded the timing of Bendo's appearance; Gilbert Burnet simply recorded:

> Being under an unlucky accident which obliged him to keep out of the way, he disguised himself so that his nearest friends could not have known him and set up in Tower Street for an Italian Mountebank, where he had a stage, and practised physic for some weeks, not without success.

Conjecture has always been about which unlucky accident this was. The smashing of sundial? The banishment from Court for handing the wrong satire to the King? But both Graham Greene and Professor Pinto convincingly linked the unfortunate death of Downs, which occurred in June 1676, to Rochester's disguise as Bendo. They cite a letter, written by Henry Savile to Rochester in August 1676. Charles II was by now deeply interested in chemistry, and was engaged in carrying out experiments with Monsieur Rabell, a French apothecary. Savile suggests in his letter that he cannot see 'a better opportunity of doing your business' (surely a reference to Rochester's returning to the King's favour), because 'now your chemical knowledge will give you entrance . . .' It is most likely, they believe, that this mention of 'chemical knowledge' is a wry dig at Dr Bendo's outrageous, and quackish medical claims.

In 1687, Thomas Alcock, who had been a servant to Rochester and had played the part of one of Bendo's assistants, sent the Earl's eldest daughter, the eighteen-year-old Anne Baynton, a New Year's gift of a manuscript book in which he gave an account of the entire episode. He explained that her father had disappeared from Whitehall to avoid 'an apparent storm that threatened the continual sunshine he had always breathed in' and that it was rumoured he had gone to France.

But Rochester had taken lodgings in a goldsmith's house in Tower Street. Having hired a number of assistants to Bendo, he decided his stage would be at nearby Crosset Fryers. The doctor's handbill, or advertisement – a work of some literary importance – was given out in the streets by 'nimble emissaries' and 'sonorous hawkers' who, said Alcock, made all the town ring with Bendo's 'extraordinary performances'. The public were soon flocking to the doctor's 'laboratory' (the lodgings in Tower Street) to catch a glimpse of the great man at work. Just as people are encouraged today by a chef who is confident enough about his cooking to do it in front of them, so these Londoners were impressed by Dr Bendo's readiness to concoct his wondrous potions in the public eye. It is even more ironic, therefore, to consider that his recipes included doses of ash, soot and urine. Alcock gave a wonderful description of the crowds staring in awe as Bendo worked 'with his scales and weights, making up medicines of all sorts and sealing them with his seal of office, giving pretended directions to his operators by his indicative gestures in a language which neither he, nor they understood one word of. Alcock and the others, dressed like 'the old witches in Macbeth', similarly kept up a patter of 'damned unintelligible gibberish'.

Bendo himself was quite a sight. He was dressed in 'an old overgrown green gown' lined with exotic furs of various colours, and he religiously wore it in memory of 'Rabelais his master'. He also sported 'an antique cap, a great reverend beard and a magnificent false medal set round with glittering pearl, rubies, and diamonds of the same cognation, hung about his neck in a massy gold-like chain of princes' metal, which the King of Cyprus (you must know) had given him for doing a signal cure upon his darling daughter, the princess Aloephangina, who was painted in a banner and hung up at his elbow'. The doctor was not fussy about what went into the medicines – 'various mixtures of ashes, soot, lime, chalk, clay, old wall, soap and indeed anything that came to hand by the assistances of a little blue verditer, red russet, white lead, yellow oaker, umber, lamblack, sheering smelt, powdered brick, pulverised slate and cornish tile' – which 'cost him nothing but taking up, for where e're he went he used to say it was all Indies'. These mixtures were presented to the public as a vast array of washes, powders, paints, ointments, antidotes, charms, elixirs, sulphurs, pills, potions, essences, lozenges, opiates and tinctures.

Bendo was also able to predict the future, interpret dreams and make all kinds of judgements just from examining moles, warts and birthmarks on the naked body. He kindly put his more modest female clients at their easy by assuring them that he had no wish, 'not for all the world', to see their markings himself, and that it would be perfectly sufficient if his wife carried out the examination later on and then reported the positions and shapes of the markings back to him. At the appointed hour the client would return and wait in the bedroom, and at length the good Mrs Bendo – a 'grave matron' – would come waddling in to make her findings. Of course, Mrs Bendo and Dr Bendo were the same person. One begins to understand why Rochester had been so confident that he could turn Elizabeth Barry into the best actress on the London stage.

It is astonishing to think that the Earl managed to attract so much attention as Bendo and yet not be suspected by anybody – but that, of course, was the whole idea of the game. Given his circumstances at the time (arrest for the murder of Downs could have led to a very long spell in the Tower), his arrogance, not usually a quality to be admired, was somehow quite sublime. There was understandable glee in Alcock's observation that Rochester deceived his 'ignorant and malicious enemies who thought he had gone to France' by selling them, their wives and their children rubbish and dirt disguised as medicine. His triumph over the society he despised could not have been more glorious.

If anything was in danger of giving him away it was not his disguise or his assistants but the handbill. It was too obviously written by a master of prose and could never have been the work of a man who claimed to have been abroad since he was fifteen. There are some typical Rochester flourishes in it, perhaps the most characteristic being his argument that in a world as hypocritical as this one the difference between the counterfeit and the original, the valiant man and the coward, the politician and the fool, and the wealthy man and the bankrupt, is to all appearances non-existent:

If I appear to anyone like a counterfeit, even for the sake of that chiefly ought I to be construed a true man, who is the counterfeit's example, his original, and that which he imploys his industry and pains to imitate and copy. Is it, therefore, my fault if the cheat, by his wits and endeavours, makes himself so like me that consequently I cannot avoid resembling him? Consider, pray, the valiant and the coward, the wealthy merchant and the bankrupt, the politician and the fool; they are the same in many things and differ but in one alone: the valiant man holds up his head, looks confidently round about him, wears a sword, courts a lord's wife and owns it; so does the coward. One only point of honour, and that's courage (which like a false metal one only trial can discover) makes the distinction.

The bankrupt walks the exchange, buys bargains, draws bills, and accepts them with the richest, whilst paper and credit are current coin: that which makes the difference is real cash, a great difference indeed, and yet but one, and that the last found out, and still till then the least perceived.

Now for the politician, he is a grave, deliberating, close, prying man: pray, are there not grave, deliberating, close, prying fools? If then the difference betwixt all these (though infinite in effect) be so nice in all appearance, will you expect it should be otherwise betwixt the false physician, astrologer, &c. and the true? The first calls himself learned doctor, sends forth his bills, gives physic and counsel, tells and foretells; the other is bound to do just as much; 'tis only your experience must distinguish betwixt them, to which I willingly submit myself. I'll only say something to the honour of the mountebank, in case you discover me to be one.

Reflect a little what kind a creature 'tis: he is one, then, who is fain to supply some higher ability he pretends to with craft; he draws great companies to him, by undertaking strange things which can never be effected.

The politician (by his example no doubt) finding how the people are taken with specious, miraculous impossibilities, plays the same game, protests, declares, promises I know not what things which he's sure can ne'er be brought about; the people believe, are deluded and pleased. The expectation of a future good, which shall never befall them, draws their eyes off a present evil; thus they are kept and established in subjection, peace and obedience, he in greatness, wealth and power: so you see the politician is, and must be a mountebank in state affairs, and the mounteback (no doubt if he thrives) is an errant politician in physic . . .

Like James Themut, the so-called High Dutch physician who conned the people of Oxford in Rochester's undergraduate days,

Bendo reeled off a number of conditions he could cure, such as scurvy, green-sickness, inflammations, and obstructions in the stomach, but while he charged for the medicines he dispensed, receiving a great deal of gold and silver, his 'affable and communicative' advice was free. Alcock explained to Rochester's daughter that Dr Bendo was not prepared to charge his fellow creatures anything for the talent he had freely received. This meant the poor were soon seeking his opinions in droves, infuriating the other apothecaries in the area, who declared that Alexander Bendo and his wretched assistants were 'all notorious thieves and had certainly robbed some interloper's cellar'.

Perhaps the Earl took Savile's advice and went to see Charles while he was working with Monsieur Rabell. Somehow or other he did gain the King's sudden permission to return to Whitehall in safety, because Alcock said that the very night after Rochester's 'ostracism' was lifted, he stunned everyone who thought he had been hiding in France by turning up 'in splendour' to a ball at the palace and was 'in as great favour as ever'. It was, remarked Alcock drily, 'the quickest voyage from France that ever man did, which was the talk and admiration of the whole town'.

The overnight disappearance of Bendo and his team sent a rumour round the town that they had been an enchanted crew of spirits who had come from, and gone back to, the land of the dead. This, said Alcock, caused the credulous patients to throw away their medicines, which they now feared were bewitched.

※ ※ ※

In the early spring of 1676, Rochester had said in a letter to Henry Savile written from High Lodge: 'I would be glad to know if the parliament be like to sit any time . . . I would make me at the session. Livy and sickness has a little inclined me to policy.' Like all drinking alcoholics he suffered from what might be called the 'tomorrow I turn over a new leaf' syndrome – although to be fair to him he did acknowledge to Savile that once he got to the capital he expected to change 'the folly' of attending parliament for a lesser one: 'whether wine or women I know not; according as my constitution serves me'. (This does not mean he planned to be unfaithful to Barry; she was probably what he had in mind by 'women'.)

Nevertheless, he had clearly been full of good intent. That he should then find himself wanted for murder a few months later was endemic of his alcoholism, which will render all constructive efforts and renewed attempts at good behaviour unsustainable until complete abstinence is undertaken. It is interesting to see, for example, that, at the start of 1677 he was similarly infused with the idea of business, and began attending the Lords with particular enthusiasm. His appearances tailed off very quickly though, from more than a dozen in March to just one in May. He was still drinking.

Most people think that alcoholism amounts to being addicted to drink and therefore getting drunk a lot. But the disease syndrome involves far more than this. Like all chronic, drinking alcoholics, Rochester was mentally ill as well as physically sick, and listed below are some of the characteristics which Professor Kenneth Blum and James Payne say they expect to find in 'the typical alcoholic'. Underneath each one is a relevant quotation from the Earl or an explanation by the author.

Restlessness, impulsiveness, anxiety.
The man who hated still life; who snatched Elizabeth Mallet at Charing Cross and who drank to wash away his cares was certainly restless, impulsive and anxious.

Selfishness, self-centredness, lack of consideration.
It is hard to know where to start. Rochester encapsulated the excessive and selfish nature of most of Charles's courtiers – but he could also show great kindness (particularly to his wife) and helped a number of aspiring writers with his patronage.

Stubbornness, ill humour, irritability, anger and rage.
There is no indication that he was a stubborn man, but his irritability can be sensed from a number of his letters and his anger was formidable (this is very often the leading characteristic of alcoholism):

> Who can abstain from satire in this age?
> What nature wants I find supplied by rage . . .

Depression, self-destructiveness, contactlessness.
The sad intervals and severe reflections he spoke of to Burnet may indicate very deep troughs of depression indeed. His self-destructiveness knew no bounds and his frequent disappearances, not just from his wife but from the Court and all those who knew him were indicative of his isolation. Rochester stood apart from everybody:

> There sighs not on the plain
> So lost a swain as I . . .

Physical cruelty, brawling, child or husband/wife abuse.
Rochester's cruelty to others was inflicted through anger and spontaneity much more than it was ever calmly pre-meditated. He did not take pleasure in causing unhappiness to others: it was just the inevitable result of his own unhappiness. We are reminded that it is rare and difficult for somebody who is unhappy with themselves to bring about happiness in others. Rochester never abused his wife or children, all of whom he adored. Brawling, however, was part of his life.

Arrogance that may lead to aggression or to coldness and withdrawal.
His arrogance was so great, that, as in the Alexander Bendo episode, he could deliberately set out to mock the world. It also usually embraced aggression:

> I'll tell of whores attacked, their lords at home;
> Bawds' quarters beaten up, and fortress won,
> Windows demolished, watches overcome,
> And handsome ills by my contrivance done . . .

And, although the Earl was essentially a very heated man, his aggresion could be cold too. As 'Tunbridge Wells' shows, he was able to be as laughingly dismissive of people as he was made angry by them. His conversion to Christianity might also be said to be connected with a contempt for the world about him.

Aggressive sexuality, often accompanied by infidelity, which may give way to sexual disinterest or impotence.
The reader can afford to smile: this is Rochester's sexual

curriculum vitae. Paradoxically, it was his puritan streak which made him so sexually aggressive. He rarely wrote about sex without sounding at odds with it, which, in turn, is why he wrote about it so much. His intrinsic holiness was in fierce conflict with the fundamental worldliness of sex. To some extent, that gives us the poet. It was said earlier that drunkenness can be a distorted form of openness, and that is why Rochester smashed, on instinct, the King's phallic sundial. His infidelity was further encouraged by the cynicism of Hobbism, which excused his instinct for promiscuity. His sexual disinterest and his impotence, which set in during 1678, were directly caused by his alcoholism. But Blum and Payne would say that his entire sexuality was governed by alcoholism, and they would probably be right.

*Lying, deceit, broken promises.
Lies and broken promises to unsuspecting women like Miss Anne Temple, the maid of honour whose head, said Anthony Hamilton, was so completely turned by Rochester 'that it was a pity to see her', were part of the Earl's technique as a lover. He was as cunning as he was inconstant. His deceit was celebrated by his relish for passing himself off in disguise as somebody else. Where he differed from most alcoholics was that he did not lie about his drinking. This was partly because of his social standing, which made him answerable to very few people, and the excess of Hobbism which made heavy drinking at Whitehall acceptable.

*Low self-esteem, shame, guilt, remorse.
Rochester's self-disgust became an increasingly blatant part of his poetry, accounting for verses like 'The Debauchee' ('I rise at eleven, I dine about two'), and his 'To the Postboy', which he wrote after the affray at Epsom. In it he combines his arrogance with guilt and a frightening degree of self-flagellation. A similar contradiction once caused him to boast to Barry of being the most fantastical odd man alive. (By fantastical he meant ridiculous, and not wonderful.) When Rochester criticised or laughed at himself, his ego demanded an audience. 'To the Postboy' begins with the verbal abuse of a servant, a characteristic which, as was noted earlier, was one of Rochester's traits:

Son of a whore, God damn you! can you tell
A peerless peer the readiest way to Hell?
I've outswilled Bacchus, sworn of my own make
Oaths would fright furies and make Pluto quake!
Iv'e swived more whores more ways than Sodom's walls
E'er know – or the college of Rome's cardinals.
Witness heroic scars! – Look here! Ne'er go!
Cerecloths and ulcers from the top to toe!
Frighted at my own mischiefs, I have fled
And bravely left my life's defender dead;
Broke houses to break chastity, and dyed
That floor with murder which my lust denied.
Pox on it; why do I speak of these poor things?
I have blasphemed my God, and libelled Kings!
The readiest way to Hell! – come, quick!

   Postboy: Ne'er stir.
          The readist way, my Lord, is by Rochester.

The Earl's low self-esteem can also be seen from the way in which he referred to himself in letters to Savile as a royal 'pimp' and a 'fool and a buffoon'. Note how hard on himself he is in the above poem (line ten) when he calls Downs his 'life's defender'. In a sense he is right, because if Downs had not been holding on to him then the officers of the watch would probably have smashed the Earl over the head instead – but it is a melodramatic term none the less.

Reduced mental and physical function; eventually blackouts.
Rochester's physical decay, including his failing eyesight, is evident, and his reduced mental faculties include the lack of judgement he showed over the frustrated duel with Mulgrave. Eventually he became unable, in 1679, to decide for himself whether 'An Essay Upon Satire' was by Mulgrave or Dryden. A few years earlier he would have known one from the other by reading a few lines.

Susceptibility to other diseases.
In the last few years of his life Rochester was riddled with disease; in a letter to Henry Savile in July 1678 he described himself as being in 'a damned relapse, brought by a fever, the stone, and

some ten diseases more, which have deprived me of the power of crawling'.

*Denial that there is a drinking problem.
We have no evidence of what he told his wife or Elizabeth Barry when they criticised his drinking.

Understandably, when researchers into alcoholism like Blum and Payne discuss the symptoms, they do not always mention that drinking alcoholics have virtues too. But they can be particularly humane, compassionate and kind people. Rochester was a doting if absent father (his letters to his son are arguably the most moving he ever wrote), a loving though unfaithful husband and was as popular among his friends as he was hated by his enemies. His alcoholism also contributed to his poetry as much as it destroyed his life.

Blum and Payne have one more characteristic which they say *always* exists: loneliness. It is one of the most striking features of the Earl's work. 'Tunbridge Wells', for example shows him in the light of a complete outsider, and in 'A Ramble in St James's Park' he is a very solitary figure indeed.

From a purely dramatic viewpoint, this satire is among his greatest works and the crudity of its language should not be allowed to detract from its subtlety. Women readers who find themselves hating him for the sentiments he expresses should be warned that it is a deliberate trap: if he could not receive the passion of love, he wanted its opposite: contempt. 'After coming to a good understanding with a new mistress, I love nothing more than a quarrel with an old one' was Rochester's stance as well as Dorimant's. Anything but dull, insipid indifference. Anything but what he called 'still-life'. 'A Ramble in St James's Park' is also the poem in which the Earl reveals that Hobbism has failed him and that he was never fit for it. Fired by the emotion of jealousy, it was surely written during the affair with Elizabeth Barry. The satire begins:

> Much wine had passed, with grave discourse
> Of who fucks who, and who does worse
> (Such as you usually do hear
> From those that diet at the Bear),

> When I, who still take care to see
> Drunkenness relieved by lechery,
> Went out into St James's Park
> To cool my head and fire my heart. . . .

While 'A Satire against Reason and Mankind' contains his most famous opening, the eight lines above are gilded with a majesty which makes his arrogance as forgivable as it is awesome. In his drunkenness, the world about him becomes grotesque, disgusting, immoral. He observes how the

> . . . rows of mandrakes tall did rise
> Whose lewd tops fucked the very skies.
> Each imitative branch does twine
> In some loved fold of Aretine,
> And nightly now beneath their shade
> Are buggeries, rapes, and incests made.

But this is a religious man speaking:

> Unto this all-sin-sheltering grove
> Whores of the bulk and the alcove
> Great ladies, chambermaids and drudges,
> The ragpicker, and hieress trudges.
> Carmen, divines, great lords and tailors;
> Prentices, poets, pimps and jailers;
> Footmen; fine fops to here arrive,
> And here promiscuously they swive.

We should not be surprised that, when the lover of the hard-hearted Elizabeth Barry spots his old flame Corinna, he is more magnetised by her contempt than he is offended by it:

> Along these hallowed walks it was
> That I beheld Corinna pass.
> Whoever had been by to see
> The proud disdain she cast on me
> Through charming eyes, he would have swore
> She dropped from heaven that very hour,

> Forsaking the divine abode
> In scorn of some despairing god.
> But mark what creatures women are:
> How infinitely vile when fair!

To his mortification, three insipid, silly fops, with 'wriggling tails', run up to her. He observes that one of them '. . . not only eats and talks/But feels and smells; sits down and walks.' He is appalled that Corinna wants anything to do with them. If the Earl had looked down on women as unintelligent ornaments then he would have blamed other men for misleading and manipulating them. But his respect for women throws chauvinism into reverse and makes him furious with Corinna for her atrocious lack of judgement. When Elizabeth Barry began sleeping with someone else he wrote to her: 'since discretion is the thing alone you are like to want, pray study to get it'. One of the fops, in 'a strain 'twixt tune and nonsense',

> Cries: 'Madam, I have loved you long since;
> Permit me your fair hand to kiss';
> When at her mouth her cunt cries 'Yes!',
> In short, without much more ado,
> Joyful and pleased, away she flew,
> And with these three confounded asses
> From park to hackney coach she passes.

For the first time in the poem he now switches the spotlight onto himself. It is as clear to him as ever that human beings are motivated by their bestial desires and should own up to it rather than mince about coquettishly as though sex is gently civilising:

> So a proud bitch does lead about
> Of humble curs the amorous rout,
> Who most obsequiously do hunt
> The savoury scent of salt-swollen cunt.
> Some power more patient now relate
> The sense of this surprising fate.
> Gods! that a thing admired by me
> Should fall to so much infamy.

Had she picked out, to rub her arse on,
Some stiff-pricked clown or well-hung parson,
Each job of whose spermatic sluice
Had filled her cunt with wholesome juice,
I the proceeding should have praised
In hope she'd quenched a fire I raised.
Such natural freedoms are but just:
There's something generous in mere lust.
But to turn damned abandoned jade
When neither head nor tail persuade;
To be a whore in understanding,
A passive pot for fools to spend in!
The devil played booty, sure, with thee
To bring a blot on infamy.

He finds all this particularly galling when, during his relationship with Corinna, he allows her to enjoy other men. But whereas in the 1660s Rochester was writing about inconstancy as though it was one of the beauties life had to offer ('Tell me no more of constancy/The frivolous pretence/Of cold age, narrow jealousy,/Disease, and want of sense') he now speaks of it with a jealous disgust. The implication is that even when he was giving Corinna permission to bed whoever she wanted, he did not find it quite as easy as he had pretended. The King's lack of concern over infidelity made him suited to Hobbism; Rochester had followed the same path when it was against his nature. These lines are an angry confession that Hobbism has let him down:

Did ever I refuse to bear
The meanest part your lust could spare?
When your lewd cunt came spewing home
Drenched with the seed of half the town,
My dram of sperm was supped up after
For the digestive surfeit water.
Full gorgèd at another time
With a vast meal of nasty slime
Which your devouring cunt had drawn
From porters' backs and footmen's brawn,
I was content to serve you up

My ballock-full for your grace cup,
Nor ever thought it an abuse
While you had pleasure for excuse . . .

Ah, but he did, he did. The rest of the poem is devoted to his manic jealousy, which he celebrates in a thoroughly self-flagellatory manner by making himself as obnoxious as he possibly can. He even implies that he is a ranting coward:

May stinking vapours choke your womb
Such as the men you dote upon!
May your depravèd appetite,
That could in whiffling fools delight,
Beget such frenzies in your mind
You may go mad for the north wind,
And fixing all your hopes upon 't
To have him bluster in your cunt,
Turn up your longing arse t'th'air
And perish in a wild despair!
But cowards shall forget to rant,
Schoolboys to frig, old whores to paint;
The Jesuits' fraternity
Shall leave the use of buggery;
Crab-louse, inspired with grace divine,
From earthly cod to heaven shall climb;
Physicians shall believe in Jesus
And disobedience cease to please us,
Ere I desist with all my power
To plague this woman and undo her.
But my revenge will best be timed
When she is married that is limed.
In that most lamentable state
I'll make her feel my scorn and hate:
Pelt her with scandals, truth or lies,
And her poor cur with jealousies,
Till I have torn him from her breech
While she whines like a dog-drawn bitch;
Loathed and despised, kicked out o'th' Town
Into some dirty hole alone,

To chew the cud of misery
And know she owes it all to me.

And may no woman better thrive
That dares profane the cunt I swive.

In the last years of his life, Rochester taught himself an arrogance which was actually designed more for self-defence that it was for attack. Like any wounded animal he retreated from others about him, but at the same time was at his most dangerous towards them if threatened. At Whitehall, he was now having to fend off the inevitable fresh charge of gross cowardice following the death of Downs. Among the most forward of his accusers was the imprudent Sir Carr Scrope, whose poem 'A Defence of Satire' taunted Rochester with the following lines:

He who can push into a midnight fray
His brave companion and then run away,
Leaving him to be murdered in the street,
Then put it off with some buffoon conceit:
Him, thus dishonoured, for a wit you own,
And count him as top fiddler of the town.

Rochester had not *pushed* anybody into 'a midnight fray'. The 'buffoon conceit' refers to is witticism in 'A Satire Against Reason and Mankind' that all men would be cowards if they dared. When he picked up his pen to deal with Scrope he thought it would be easy as brushing away flies:

To rack and torture thy unmeaning brain
In Satire's praise to a low, untuned strain,
In thee was most pertinent and vain,
When in thy poem we more clearly see
That satire's of divine authority:
For God made one of Man when he made thee ...

But Scrope was made of sterner stuff and came back at the Earl with the following epigram:

Rail on, poor feeble scribbler; speak of me
In as bad terms as the world speaks of thee.
Sit swelling in thy hole, like a vexed toad,
And, full of pox and malice, spit abroad.
Thou can'st hurt no man's fame with thy ill word:
Thy pen is full as harmless as thy sword

'Swelling in thy hole, like a vexed toad' referred, of course, to Rochester's existence in High Lodge. The epigram as a whole was rather too clever and cutting for Rochester's liking. His last word on Scrope, a satire called 'On Poet Ninny', was his most brutal. In it he declared that the man's libels could never be as offensive as his appearance and personality were:

. . . Born to no other but thy own disgrace,
Thou art a thing so wretched and so base
Thou canst not even offend but with thy face;
And dost at once a sad example prove
Of harmless malice and of hopeless love,
All pride and ugliness! Oh, how we loathe
A nauseous creature so composed of both! . . .
Thou art below being laughed at; out of spite,
Men gaze upon thee as a hideous sight,
And cry: 'There goes the melancholy knight!'
There are some modish fools we daily see,
Modest and dull: why, they are wits to thee!
For, of all folly, sure the very top
Is a conceited ninny and a fop;
With face of farce, joined to a head romancy,
There's no such coxcomb as your fool of fancy.
But 'tis too much on so dispised a theme:
No man would dabble in a dirty stream.

The worst that I could write would be no more
Than what thy very friends have said before.

At the same time, the Earl was having to deal with attacks from Mulgrave. That there had already been a war of words between them is clear from the opening lines of Rochester's poem 'My

Lord All-Pride', which appeared in the late 1670s. Now that he was being accused of cowardice again, he drew, in the fourth line, on their frustrated duel in 1669 and slung the same taunt back:

> Bursting with pride, the loathed impostume swells;
> Prick him, he sheds his venom straight and smells,
> But 'tis so lewd a scribbler, that he writes
> With as much force to nature as he fights;
> Hardened in shame, 'tis such a baffled fop
> That every schoolboy whips him like a top.
> And, with his arm and head, his brain's so weak
> That his starved fancy is compelled to rake
> Among the excrements of others' wit
> To make a stinking meal of what they shit;
> So swine, for nasty meat, to dunghill run,
> And toss their gruntling snouts up when they've done.
> Against his stars the coxcomb ever strives,
> And to be something they forbid, contrives.
> With a red nose, splay foot, and goggle eye,
> A ploughman's looby mien; face all awry;
> With stinking breath and every loathsome mark
> The Punchinello sets up for a spark . . .

But the Epsom incident did not offend Mulgrave and Scrope; it enhanced Rochester's notoriety to such a degree that in 1677 he was calling himself 'a man whom it is the great mode to hate'. Rumour was now linking him to every fresh scandal and his name was as much the talk of the town as Dr Bendo's had been. On the night of 23 May 1677, for example, a French cook was stabbed at a house in which Rochester was dining, and the following day it was assumed by many at Whitehall that the Earl was the culprit. Savile did his best to prevent the rumour from spreading beyond London. In a letter to Viscount Halifax he wrote:

Last night, also, Du Puis, a French cook in the Mall, was stabbed for some pert answer by one Mr Floyd, and because my Lord Rochester and my Lord Lumley were supping in the same house, though in both different rooms and companies, the good nature of the town has reported it all this day that his Lordship was the stabber. He desired me therefore to write to you to stop that report from going northward, for he says if it once get as far as York, the truth will not be believed under two or three years.

Four months later Savile was one of those who heard a widespread rumour in London that Rochester and others had been gallavanting around Woodstock Park in the nude – on the day of the Sabbath, no less. Unlike the other gossips, he did his friend the justice of seeking out the facts. In his letter to the Earl, whom he had heard was ill again, he said he wanted 'to know the truth from yourself, who, alone, do speak true concerning yourself'. The rest of the world, commented Savile, was not only 'apt to believe' but was 'very ready to make lies concerning you'.

In tones of tired amusement, Rochester, describing himself as the most unsolid of fleshy fry, said in his reply:

For the hideous deportment, which you have heard of concerning running naked, so much is true: that we went into the river somewhat late in the year and had a frisk for forty yards in the meadow to dry ourselves.

The King and his brother James would have done as much, he believed, as would the Lord Chancellor and the Archbishops of Canterbury and York when they were schoolboys. Then he remembers some indiscreet behaviour by Henry Savile himself:

And now, Mr Savile, since you are so pleased to quote yourself for a grave man and the number of the scandalized, be pleased to call to mind the year 1676, when two large fat nudities led the coranto round Rosamund's fair fountain while the poor violated nymph wept to behold the strange decay of manly parts . . .

Even when he was joking, Rochester would point to hypocrisy.

In spite of his own undramatic explanation, the story inevitably became part of the Rochester legend, so that nearly fifty years later Thomas Hearne was declaring that the Earl:

used sometimes, with others of his companions, to run naked, and particularly they did so once in Woodstock Park, upon a Sunday in the afternoon, expecting that several of the female sex would have been spectators, but not one appeared. The man that stripped them and pulled off their shirts, kept the shirts, and did not deliver them any more, going off with them before they finished the race.

In the same letter to Savile, written in October, Rochester declared himself 'almost blind, utterly lame and scarce within reasonable hopes of ever seeing London again'. His physical decay can even be detected from two of the surviving portraits of him. The one on the cover of this book was painted in the 1660s by Sir Peter Lely, quite possibly upon the Earl's appointment as Gentleman of the Bedchamber in March 1667. He looks fit, noble, sober and dashing. By the time the famous portrait of him crowning a monkey with a laurel was painted in the 1670s (it is attributed to Jacob Huysmans), his looks had begun to fade. He is fatter in the face, a little wan and the eyes are noticeably heavy. It seems as though a monkey really did sit with Rochester for this portrait: in a letter to Savile he said that most human affairs are 'carried on at the same nonsensical rate, which makes me, who am now grown superstitious, think it a fault to laugh at the monkey we have here when I compare his condition with mankind'.

❖ ❖ ❖

The tense and dissatisfied relationship between Rochester and his wife was not helped by his mother's decision to move from Ditchley to Adderbury, probably in 1677. That was the year her grandson, Sir Edward Lee, married at the age of fourteen and became master of the old house in which the Earl had been taught by Mr Giffard. Rochester was at Adderbury when the move took place and his wife was at her estate in Somerset; the power his mother wielded within the family – and particularly over him – is clear from the way in which he broke the news in a letter to Enmore. He does not sound as though he has had a say in the matter himself, and can only promise his wife that he will continue to do his best to make her happy. His mother had previously indicated that she would not be moving to Adderbury, but the

> alteration of my mother's resolutions, who is now resolved against ever moving from hence, puts me upon some thoughts which were almost quite out of my head; but you may be sure I shall determine nothing that does not tend as much to your real happiness as lies in my power. I have therefore sent you this letter to prepare you for a remove first hither, and afterwards as fate shall direct, which is, I find, the true disposer of things, whatever we attribute to wisdom or providence. . . .

Considering that relations between Rochester's wife and mother were difficult, his motives for binding them together after his death are suspect. It has been suggested that he did this because he was anxious they should reconcile their differences, but, given the attention he pays to jealousy in his poetry, that emotion is a likelier reason. In his will he stated that the purpose of making them joint guardians of his son Charles, until the boy was twenty-one was 'for the better assurance of a happy correspondency' between them. However, this was conditional on his wife remaining unmarried and living 'friendlily' with his mother. If she decided to 'marry or wilfully separate herself from my mother, her guardianship shall determine'. That he was prepared to part his wife from their son indicates a more burning motive than a wish to see harmony in the household, but it was of little consequence, since Charles only survived his father by sixteen months and Rochester's wife died soon afterwards of an 'apoplexy'.

Of course, his nationwide reputation for debauchery, violence, cowardice and, according to some, murder, did nothing to please his mother-in-law. He began to dread her yearly visits to Adderbury, and eventually, in a welter of anger, despair and the usual self-hatred, he wrote to his wife, who had now been complaining, he said, for three years, and very unkindly described death as a surer friend than she was:

> My most neglected wife, till you are a much respected widow
> I find you will scarce be a contented woman, and to say no

more than the plain truth I do endeavour so fairly to do you that last good service that none but the most impatient would refuse to rest satisfied. What even angel enemy to my repose does inspire my Lady Warre to visit you once a year and leave you bewitched for eleven months after? I thank my God that I have the torment of the stone upon me, (which are no small ones), rather than that unspeakable one of being an eye-witness to your uneasiness. Do but propose to me any reasonable thing upon earth I can do to set you at quiet, but it is like a mad woman to lie roaring out of pain and never confess in what part it is; these three years have I heard you continually complain, nor has it ever been in my power to obtain the knowledge of any considerable cause with confidence. I shall not have the like affliction three years hence, but that repose I'll owe to a surer friend than you; when that time comes you will grow wiser, though I fear not much happier.

But his wife could fight her corner in the sure knowledge that it was she, not he, who was wronged, and when she did choose to explain her pain she could be extremely articulate:

If I could have been troubled at anything when I had the happiness of receiving a letter from you I should be so because you did not name a time when I might hope to see you: the uncertainty of which very much afflicts me. Whether this odd kind of proceeding be to try my patience or obedience I cannot guess, but I will never fail of either where my duty to you require them. I do not think you design staying at Bath now that it is like to be so full, and God knows when you will find in your heart to leave the place you are in. Pray consider with yourself whether this be a reasonable way or proceeding and be pleased to let me know what I am to expect, for there being so short a time betwixt this and the sitting of the Parliament I am confident you will find so much business as will not allow you to come into the country. Therefore pray lay your commands upon me what I am to do, and, though it be to forget my children and the long hopes I have lived of seeing you, yet I will endeavour to

obey you or in the memory only torment myself without
giving you the trouble of putting you in mind that there lives
such a creature as your humble —.

Such reasonable language from such a good wife can only
torment the unfaithful husband's conscience still further. She
could speak to him in much stronger terms than this though,
drawing from him the petulant assertion that 'heroic resolutions in
women are things of the which I have never been transported with
great admiration, nor can be if my life lay on't, for I think it is a
very impertinent virtue'. The punishment he gave her for such
impertinence was veiled under a show of gallantry: 'I have too
much respect for you to come near you whilst I am in disgrace,
but when I am a favourite again I will wait on you.'

These wranglings did not affect Rochester's love for his
children, and in particular for his son Charles. Had he survived to
see the boy die at the age of ten, his reaction might have been
similar to that of the King's at the news of Minette's death. Once,
when his wife was staying at her Enmore estate, he was charged
with looking after Charles at High Lodge. The boy fell ill though,
and so his father sent him back to Adderbury where he could be
looked after by the dowager Countess. Rochester then set off for
London. From the following letter it is clear that his wife had been
angry when she heard about this down in Somerset. Perhaps she
had not been ready to believe there was anything wrong with her
son, and that Rochester had been seeking an excuse for going off
to the capital.

It were very unreasonable should I not love you whilst I
believe you a deserving good creature. I am already so weary
of this place [London] that upon my soul I could be content
to pass my winter at Cannington [in Somerset], though I
apprehend the tediousness of it for you. Pray send me word
what lies in my power to do for your service and ease here or
wherever else you can imploy me, and assure yourself I will
neglect your concern no more than forget my own. 'Twas
very well for your son, as ill as you took it, that I sent him to
Adderbury, for it proves at last to be the King's Evil
[scrofula] that troubles him and he comes up to London this

week to be touched. My humble service to my Aunt Rogers and Nann. I write in bed and afraid you can't read it.

Two very beautiful letters from Rochester to his son, both written in the late 1670s, have survived. In them he encourages the child to be honest, dutiful and God-fearing. He is desperate that the boy should not take after him. Having appointed a tutor to Charles it seems the Earl then gave the man the following letter to pass on to him:

I hope Charles, when you receive this, and know that I have sent this gentleman to be your tutor, you will be very glad to see I take such care of you, and be very grateful: which is best shown in being obedient and diligent. You are now grown big enough to be a man, if you are wise enough, and the way to be truly wise is to serve God, learn your books, and observe the instructions of your parents first, and next your tutor. According as you employ that time, you are to be happy or unhappy for ever. But I have so good an opinion of you that I am glad to think you will never deceive me. Dear child, learn your book and be obedient, and you shall see what a father I will be to you. You shall want no pleasure while you are good. And that you may be so are my constant prayers.
                                   Rochester.

Rochester could remember how, when he was Charles's age, he had waited with excitement in Paris for his father to arrive. He had also, as Clarendon said at the time, loved receiving his father's letters. Now he wanted his own son to write more often – and he hinted at that while Charles was being looked after by the dowager Countess:

Charles, I take if it very kindly that you write to me (though seldom) and wish heartily you would behave yourself so, as that I might show how much I love you without being ashamed. Obedience to your grandmother, and those who instruct you in good things, is the way to make you happy here and forever. Avoid idleness, scorn lying, and God will bless you: for which I pray.
                                   Rochester.

Of course, there was one other letter to be written. By the late 1670s Rochester had acquired quite enough 'chemical knowledge' (to quote Henry Savile) to appreciate that the 'surer friend' of death was close now. As we shall see, the poet who believed that we need not fear another hell was not, at this stage, unduly bothered about dying either. It was of more importance to him that he wrote a letter to his wife giving her the satisfaction, at least, of knowing that *he knew* she had always been too good for him. Lady Rochester had waited for this confession for far too long, and her husband sent it with a gentleness which was as typical of him as the burning jealousy which prevented her from marrying again:

'Tis not an easy thing to be entirely happy, but to be kind is very easy, and that is the greatest measure of happiness. I say not this to put you in mind of being kind to me; you have practised that so long that I have a joyful confidence you will never forget it; but to show that I myself have a sense of what the methods of my life seem so utterly to contradict. I must not be too wise about my own follies, or else this letter had been a book, dedicated to you, and published to the world.

❧ ❧ ❧

Elizabeth Barry became pregnant in the spring of 1677, but for Rochester the relationship remained as frustrating and unhappy as ever. There were times when she could encourage him with a display of warmth and good humour, and his short letter: 'Madam, you are stark mad and therefore the fitter for me to love, and that is the reason, I think, I can never leave to be your humble servant', shows that the affair had its moments of light-heartedness; but besides Barry's unpredictable temperament ('Madam, I found you in a chiding humour today and so I left you'), Rochester also had to contend with her interfering friend 'Mrs R', who may have been either the 'lean' one or the 'fat' one:

So much wit and beauty as you have should think of nothing less than doing miracles; and there cannot be a greater than to continue to love me . . . but to pick out the wildest and most fantastical odd man alive and to place your kindness there, is an act so brave and daring as will show the greatness of your spirit, and distinguish you in love, as you are in all things else, from womankind. Whether I have made a good argument for myself, I leave you to judge, and beg you to believe me whenever I tell you what Mrs R is, since I give an account of her humblest servant. Remember the hour of strict account, when both hearts are to be open, and we obliged to speak freely, as you ordered it yesterday, for so I must ever call the day I saw you last, since all time between that and the next visit is no part of my life, or at least like a long fit of the falling-sickness wherein I am dead to all joy and happiness.

Suddenly he is interrupted:

Here's a damned impertinent fool bolted in, that hinders me from ending my letter. The plague of —— take him, and any man or woman alive that takes my thoughts off of you. But in the evening I will see you and be happy in spite of all the fools in the world.

Inevitably, his drinking accounted for angry, irrational outbursts which only did further damage to the relationship. 'I cannot but confess, with an humble and sincere repentance, that I have hitherto lived very ill; receive my confession and let the promise of my future zeal and devotion obtain my pardon for last night's blasphemy against you, my Heaven.' Such promises from an alcoholic are usually worth ignoring.

One serious mistake Rochester appears to have made with Barry was to try and persuade her to leave the stage. Like many ambitious young actors she was quite prepared to put her career ahead of any love affair; it was the former which had led to the latter in the first place. Although the Earl was so involved in the London theatre, he had no time for the egotism and silliness of those who worked in it – and to sit watching such a beloved mistress acting before crowds of leering fops was to see her selling her very self:

> Leave this gaudy, gilded stage,
> From custom more than use frequented,
> Where fools of either sex and age

Crowd to see themselves presented.
To love's theatre, the bed,
Youth and beauty fly together
And act so well it may be said
The laurel there was due to either.
'Twixt strife of love and war the difference lies in this:
When neither overcomes, love's triumph greater is.

Now nearly finished, Rochester was bed-ridden at High Lodge when, in December 1677, Savile broke him some news he had heard from the King the night before:

> . . . your Lordship has a daughter borne by the body of Mrs Barry, of which I give your honour joy. I doubt she does not lie in much state, for a friend and protectress of hers in the Mall was much lamenting her poverty very lately, not without some gentle reflections on your Lordship's want either of generosity or bowels towards a lady who had not refused you the full enjoyment of her charms.

Savile, never sycophantic to Rochester, seems to think that this friend of Mrs Barry's had a point – but it was now more than the Earl could do to look after himself. In his condition the most he could manage was to send her a box of 'trifles' and a letter, not without wit, in which he said he was hopeful of seeing her soon:

> Your safe delivery has delivered me too from fears for your sake which were, I'll promise you, as burthensome to me as your great belly could be to you. Everything has fallen out to my wish, for you are out of danger and the child is of the soft sex I love. Shortly my hopes are to see you, and in a little while after to look on you with all your beauty about you. Pray let nobody but yourself open the box I sent you. I did not know, but that in lying-in you might have use of those trifles. Sick and in bed as I am, I could come at no more of 'em.

There is some uncertainty over the identity in Rochester's will of 'an infant child by the name of Elizabeth Clerke' who was to receive an annuity, bound to the manor of Sutton-Mallet, of £40 for the rest of her life. What has caused the confusion is the allegation by Captain Alexander Smith that Rochester had a child in the country by a Madam Clark. Ridiculously, he claimed that the Earl raped this girl while her grandmother helped by holding her legs down. During the rape, said Smith, the Earl recited the lines:

> Though round my bed the fumes plant their charms,
> I'll break them with Jocasta in my arms:
> Clasped in the folds of love, I'll wait my doom;
> And act my joys, though thunder shakes the room.

However absurd rumours become they tend to have at least a tincture of truth behind them, and one certainly wonders why a daughter by Mrs Barry, though definitely called Elizabeth, should have acquired the surname 'Clerke'. (She died shortly before reaching adulthood.) So *was* there another child? It can only be said that Smith's appetite for salacious gossip makes him most untrustworthy and that 'Elizabeth Clerke' is *likelier* to have been Mrs Barry's daughter than anybody else's.

Shortly after the birth, Rochester discovered that Mrs Barry had another lover. Shocked, despairing and drunk, he sat writing to her at three o'clock in the morning and told her that his anger, spleen, revenge and shame could not make him disown the great truth 'that I love you above all things in the world'.

> I thank God I can distinguish; I can see very woman in you and from yourself am convinced I have never been in the wrong in my opinion of women. 'Tis impossible for me to curse you, but give me leave to pity myself – which is more than ever you will do for me. You have a character and you maintain it, but I am sorry you make me an example to prove it. It seems, as you excel in everything you scorn to grow less in that noble quality of using your servants very hardly . . .

In the 1660s, when he was healthy and drink had not diseased his mind, he had written one of his most stunning lyrical poems about the sheer impossibility of fidelity in a world subjected to continual change, and the untenable nature of time:

All my past life is mine no more;
The flying hours are gone,
Like transitory dream given o'er
Whose images are kept in store
By memory alone.

Whatever is to come is not:
How can it then be mine?
The present moment's all my lot,
And that, as fast as it is got,
Phyllis, is wholly thine.

Then talk not of inconstancy,
False hearts, and broken vows;
If I, by miracle, can be
This livelong minute true to thee,
'Tis all that heaven allows.

Ten years later he no longer believed in Hobbism. He had learnt the hard way that far from being something beautiful, inconstancy brought more jealousy and destruction than it could ever bring happiness. The following lines are open to more than one interpretation, but they were written with bitter sarcasm:

'Tis not that I am weary grown
Of being yours, and yours alone,
But with what face can I incline
To damn you to be only mine?
You, whom some kinder power did fashion,
By merit and by inclination,
The joy at least of one whole nation.

Let meaner spirits of your sex
With humbler aims their thoughts perplex,
And boast if by their arts they can
Contrive to make one happy man;
Whilst, moved by an impartial sense,
Favours, like nature, you dispense
With universal influence.

See, the kind seed-receiving earth
To every grain affords a birth.
On her, no showers unwelcome fall:
Her willing womb retains 'em all.
And shall my Celia be confined?
No! Live up to thy mighty mind
And be the mistress of mankind.

Helpless to contain his pain, Rochester lashed out at Elizabeth Barry like a cornered, wounded animal. With a hatred so easily bourne out of passionate love, he now sought to inflict the same degree of anger and misery that he was feeling himself, on the woman who had been 'dearest of all that ever was dearest to me'. It was easy. He had abducted somebody once before.

He took the child. Then he wrote a bitingly clever letter to Barry, suggesting that he had no alternative but to look after their daughter himself, since it was a duty her mother was unfit to perform.

I am far from delighting in the grief I have given you by taking away the child, and you, who made it so absolutely necessary for me to do so, must take that excuse from me for all the ill nature of it. On the other side, pray be assured, I love Betty so well that you need not apprehend any neglect from those I employ, and I hope very shortly to restore her to you a finer girl than ever. In the mean time you would do well to think of the advice I gave you, for how little show soever my prudence makes in my own affairs, in yours it will prove very successful if you please to follow it, and since discretion is the thing alone you are like to want, pray study to get it.

His bitterness, combined with his failing libido, ensured that there would be no more affairs of the heart. It is by no means certain that he even spoke to Elizabeth Barry again. What he needed to do now was to forget his despair in the only way he had ever known. The five years of continuous drunknness reached a frightening crescendo, and if he really believed that drink could supplant the unhappiness which he thought womankind had brought him then he was deceiving himself as only the alcoholic can:

Love a woman? You're an ass!
'Tis a most insipid passion
To choose out for your happiness
The silliest part of God's creation.

Let the porter and the groom,
Things designed for dirty slaves,
Drudge in fair Aurelia's womb
To get supplies for age and graves.

Farewell, woman! I intend
Henceforth every night to sit
With my lewd, well-natured friend,
Drinking to engender wit.

Then give me health, wealth, mirth and wine,
And, if busy love entrenches,
There's a sweet, soft page of mine,
Does the trick worth forty wenches.

Rochester proceeded to make himself so ill that by the spring of
1678 it was widely believed that he was dead.

10

ROSIDORE'S REPRIEVE

For my own part I'm taking pains not to die, without
knowing how to live on when I have brought it about.

Rochester, writing to Savile

When the playwright Nathaniel Lee, one of Rochester's
more grateful protégés, produced his comedy *The
Princess of Cleve* in September 1681, fourteen months
after the Earl's death, he reminded Londoners that, having already
fooled them all as Dr Bendo, Rochester bamboozled them again in
the spring of 1678 by recovering from a sickness which they
assumed at the time had killed him. In tribute to the man who had
helped his career as a dramatist, Lee created the character of
Count Rosidore, who is eulogised by Nemours and the Vidame of
Chartres in the following exchange:

Vidame: He that was the life, the soul of pleasure
          Count Rosidore, is dead.

Nemours: Then we may say
          Wit was and satyr is a carcass now.
          I thought his last debauch would be his death
          But is it certain?

Vidame: Yes; I saw him dust.
          I saw the mighty thing a nothing made;

> Huddled with worms, and swept to that cold den
> Where Rosidore is now but common clay,
> Whom every wiser emmet bears away
> And lays him up against a winter's day.

If anyone in the audience was still unsure about who Count Rosidore represented, Lee left them in no doubt with the sentiments he poured out through Nemours:

> He was the spirit of wit and had such an art in gilding his failures that it was hard not to love his faults. He never spoke a witty thing twice, though to different persons. His imperfections were catching and his genius was so luxuriant that he was forced to tame it with a hesitation in his speech to keep it in view. But oh! how awkward; how insipid, how poor and wretchedly dull is the imitation of those that have all the affectation of his verse and none of his wit.

It is an epitaph which bears a close comparison with what the Earl's friend Robert Wolseley said about him in the preface of *Valentinian*:

> He had a wit that was accompanied with an unaffected greatness of mind and a natural love to justice and truth; a wit that was in perpetual war with knavery, and ever attacking those kind of vices most whose malignity was like to be most diffusive . . . Never was his pen drawn but on the side of good sense, and usually employed like the arms of the ancient heroes, to stop the progress of arbitrary oppression and beat down the brutishness of headstrong will; to do his King and country justice upon such public state thieves as would beggar a Kingdom to enrich themselves . . . These were the vermin whom (to his eternal honour) his pen was continually pricking and goading. A pen, if not so happy in the success, as generous in the aim, as either the sword of Theseus or the club of Hercules; nor was it less sharp than that, or less wieghty than this . . .

Nemour's question to Vidame, 'But is [his death] certain?' must have raised a laugh from Dorset Garden Theatre audiences for, in

April 1678, Rochester's demise seemed certain enough for Anthony Wood to confirm in his journal that, 'About 18 April, John, Earl of Rochester, died at London aged 28 or thereabouts.' On 25 April there was rather different news from Sir Ralph Verney's son, John: 'Lord Rochester has been very ill and is very penitent, but is now bettering.' Finally, there is Rochester himself, now more bored with the myth of himself than ever, telling Savile in weary tones that he too had

> received the unhappy news of my own death and burial. But hearing what heirs and successors were decreed me in my place, and chiefly in my lodgings, it was no small joy to me that these tidings prove untrue. My passion for living is so increased that I omit no care of myself, while before I never thought life the trouble of taking. The King, who knows me to be a very ill-natured man, will not think it an easy matter for me to die now I live chiefly out of spite. Dear Mr Savile; afford me some news from your land of the living.

Those are hardly the words of a man running scared, and yet most people, including historians and commentators on the age in general, make the easy assumption that Rochester turned to Christianity because he was frightened of dying. This is rubbish. The man's cynicism and indifference to almost everything was so deep that, according to his eventual confessor, Gilbert Burnet, Rochester only suffered the presence of priests at his bedside during this near-fatal illness in order to satisfy those who still loved him:

> . . . in the sickness which brought him so near death before I first knew him, when his spirits were so low and spent that he could not move nor stir, and *he did not think to live an hour*, he said his reason and judgement were so clear and strong that from thence, he was fully persuaded that death was not the spending or dissolution of the soul, but only the separation of it from matter. He had, in that sickness, great remorses for his past life, but he afterwards told me, they were rather *general and dark horrors than any convictions of sinning against God*. He was sorry he had lived so as to waste his strength so soon, or that he had brought such an ill

245

name upon himself, and had an agony in his mind about it, *which he knew not well how to express.* But at such times, though he complied with his friends in suffering divines to be sent for, he said he had no great mind to it, and that it was but a piece of his breeding, to desire them to pray by him, in which he joined little himself.

(All the italics are the author's.)

The reason Rochester's 'reason and judgement were so clear and strong' during this illness is that it sobered him up. We do not know for how long he was in bed, but the letter to Savile quoted above was written by a man who, for the first time in five years, was totally sober. It has already been noted that the alcoholic who enters abstinence experiences a shock of realising just how serious life really is. There can be a tremendous and nasty feeling of sheer *pressure*. In his sobriety, the Earl's existence embraced all these feelings: anxiety, sadness, guilt, tenseness, unbearable loneliness, moroseness, introversion, worry and frustration. The degree of contemplation and retrospection becomes so acute that, without professional help, the newly recovering alcoholic will run a serious risk of a mental breakdown. In trying to beat what was earlier described as one of the world's most hidden illnesses, the alcoholic also goes through a period of self-recognition and self-evaluation.

It was sobriety, and never fear, which turned Rochester towards God.

Rochester did suffer lapses back into alcoholism between now and his death in the summer of 1680 though. '. . . it is a miraculous thing when a man half in the grave cannot leave off playing the fool and the buffoon', he wrote to Savile in the summer of 1678, before adding, 'but so it falls out to my comfort!' He was not being as foolish as he thought, for the alternative discomfort of going entirely *without* drink could have caused him to lose his mind. In the meantime his mood of high seriousness when he was *not* playing the fool and the buffoon prompted the following observation from his friend Robert Wolseley:

I must not here forget that a considerable time before his last sickness his wit began to take a more serious bent and to frame and fashion itself to public business. He began to inform himself of the wisdom of our laws and the excellent constitution of the English Government, and to speak in the House of Peers with general approbation. He was inquisitive of all kinds of histories that concerned England, both ancient and modern, and set himself to read the Journals of Parliament Proceedings. In effect, he seemed to study nothing more than which way to make that great understanding God had given him most useful to his country, and I am confident, had he lived, his riper age would have served it as much as his youth had diverted it.

To live 'chiefly out of spite' is, of course, no way to live at all and will prove unsustainable to all but the most malevolent. Rochester was not as malevolent as he sometimes needed to believe, and it was a search for life's meaning, not spite, which kept him alive until the summer of 1680.

In order to stop drinking altogether, the alcoholic has to reach what is commonly called 'the bottom'. This moment – the sudden realisation that alcohol can no longer be allowed to be the ruin of life – has been described by many former drinkers in almost religious terms; as though it were like being 'born again'. For some alcoholics it occurs after just one too many misdemeanours; for others it might result from having done something dreadful. But for most, it never occurs at all.

There can also be many false 'bottoms' along the route to the final one, and we have already noted that Rochester had promised Elizabeth Barry he was going to reform; that in 1676 'Livy and sickness' had supposedly inclined him to 'policy'; that the following year he briefly stepped up his appearances at the House of Lords. Although his *general* conduct really did change now, there were still many lapses.

He began to fluctuate between long periods of high seriousness (sobriety) and short bursts of flippancy (drunkenness). He could quote Falstaff on the subject of drinking when he was in the latter mood, but when he was sober and had a pen in his hand, he recognised that personally, he could no longer play an active part in the world of excess:

As some brave admiral, in former war
Deprived of force, but pressed with courage still,
Two rival fleets appearing from afar,
Crawls to the top of an adjacent hill;

From whence, with thoughts full of concern, he views
The wise and daring conduct of the fight,
Whilst each bold action to his mind renews
His present glory and his past delight;

From his fierce eyes flashes of fire he throws,
As from black clouds when lightning breaks away;
Transported, thinks himself amidst the foes,
And absent, yet enjoys the bloody day;

So, when my days of impotence approach,
And I'm by pox and wine's unlucky chance
Forced from the pleasing billows of debauch
On the dull shore of lazy temperance,

My pains at least some respite shall afford
While I behold the battles you maintain
When fleets of glasses sail about the board,
From whose broadsides volleys of wit shall rain.

Nor let the sight of honourable scars
Which my too forward valour did procure,
Frighten new-listed soldiers from the wars:
Past joys have more than paid what I endure.

Should any youth worth being drunk prove nice,
And from his fair inviter meanly shrink,
'Twill please the ghost of my departed vice
If, at my counsel he repent and drink.

Or should some cold-complexioned sot forbid,
With his dull morals, our bold night alarums,
I'll fire his blood by telling what I did
When I was strong and able to bear arms.

I'll tell of whores attacked, their lords at home;
Bawds' quarters beaten up and fortress won;
Windows demolished, watches overcome;
And handsome ills by my contrivance done.

Nor shall our love-fits, Chloris, be forgot,
When each the well-looked linkboy strove t'enjoy,
And the best kiss was the deciding lot
Whether the boy fucked you, or I the boy.

With tales like these I will such thoughts inspire
As to important mischief shall incline:
I'll make him long some ancient church to fire,
And fear no lewdness he's called to by wine.

Thus, statesmanlike, I'll saucily impose,
And, safe from action, valiantly advise;
Sheltered in impotence, urge you to blows,
And, being good for nothing else, be wise.

The impotence which Rochester mentions twice in the above poem, 'The Maimed Debauchee', was ironically being enhanced by his sobriety. After such a long period of drunkenness it would have been remarkable if he had not experienced, upon ceasing to drink, a sudden and complete loss of sexual interest or drive. This is usually recoverable after some months of abstinence but, since the Earl kept returning to drink intermittently, he was perpetuating the whole cycle.

In the summer of 1678 he sounds, in his letters, as though he had come to terms with death, if not life. Sobriety meant that his cynicism could now sometimes bear the mark of a tired, passive disillusionment rather than the old anger of fire. In June, he declared to Savile that he had not renounced business. 'Let abler men try it', though only the year before he had acted as trustee to Nell Gwyn. It was in a mood of grim realism that he told Savile what his advice to Nell had always been:

Take your measures just contrary to your rivals, live in peace with all the world, and easily with the King. Never be so ill-natured to stir up his anger against others, but let him forget the use of a passion which is never to do you good. Cherish his love wherever it inclines, and be assured you can't commit greater folly than pretending to be jealous; but, on the contrary, with hand, body, head, heart and all the faculties you have, contribute to his pleasure all you can, and comply with his desires throughout: and, for new intrigues, so you be at one end 'tis no matter which: make sport when you can, at other times help it.

One month later 'the undefaced angel' surfaced again and Rochester sent a letter of floating lyricism to prove it. Savile had written to him from Madam Fourcard's baths in Leather Lane, where he was sweating out the pox in the company of, among others, the Earl's old flame Jane Roberts. (A clergyman's daughter, the beautiful Jane was to die of her condition within the year.) With them, laughed Savile, was Will Fanshawe, one of Rochester's disreputable drinking companions. Three rogues in the same basket. Alone – apart from his servants – at High Lodge, the Earl sat back and remembered his own days at Madam Fourcard's nine years earlier; he recalled the awful strictness of Barten and Ginman, who helped to run the place. And he had never forgotten Jane. He picked up his pen with the gentle retrospection of a 'maimed debauchee':

Were I as idle as ever, which I should not fail of being, if health permitted I would write a small romance and make the sun, with her dishevelled rays, gild the tops of the palaces in Leather Lane. Then should those vile enchanters, Barten and Ginman, lead forth their illustrious captives in chains of quicksilver, and, confining 'em by charms to the loathsome banks of a dead lake of diet-drink, you, as my friend, should break the horrid silence and speak the most passionate fine things that ever heroic lover uttered; which, being softly and sweetly replied to by Mrs Roberts, should rudely be interrupted by the envious F——. Thus would I lead the mournful tale along, till the gentle reader bathed with the tribute of his eyes the names of such unfortunate lovers; and this, I take it, would be a most excellent way of celebrating the memories of my most pocky friends, companions and mistresses. But it is a miraculous thing – as the wise have it – when a man half in the grave cannot leave off playing the fool and the buffoon; but so it falls out to my comfort. For at this moment I am in a damned relapse, brought by a fever, the stone and some ten diseases more, which have deprived me of the power of crawling, which I happily enjoyed some days ago. And now, I fear, I must fall, that it may be fulfilled which was long since written for instruction in a good old ballad:

> But he who lives not wise and sober.
> Falls with the leaf, still, in October.

About which time, in all probability, there may be a period added to the ridiculous being of your humble servant
                              Rochester.

Like all great writers, Rochester could drop magical phrases from his pen such as 'dishevelled rays'; 'chains of quicksilver'; 'vile enchanters'; with consummate ease.

This summer of 1678 was a period of tremendous reflection for the Earl. If he was not actually ill all the time then he was certainly not a well man either, and physical disability will only fuel contemplation. His loneliness was chronic; his unhappiness deep. A confession of platonic love is always helped by melancholy. To Savile he wrote:

'Tis not the least of my happiness that I think you love me, but the first of all my pretensions is to make it appear that I faithfully endeavour to deserve it. If there be a real good upon earth, 'tis in the name of friend, without which all others are merely fantastical. How few of us are fit stuff to make that thing; we have daily the melancholy experience. However, dear Harry, let us not give out, nor despair of bringing that about, which, as it is the most difficult and rare accident of life, is also the best; nay, perhaps, the only good one. This thought has so entirely possessed me since I am come into the country . . .

He had attended the House of Lords in sporadic bursts since 1667, but now he was ready to make a speech of some gravity. By 1678 the reign of Charles II had lost much of its frivolity and even the wits, prompted by age, were looking more serious. That summer, Savile told Rochester he was being dispatched as a diplomat to France in the company of 'Embassador Extraordinary', Lord Sunderland. In his sobriety, the Earl was moving with these times, and after a man called Christopher Kirby came forward to tell the King that a Jesuit plot existed to kill him, Rochester, writing to his wife from London, told her that 'things are now reduced to the extremity on all sides that a man dares not turn his back for fear of being hanged'. What had really shaken the capital was not the evidence being given to the Privy Council by one Titus Oates, but the apparent murder of a Protestant magistrate called Sir Edward Berry Godfrey, whose battered body was found on Primrose Hill in the middle of October. Panic, fear and anti-Catholic rumour coursed through the town. But when a bill was put before Parliament to exclude Charles's brother, the Catholic and presumptive heir, James, from ever taking the throne, Rochester stood up in the Lords and showed that in sobriety his thought could be measured, cautious and far from impetuous:

Mr Speaker, sir; although it hath been said that no good Protestant can speak against this Bill, yet, sir, I cannot forbear to offer some objections against it. I do not know that any of the King's murderers were condemned without being heard, and must we deal thus with the brother of our King? It is such a severe way of proceeding that I think we cannot answer it to the world, and therefore it would consist much better with the justice of the House to impeach him and try him in a formal way, and then cut off his head – if he deserve it. I will not offer to dispute the power of Parliaments, but I question whether this law, if made, would be good in itself. Some laws have a natural weakness with them. I think that by which the old Long Parliament carried on their rebellion was judged afterward void in law, because there was a power given which could not be taken from the Crown. For aught I know, when you have made this law it may have the same flaw in it. If not, I am confident there are a loyal party which will never obey but will think themselves bound by their oath of allegiance and duty to pay obedience to the Duke (if ever he should come to be King) which must occasion a civil war. And, sir, I do not find that the proviso that was ordered to be added for the security of the Duke's children is made strong enough to secure them, according to the debate of the House; it being liable to many objections, and the more because the words Presumptive Heir of the Crown are industriously left out, though much insisted upon when debated here in the House. Upon the whole matter, my humble motion is, that the bill may be thrown out.

Rochester had personal reasons for wanting to see this Catholic witch hunt die; he had overseen his wife's conversion to the Church of Rome – quite probably because the heir to the throne was a Catholic himself, and he wished to secure her future, along with his children's.

✤ ✤ ✤

If there is a secret to defeating alcoholism, it lies in the whole idea of *acceptance*. Alcoholics have to teach themselves that, if you take on the world, you lose. Rochester's sobriety was still be governed by a bitter darkness, and the man who wrote the following lines into Fletcher's *Valentinian* had to teach himself to change the things that could be changed, accept the things which could not be changed, and acquire the wisdom to know the difference. This was utterly beyond him for as long as he did not trust in God:

> Supreme first causes: you, whence all things flow,
> Whose infiniteness does each little fill;
> You, who decree each seeming chance below,
> So great in power were you as good in will,
> How could you ever have produced such an ill?
>
> Had your eternal mind been bent to good,
> Could human happiness have proved so lame?
> Rapine, revenge, injustice, thirst of blood,
> Grief, anguish, horror, want, despair and shame,
> Had never found a being, nor a name . . .

Alcoholism is a peculiarly religious condition, because without trusting in a higher power, without a governing body to make sense of everything, without *spirituality*, the world will seem valueless through the drinker's eyes. There is a universal streak of thinking at work here; not a worldly one, and Rochester's brilliant poem 'Upon Nothing' was directly influenced by the illness which was now making his life a living hell.

> Nothing! thou elder brother even to Shade;
> Thou hadst a being ere the world was made,
> And, well fixed, art alone of ending not afraid.
>
> Ere Time and Place were, Time and Place were not,
> When primitive Nothing Something straight begot;
> Then all proceeded from the great, united, What.
>
> Something, the general attribute of all;
> Severed from thee, its sole original,
> Into thy boundless self must undistinguished fall.
>
> Yet Something did thy mighty power command,
> And from thy fruitful Emptiness's hand
> Snatched men; beasts; birds; fire; water; air and land.
>
> Matter, the wickedest offspring of thy race,
> By Form assisted, flew from thy embrace,
> And rebel Light obscured thy reverend dusky face.
>
> With Form and Matter, Time and Place did join;
> Body, thy foe, with these did leagues combine
> To spoil thy peaceful realm, and ruin all thy line.
>
> But turncoat Time assists the foe in vain,
> And, bribed by thee, destroys their short-lived reign,
> And to thy hungry womb drives back thy slaves again.
>
> Though mysteries are barred from laic eyes,
> And the divine alone with warrant pries
> Into thy bosom, where the truth in private lies,

Yet this of thee the wise may truly say:
Thou from the virtuous nothing does delay,
And, to be part of thee, the wicked wisely pray.

Great Negative; how vainly would the wise
Inquire; define; distinguish; teach; devise;
Didst thou not stand to point their blind philosophies!

Is or Is Not, the two great ends of Fate,
And True or False, the subject of debate,
That perfect or destroy the vast designs of state –

When they have racked the politician's breast,
Within thy bosom most securely rest,
And when reduced to thee, are least unsafe and best.

But Nothing, why does Something still permit
That sacred monarchs should in council sit
With persons highly thought at best for nothing fit,

While weighty Something modestly abstains
From princes' coffers, and from statesmen's brains,
And Nothing there like stately Nothing reigns?

Nothing! who dwellst with fools in grave disguise,
For whom they reverend shapes and forms devise.
Lawn sleeves and furs and gowns, when they like thee look wise,

French truth; Dutch prowess; British policy;
Hibernian learning; Scotch civility;
Spaniards' dispatch; Danes' wit are mainly seen in thee;

The great man's gratitude to his best friend,
Kings' promises, whores' vows – towards thee they bend,
Flow swiftly into thee, and in thee ever end.

   Although Rochester had begun to believe in the existence of the
soul, during the spring illness in which he had 'dried out', this did
not necessarily mean a God existed too. It did, however, prompt

the quest for God, or a Higher Power. His desire to 'find out' gradually became ravenous – and what at first stood in his way was the inability to believe in a God who could possibly allow the world to be so full of grief, horror and despair.

Rochester was on the right path however. The alcoholic's chances of recovering *without* discovering a positive sense of spirituality are negligible. Statistics show that in America (which is starting to treat alcoholism with a seriousness the British government might think it prudent to follow), out of all the alcoholics who have lasted a year without drink, and who proudly declare they will manage a second year of sobriety, only forty per cent will succeed. And these are people who think they are committed. In our own society, people like Sir Anthony Hopkins, Barry Humphries and Jimmy Greaves (to name only the most famous) are heroes, because they have rediscovered themselves against all the odds, and are winning the most important fight of their lives. In the seventeenth century, the Earl of Rochester lost his own fight because he literally could not meet the deadline. There does come a moment when it is all too late. Rochester ran out of time because he would not stop asking the same questions. He would not *accept*. In the autumn of 1679 he fell seriously ill again and, while this sickness accelerated his quest, his own intellect and anger stood in the way of a swift understanding. It is quite peculiar that the religious Graham Greene, of all people, should have said: 'To forswear wine and women might have saved him'. It had nothing to do with wine and women any more. The man who wrote 'Upon Nothing' was on another plane now. He was writing to his son in the desperate hope that the boy would be God-fearing. What he did not bother to add was that his hopes for himself were the same, and just as desperate.

But this second near-fatal illness did make a difference. Jane Roberts, the royal mistress who had asked the King to take her back from the Earl in the early 1670s, had died of the pox – and she had repented of all her sins before a priest, one Gilbert Burnet. Rochester had been very fond of Jane, and news of her confessions to Burnet was partly what prompted him to pick up Burnet's book *The History of the Reformation*. According to Burnet:

The occasion that led me into so particular a knowledge of him was an intimation given me by a gentleman of his acquaintance of his desire to see me. This was some time in October, 1679, when he was slowly recovering out of a great disease.

We should take stock here, and remember that Rochester called for the priest when he was *recovering* – not declining.

He had understood that I often attended on one well known to him that died the summer before; he was also then entertaining himself with the first part of *The History of the Reformation*, then newly come out, with which he seemed not ill pleased: and we had accidentally met in two or three places some time before. These were the motives that led him to call for my company. After I had waited on him once or twice, he grew into that freedom with me as to open to me all his thoughts, both of religion and morality, and to give me a full view of his past life, and seemed not uneasy at my frequent visits.

During the previous winter, of 1678, Rochester had held discussions with a man of greater intellect that Burnet, the twenty-four-year-old deist Charles Blount, son of the philosopher Sir Henry Blount. Quite why Rochester eventually opted for Burnet's 'counselling' instead of Blount's remains unclear, for he was impressed enough by the latter's opinions to send him the following bleak-minded version of a Seneca chorus:

> After death, nothing is, and nothing; death;
> The utmost limit of a gasp of breath.
> Let the ambitious zealot lay aside
> His hopes of heaven, whose faith is but his pride;
> Let slavish souls lay by their fear.
> Nor be concerned which way nor where
> After this life they shall be hurled.
> Dead, we become the lumber of the world,
> And to that mass of matter shall be swept
> Where things destroyed with things unborn are kept.
> Devouring time confounds body and soul.
> For Hell and the foul fiend that rules

> God's everlasting fiery jails,
> Devised by rogues; dreaded by fools,
> With his grim, grisly dog that keeps the door,
> Are senseless stories; idle tales;
> Dreams, whimseys and no more.

In his reply to Rochester, sent in early February 1679, Blount cleverly suggested that a man who could write poetry as well as this, was proof of God's existence:

> My Lord,
> I had the honour yesterday to receive from the hands of an humble servant of your Lordship's your most incomparable version of that passage of Seneca's, where he begins with – Post mortem nihil est, ipsaque mors nihil, &c. – and must confess, with your Lordship's pardon, that I cannot but esteem the translation to be, in some measure, a confutation of the original; since what less than a divine and immortal mind could have produced what you have there written? Indeed, the hand that wrote it may become *lumber*, but sure, the spirit that dictated it can never be so. No, my Lord; your mighty genius is a most sufficient argument of its own immortality, and more prevalent with me than all the haranges of the parsons or sophistry of the schoolmen. . . .

⚜ ⚜ ⚜

At the end of 1679, when Rochester was sick in the country, John Dryden was viciously assaulted in Covent Garden by, as the current newsletter *Domestic Intelligence Number 49* had it:

> three persons who called him rogue and son of a whore, knocked him down and dangerously wounded him, but upon his crying out murder, they made their escape. It is conceived they had their pay before hand, and designed not to rob him, but to execute on him some feminine if not popish vengeance.

Nobody has ever discovered with certainty who instigated this attack on Dryden, but public opinion at the time pointed strongly at

Louise de Kéroualle, the Duchess of Portsmouth. She had good reason to feel angry with the Poet Laureate, for he was assumed to have been the author of 'An Essay on Satire' which included the lines:

> Nor shall the royal mistresses be named.
> Too ugly, or too easy to be blamed. . . .
> Was ever prince by two at once misled;
> False; foolish; old; ill-natured and ill-bred?

The other royal mistress was Nell Gwyn, but she was never suspected as being the organiser of the attack. The reasons for this were simple: first, she was a famously easy-going person and, more importantly, she was not a Catholic. Louise de Kéroualle was, and the hysterical antipathy for the Church of Rome which swept England after the Popish Plot of 1678 ensured that most commentators, like Narcissus Luttrell, thught the attack had been 'done by order of the Duchess of Portsmouth; she being abused in a late libel . . . of which Mr Dryden is suspected to be the author'.

But, inevitably, there were those who blamed Rochester for the drubbing of Dryden. Rochester had also come in for criticism in 'An Essay on Satire':

> Rochester I despise for's mere want of wit,
> Though thought to have a tail and cloven feet;
> For while he mischief means to all mankind,
> Himself alone the ill effects does find. . . .

The author continued in the same vein, calling the Earl a hypocrite, a coward and, finally, a bad writer:

> Sometimes he has some humour; never wit:
> And if it rarely, very rarely hit,
> 'Tis under such a nasty rubbish laid,
> To find it out's the cinder woman's trade . . .
> So lewdly dull his idle works appear,
> The wretched texts deserve no comments here.

Rochester's response to Savile, upon reading these lines, appears to have been one of detached amusement, not anger.

I have sent you herewith a libel, in which my own share is not the least. The King, having perused it, is no ways dissatisfied with his. The author is apparently Mr Dryden, his patron my Lord Mulgrave having a panegyric in the midst . . .

(The irony of the situation is that, in fact, Mulgrave wrote the satire, in which Dryden had a hand, and not the other way round.)

Yet the voices accusing Rochester of the cowardly assault on Dryden have grown louder over the centuries, not least because of the discovery of the infamous letter to Henry Savile, in which the Earl refers to forgiving Dryden and leaving the 'repartee to Black Will with a cudgel'. This letter, because it appeared to be a literal reference to what ensued, was always presumed to have been written around the time of the attack. But Professor J.H. Wilson, in the middle of this century, proved that the letter had been written three years previously, when Dryden had chosen Mulgrave over Rochester as patron and Rochester had insulted Dryden in his 'An Allusion to Horace'. Dryden had first taken his revenge in his preface to the play *All for Love*, in 1678, when he called the Earl a 'rhyming judge of the twelvepenny gallery' and a 'legitimate son of Sternhold [the standard form of abuse to a bad poet]'. Rochester never bothered to respond to this; would he have had Dryden beaten maliciously, believing him to have written similar comments, a year later?

Another theory, put forward by Graham Greene, was that Rochester and the Duchess of Portsmouth had colluded in the attack. However, the two were hardly on speaking terms by 1679, a fact contributed to by Rochester's description of the Duchess, in 'A Dialogue', as having 'prick in cunt, though double-crammed'. A woman described thus tends not to smile upon her accuser.

The idea that Rochester did orchestrate the cudgelling of Dryden, along with the accusation that he persecuted the playwright Otway, is one that has taken firm hold. Sir Edmund Gosse was ready to believe the worst of the Earl:

his habitual drunkenness may be taken as an excuse for the physical cowardice for which he was notorious . . . so sullen was his humour, so cruel his pursuit of pleasure, that this figure seems to pass through . . . his times, like that of a veritable devil.

Shortly after Rochester's death, Samuel Woodford wrote the following lines:

> Madness and follies, which how ere begun,
> Were not by Rochester sustained alone,
> Though he almost alone, the burden bore
> Beside the monstrous pack, which were his own.

The trap of using Rochester as a scapegoat for every inexplicable mishap of the Restoration period continues to gape, and it is important to consider the Earl's own nature. He was vicious and cruel in his satires and malicious in his written attacks, but would this man, the master of the pen, have resorted to coldly commissioning a physical assault on an enemy? Rochester had always played the game, responding to libel with libel: would he have paid others to take his revenge? And, finally, would he have enhanced his own reputation for cowardice by having Dryden attacked? The reader must judge.

11

CREDO

I was not long in his company when he told me, he should treat me with more freedom than he had ever used to men of my profession. He would conceal none of his principles from me, but lay his thoughts open without any disguise . . .

Gilbert Burnet

Rochester's long discussions with Gilbert Burnet in London, during the winter of 1679, took on the form of psychoanalysis. The Earl had a great deal to confess about himself, and even more to understand. Burnet was the more passive figure, coaxing his 'patient', politely disagreeing with him and, above all, encouraging him. Rochester's nervousness is apparent from Burnet's remark that 'our freest conversation was when we were alone, yet upon several occasions other persons were witnesses to it'. Burnet makes it clear that the Earl told him certain things about his past behaviour which remained a secret between the two of them, and that Rochester was not happy for some of these confessions to be heard by anyone other than the priest. This was an intensely private business.

'I followed him with such arguments as I saw were most likely to prevail with him,' wrote Burnet, 'and my not urging other reasons proceeded not from any distrust I had of their force, but from the necessity of using those that were most proper for him . . . he was in the milk-diet, and apt to fall into hectical fits; an accident weakened him, so that he thought he could not live long.' This was remarkably sensitive and 'modern' thinking: Burnet, the future Bishop of Salisbury, was not going to make the mistake of ramming the name of God down Rochester's throat; the game he played instead was a waiting one. 'As to the Supreme Being', wrote Burnet, 'he had always some impression of one, and professed often to me that he had never known an entire atheist who fully believed there was no God. Yet when he explained his notion of this Being, it amounted to no more than a vast power . . .'

They talked about three general subjects: morality, natural religion and revealed religion. Rochester confessed to seeing the necessity of morality in order to ensure the good government of the world and for the preservation of health, life and friendship. He was

> very much ashamed of his former practices, rather because he had made himself a beast, and had brough pain and sickness on his body, and had suffered much in his reputation, than from any deep sense of a supreme being or another state: but so far this went with him, that he resolved firmly to change the course of his life . . .

It is interesting to consider that these dialogues between Rochester and Burnet anticipated directly the twelve steps to discovery espoused by Alcoholics Anonymous:

1 We admitted we were powerless over alcohol; that our lives had become unmanageable.
2 Came to believe that a Power greater than ourselves could restore us to sanity.
3 Made a decision to turn our will and our lives over to the care of God *as we understood Him*.
4 Made a searching and fearless moral inventory of ourselves.
5 Admitted to God, to ourselves, and to another human being the exact nature of our wrongs.
6 Were entirely ready to have God remove all these defects of character.
7 Humbly ask Him to remove our shortcomings.
8 Made a list of all persons we had harmed, and became willing to make amends to them all.

9 Made direct amends to such people wherever possible, except when to do so would injure them or others.
10 Continued to take a personal inventory and when we were wrong promptly admitted it.
11 Sought through prayer and meditation to improve our conscious contact with God *as we understood Him*, praying only for knowledge of His will for us and the power to carry that out.
12 Having had a spiritual awakening as the result of these steps, we tried to carry this message to alcoholics and to practice these principles in all our affairs.

In a perverse way, the drinking alcoholic is very strong – because he or she tends to regard the world, just as Rochester had done, as a tiny, vacuous and pointless place. Alcoholics do not accept life: they fight it. One critic this century – Anne Righter – observed that Rochester's conversion involved the complete collapse of his personality, and that he 'effectively ceased to be Rochester'. This is a misunderstanding of the process of acceptance which the Earl, now sober, was going through. He had not lost his personality at all: it was just that the familiar strength had been more brittle than most people suspected.

The Hobbist in the Earl broke back out with his assertion that it was unreasonable to imagine that appetite had been put into man only for it to be restrained. According to Burnet,

Upon this he told me the two maxims of his morality then were, that he should do nothing to the hurt of any other, or that might prejudice his health, and he thought that all pleasure, when it did not interfere with these, was to be indulged as the gratification of our natural appetites . . . this he applied to the free use of wine and women.

It was typically self-deceiving of Rochester to imply that his 'morality' did nothing to hurt others. He had been hurting others all his life.

Burnet's answer to all this was inevitable. He said that,

if appetites being natural was an argument for the indulging them, then the revengeful might as well allege it for murder, and the covetous for stealing . . . and why should we not as well think that God intended our brutish and sensual appetites should be governed by our Reason, as the fierceness of beasts should be managed and tamed by the wisdom, and for the use of Man?

Rochester told his confessor that those who believed in God were happy, but that it was not within every man's power.

He did acknowledge the whole system of religion, if believed, was a greater foundation of quiet than any other thing whatsoever: for all the quiet he had in his mind, was that he could not think so good a Being as the Deity would make him miserable. I asked if when by the ill course of his life he had brought so many diseases on his body, he could blame God for it: or expect that he should deliver him from them by a miracle. He confessed there was no reason for that: I then urged, that if sin should cast the mind by a natural effect, into endless horrors and agonies, which being seated in a Being not subject to Death, must last for ever, unless some Miraculous Power interposed, could he accuse God for that which was the effect of his own choice and ill life.

This seems to have thrown the Earl, who said that he did not understand the business of inspiration. 'Why was not a man made a creature more disposed for religion, and better illuminated? . . . If a man says he cannot believe, what help is there?'

To this I answered, that if a man will let a wanton conceit possess his fancy against these things and never consider the evidence for religion on the other hand, but reject it upon a slight view of it, he ought not to say he cannot, but he will not believe: and while a man lives an ill course of life, he is not fitly qualified to examine the matter aright. Let him grow calm and virtuous, and upon due application examine things fairly . . .

Rochester was terrified of committing himself to something which was not true, but in using his reason to try and find God, as opposed to trusting in faith, he was making things doubly difficult for himself. It is also a great irony that a man who had laughed at reason for so long should now be applying it in such a way. He told Burnet that there was:

> nothing that gave him, and many others, a more secret encouragement in their ill ways, that those who pretended to believe, lived so that they could not be thought to be in earnest, when they said it. For he was sure religion was either a mere contrivance, or the most important thing that could be. So that if he once believed, he would set himself in great earnest to live suitably to it. The aspirings that he had observed at Court, of some of the Clergy, with the servile ways they took to attain to preferment, and the animosities among those of several parties, about trifles, made him often think they suspected the things were not true, which in their sermons and discourses they so earnestly recommended. Of this he had gathered many instances.

('Is there a churchman who on God relies:/Whose life, his faith and doctrine justifies?')

Yet no matter how much the Earl doubted, he kept returning to the idea of changing. God or no God, he now wanted to live cleanly.

> He saw vice and impiety were as contrary to humane society, as wild beasts let loose would be, and therefore he firmly resolved to change the whole method of his life: to become strictly just and true, to be chaste and temperate, to forbear swearing and irreligious discourse, to worship and pray to his maker: and that though he was not arrived at a full persuasion of Christianity, he would never employ his wit more to run it down, or to corrupt others.

Without a spiritual rebirth, Rochester's alcoholism made such vows quite impossible to undertake, and when he left Burnet in April 1680 for Newmarket, he drank again. Though nearly blind, he stood among the cheering crowds to watch the horse-racing, raised his glass with King Charles II for the last time and made a blazing farewell to his society. But, as he set off for his wife's estate at Enmore, via a quick stop at High Lodge, a mood of terrible turmoil began to settle upon him. His poem 'The Wish', in which he expresses a desire to return to the womb, where, 'steeped in lust, nine months I would remain' and then 'boldly fuck my passage out again' is very dangerous indeed and hints strongly at suicidal thoughts. He stepped up his anger and spoke of goodbyes:

> Tired with the noisome follies of the age,
> And weary of my part, I quit the stage;
> For who in life's dull farce a part would bear,
> Where rogues, whores, bawds, all the head actors are?
> Long I with charitable malice strove,
> Lashing the Court, those vermin to remove,
> But thriving vice under the rod still grew,
> As aged letchers whipped, their lust renew;
> What though my life hath unsuccessful been
> (For who can this Augean stable clean?)
> My generous end I will pursue in death,
> And at mankind rail with my parting breath . . .

This poem, 'Rochester's Farewell', is of dubious authenticity, but Professor Pinto had no doubt that these opening lines at least were by the Earl. Note the use of the 'dull' in line three which, taken as a whole, is reminiscent of Hamlet's question: 'Who would fardels bear, to grunt and sweat under a weary life . . .'

Quite why Rochester wanted to go into the West Country is uncertain – he may have been visiting his wife – but, during the journey, said Burnet, he argued 'with greater vigour against God and religion than ever he had done in his life before'. He was 'resolved to run them down with all the arguments and spite in the world'.

When he reached Enmore, he collapsed.

According to Burnet, it was the discomfort of the coach journey which prompted his final sickness.

This heat and violent motion did so inflame an ulcer, that was in his bladder, that it raised a very great pain in those parts: yet he with much difficulty came back by Coach to the lodge at Woodstock Park. He was then wounded both in body and mind: he understood physic and his own constitution and distemper so well, that he concluded he could hardly recover: for the ulcer broke and vast quantities of purulent matter passed with his urine.

By the time 'Mr Baptist' and his colleagues came out of the front door at High Lodge to meet the approaching carriage, he who was 'so proud, so witty and so wise', was incapable, at the age of thirty-three, of walking unaided. Gaunt, shocked and ravaged like an ancient bird of prey, he knew, as he tottered towards the canopy bed which haunts the house to this day, that 'after a search so painful and so long', all his life he had been in his despair and his acceptance of everything made way for Christ. Burnet wrote:

> Now the hand of God touched him, and as he told me, it was not only a general dark melancholy over his mind, such as he had formerly felt; but a most penetrating cutting sorrow. So that though in his body he suffered extreme pain for some weeks, yet the agonies of his mind sometimes swallowed up the sense of what he felt in his body.

What completed the breakdown and finalised a belief in another, better world, was the reading of the 53rd chapter of Isaiah by his mother's chaplain. These passages, as Robert Parsons told him, were prophetical of the sufferings of Christ. They included the lines:

> He is despised and rejected of men; a man of sorrows, and acquainted with grief . . . Surely he hath borne our griefs, and carried our sorrows; yet we did esteem him stricken; smitten of God; and afflicted . . .

Rochester told Burnet that as he listened to the chapter being read,

> he felt an inward force upon him, which did so enlighten his mind and convince him, that he could resist it no longer. For the words had an authority which did shoot like rays or

beams in his mind; so that he was not only convinced by the reasonings he had about it, which satisfied his understanding, but by a power which did so effectually constrain him, that he did ever after as firmly believe in his Saviour, as if he had seen him in the clouds.

In slipping away from the world he hated, Rochester paid loving attention to his wife and his children: at the end of May he took the Sacraments with his wife and instructed her to turn back from the Church of Rome. He told Burnet that his pleasure in taking the Holy Sacrament had been increased

> by the pleasure he had in his Lady's receiving it with him, who had been for some years misled into the Communion of the Church of Rome, and he himself had been not a little instrumental in procuring it, as he freely acknowledged. So that it was one of the joyfullest things that befell him in his sickness, that he had seen that mischief removed, in which he had so great a hand . . .

However frayed Rochester's nerves were, his mind was clear enough for him to have a 'vivacity in his discourse that was extraordinary, and in all things like himself'. He called for his children repeatedly, and 'spoke to them with a sense and feeling that cannot be expressed in writing'.

His habit of swearing was harder to break.

> He had acknowledged to me the former winter that he abhorred it as a base and indecent thing, and had set himself much to break it off: but he confessed that he was so overpowered by that ill custom, that he could not speak with any warmth without repeated oaths . . . once, he was offended with the delay of one that he thought made not haste enough, with somewhat he called for, and said in a little heat, 'that damned fellow'. Soon after, I told him, I was glad to find his style so reformed, and that he had so entirely overcome that ill habit of swearing – only that word of calling 'damned', which had returned upon him, was not decent. His answer was: 'Oh that language of fiends, which was so

familiar to me, hangs yet about me. Sure none has deserved more to be damned than I have done.' And after he had asked God pardon for it, he desired me to call the person to him, that might ask him for forgiveness: but I told him that was needless for he said it of one that did not hear it, and so could not be offended by it.

Choked with emotion, his mother wrote to her sister, Lady St John, and declared:

Oh sister, I am sure, had you heard the heavenly prayers he has made, since this sickness; the extraordinary things he has said, to the wonder of all that has heard him, you would wonder, and think that God alone must teach him, for no man could put into him such things as he says . . .

By the time Rochester made his public recantation on 19 June, calling in even the piggard boy to observe his confessions and his conversion, the word in London was that he had died. Gilbert Burnet received the same news, writing to Henry Savile's brother, Lord Halifax, to say that 'Will Fanshawe just now tells me, letters are come from the Earl of Rochester, by which it seems he must be dead by this time . . . since Mr Fanshawe told me this I hear he is dead.' When Burnet realised the Earl was, in fact, still alive, he wrote to Halifax again on 12 June:

The Earl of Rochester lives still, and is in a probable way of recovery, for it is thought all that ulcerous matter is cast out. All the town is full of his great penitence, which, by your Lordship's good leave, I hope flows from a better principle than the height of his fancy . . .

The implication here is that if Rochester survived, he might relapse into debauchery. It is more than likely that there would have been momentary drops back into alcoholism, and the Earl knew it. He told Burnet during one visit that

he was contented either to die or live, as should please God, and though it was a foolish thing for a man to pretend to choose whether he die or live, yet he wished rather to die. He knew he could never be so well, that life should be comfortable to him. He was confident he should be happy if he died, but he feared if he lived, he might relapse. And then said to me, 'In what a condition shall I be if I relapse after all this?'

Aghast at the rumour that he had converted, the Court – which had withdrawn to Windsor – sent Will Fanshawe to the Lodge. 'Sir', said the Earl to his old drinking partner,

It is true you and I have been very lewd and profane together, and then I was of the opinion you mention; but now I am quite of another mind, and happy am I that I am so. I am very sensible how miserable I was whilst of another opinion. You may assure yourself that there is a judged future state . . . I am not mad, but speak the words of truth and soberness.

Fanshawe is said to have left trembling. Meanwhile, one of the numerous doctors attending Rochester, Dr Shorter, fetched 'a deep sigh' and told Dr Radcliff: 'Well, I can do him no good, but he had done me a great deal.' After the Earl's death, Shorter, a libertine himself, turned to the Catholic Church.

Rochester's mother was worried that his ramblings whilst under the influence of laudanum might make others think he had lost his mind. 'Truly, sister, I think I may say, without partiality, that he has never been heard say, when he speaks of religion, an insensible word, nor of anything else; but one night, of which I writ you word, he was disordered in his head; but then he said no hurt; only some little ribble-rabble.' When she heard that Fanshawe had returned to the Court with the news that Rochester was now insane, she was furious.

I hear Mr Fanshawe reports my son is mad, but I thank God, he is far from that. I confess for a night and part of a day, for want of rest, he was a little disordered; but it was long since Mr Fanshawe saw him. When he reproved him for his sinful life, he was as well in his head as ever he was in his life, and so he is now, I thank God. I am sure, if you heard him pray, you would think God had inspired him with true wisdom indeed, and that neither folly or madness comes near him. I wish that wretch Fanshawe had so great a sense of sin as my poor child has . . .

On 15 June, John Cary was reporting that 'My Lord Rochester hath been ill a great while and continueth so still. He is advised to drink asses' milk and wants a good one that gives milk . . .' and one month later he was saying the patient 'continues very weak and ill'. Hopes that the Earl might rally were dashed when he began passing matter in his urine. This, truly, was the 'debt to pleasure' which he had mentioned in 'The Imperfect Enjoyment'.

Burnet returned to High Lodge on 20 July and was appalled by Rochester's condition:

. . . all hope of recovery was gone. Much purulent matter came from him with his urine, which he passed always with some pain, but one day with inexpressible torment. Yet he bore it decently, without breaking out into repinings or impatient complaints. He imagined he had a stone in his passage, but, it being searched, none was found. The whole substance of his body was drained by the ulcer, and nothing was left but skin and bone, and, by lying much on his back, the parts there began to mortify . . .

Burnet continued:

I ought to have left him on Friday, but, not without some passion, he desired me to stay that day. There appeared no symptom of present death, and a worthy physician then with him told me that though he was so low that an accident might carry him away on a sudden, yet without that, he thought he might live yet some weeks. So on Saturday at four of the clock in the morning, I left him, being the 24th of July. But I durst not take leave of him, for he had expressed so great an unwillingness to part me the day before that if I had not presently yielded to one day's stay it was likely to have given him some trouble. Therefore I thought it better to leave him without any formality. Some hours after, he asked for me, and when it was told him I was gone, he seemed to be troubled and said: 'Has my friend left me? Then I shall die shortly.' After that he spoke but once or twice till he died. He lay much silent. Once, they heard him praying very devoutly. And on Monday, about two of the clock in the morning, he died, without any convulsion or so much as a groan.

EPILOGUE

As on his death-bed gasping Strephon lay,
Strephon; the wonder of the plains;
The noblest of th' Arcadian swains;
Strephon the bold; the witty and the gay:
With many a sigh, and many a tear he said,
Remember me, ye shepherds, when I'm dead.

Thomas Flatman,
'On the Death of my Lord Rochester'

When the Earl of Rochester died, his society rose to meet him. Aphra Behn, Anne Wharton, Samuel Woodford and Thomas Flatman were among those who appreciated that, while the Earl had been so idle a rogue, he had also been so useful a person.

Quite apart from his massive contribution to English literature, Rochester, by dint of living out his art, gave full vent to our most fundamental hopes and fears. He did not know how to hold anything back, and his lines

I cannot change as others do,
Though you unjustly scorn,
For this poor swain who sighs for you
For you alone was born

can even be interpreted as a message to us. His contemporaries, for the most part, recognised that he had taken on their worst characteristics as well as their best ones, and that he had died, in a sense, as a martyr to the reign. It is impossible for any writer to put across, properly, the man's physical presence, and one thing which the elegies that mourned his death drew on was his sheer beauty. Aphra Behn actually went as far as calling him god-like.

Rochester could be, in a dark mood, quite incredibly intimidating. Tall, lean and gaunt, he could outstare the worse of his accusers with just a glint of hatred in the eyes. But, when he was feeling happier, no man was ever more charming, sparkling or seductive. These are just a few of Aphra Behn's lines:

> Mourn, mourn, ye muses; all your loss deplore:
> The young, the noble Strephon is no more.
> Yes; yes; he fled quick as departing light,
> And ne'er shall rise from death's eternal night . . .
> His name's a genius that would wit dispense,
> And give the theme a soul; the words a sense.
> But all fine thought that ravished when it spoke,
> With the soft youth eternal leave has took;
> Uncommon wit that did the soul o'ercome,
> Is buried all in Strephon's worshipped tomb;
> Satire has lost its arts; its sting is gone;
> The fop and cully now may be undone.
> That dear instructing rage is now allayed,
> And no sharp pen dares tell 'em how they've strayed.
> Bold as a God was every lash he took,
> But kind and gentle the chastising stroke.
> Mourn, mourn, ye youths, whom fortune has betrayed:
> The last reproacher of your vice is dead.

While the Earl of Mulgrave continued to whinge and whine about 'nauseous songs by the late convert made', most other writers chose to testify that they had been in the presence of someone extraordinary. Anne Wharton:

> He civilised the rude, and taught the young,
> Made fools grow wise; such artful music hung
> Upon his useful, kind, instructing tongue.
> His lively wit was of himself a part;
> Not, as in other men, the work of art
> For, though his learning, like his wit, was great,
> Yet sure all learning came below his wit . . .

An anonymous admirer wrote this epitaph:

> Here lies the Muses' darling, and the son
> Of great Apollo, who such praise won
> Upon this mole-hill globe, that Heaven thought fit
> He raised on high should in bright mansions sit,
> And safely thence upon the world look down,
> Whilst ever radiant wreaths his temples crown.
> The loss is ours; from Earth Heaven won the prize;
> His body's here, but soul above the skies.

Samuel Holland:

> Under this tomb we do inter
> The ashes of great Rochester,
> Whose pointed wit – his worst of crimes –
> So justly lashed our foppish times.
> Let none too rigorous censures fix;
> Great errors with great parts will mix.
> How broad soe'er his faults be shown,
> His penitence as large was known.
> Forbear then! – and let you and I
> By him, at least, learn how to die.

Another anonymous tribute:

> Satan rejoiced to see thee take his part;
> His malice not so prosperous as thy art.
> He took thee for his pilot to convey
> Those easy souls he spirited away.
> But to his great confusion saw thee shift
> Thy swelling sails, to take another drift,
> With an illustrious train, imputed his,
> To the bright region of eternal bliss.

But the most spectacular tribute to the man who asked his mother to burn all his letters, papers and poems upon his death, came from Elizabeth Barry. Rochester's reworking of *Valentinian* was first staged in 1684 – to great critical success – and at the first performance it was Mrs Cook who came forward to speak a prologue by Aphra Behn. The same actress gave a different prologue on the second day too.

On the third, the Queen of the London stage took her turn with yet another anonymously written tribute. Mrs Barry was as famed for being the greatest subject of Rochester's passion as she was for being a superb actress, and to walk forward before those rows of beady eyes took tremendous bravery. But it was something she wanted to do, and she delivered the message with an aplomb the man himself had taught her to acquire. The age was about to close: the King would soon die from a stroke, uttering the immortal phrase 'Let not poor Nelly starve'; Buckingham would be dead in a few years; Sir Carr Scrope, that 'purblind knight' who so offended the Earl, had already made his departure. There were new faces in this audience; faces which Rochester would not have recognised: but his name was already a legend among them.

Centre stage, Elizabeth Barry spoke first of two 'wit-consuls' who had ruled the former stage – Shakespeare and Fletcher – who with 'every passion did the mind engage'. Then, as she stood in the flickering candle-light, she paused before speaking these lines:

> Now joins a third, a genius as sublime
> As ever flourished in Rome's happiest time.
> As sharply could he wound; as sweetly engage;
> As soft his love; as divine his rage.
> He charmed the tenderest virgins to delight,
> And with his style did fiercest blockheads fright.
> Some beauties here, I see,
> Though now demure, have felt his powerful charms
> And languished in the circle of his arms.
> But for ye fops, his satire reached ye all,
> And under his lash your whole vast herd did fall.
> Oh fatal loss! That mighty spirit's gone!
> Alas! His too great heat went out too soon!
> So fatal is it vastly to excel;
> Thus young, thus mourned, his loved Lucretius fell.
>
> And now, ye little sparks who infest the pit,
> Learn all the reverence due to sacred wit.

Disturb not with your empty noise each bench,
Nor break your bawdy jests to the orange-wench;
Nor in that scene of fops, the gallery,
Vent your no-wit, and spurious raillery:
That noisy place, where meet all sort of tools,
Your huge fat lovers and consumptive fools;
Half-wits; and gamesters; and gay fops, whose tasks
Are daily to invade the dangerous masks:
And, ye little brood of poetasters,
Amend, and learn to write, from these your Masters.

BIBLIOGRAPHY

Adlard, John, Ed. *The Debt to Pleasure.*

Alcock Thomas. *The Famous Pathologist or the Noble Mountebank*, ed. V. de Sola Pinto, 1961.

Aubrey, John. *Brief Lives*, Woodbridge, 1982.

Balfour, Sir Andrew, M.D. *Letters Written to a Friend*, Edinburgh, 1700.

Beer, E.S. de. *The Diary of John Evelyn* (six volumes), Oxford, 1955.

Blount, Charles. *Miscellaneous Works, The Oracle of Reason*, London, 1695.

Blum, Professor Kenneth and Payne, James E. *Alcohol and the Addictive Brain*, New York, 1991.

Brett, Arthur. *Charles II and his Court*, 1910.

Bryant, Sir Arthur. *The England of Charles II*, 1955.

Buckingham, John, Duke of. *Works* (two volumes), The Hague, 1726.

Burnet, Gilbert. *Some Passages of the Life and Death of the Right Honourable John Earl of Rochester*, London, 1680.

Calendar of State Papers Domestic (Reign of Charles II).

Carte, Thomas. *A Collection of Original Letters and Papers* (two volumes), 1739.

Cibber, Colley. *An Apology for the Life of Mr Colley Cibber*, London, 1889.

Curll, E. *History of the English Stage*, London, 1741.

Davies, Godfrey. *The Restoration of Charles II, 1658–1660*, 1955.

Defoe, Daniel. *Journal of the Plague Year.*

Dennis, John. *Critical Works of John Dennis* (two volumes), Oxford, 1927.

Dictionary of National Biography.

Domestick Intelligence.

Downes, John. *Roscius Anglicanus*, 1708.

Etherege, Sir George. *Dramatic Works* (two volumes), Oxford, 1927.

Farley Hills, David. *Rochester, The Critical Heritage.*

Fraser, Antonia. *King Charles II*, London, 1979.

Gadbury, John. *Ephemeris or a Diary*, London, 1698.

Gardner, Helen, Ed. *The New Oxford Book of English Verse*, 1992.

Gepp, H.J. *Adderbury*, Banbury, 1924.

Gildon, Charles, Ed. *Familiar Letters: Volume Two, containing thirty six letters by the Rt. Hon. John, late Earl of Rochester*, London, 1697.

Greene, Graham, *Lord Rochester's Monkey*, London, 1974.

Ham, Roswell, *Otway and Lee*, 1931.

Hamilton, Anthony. *Memoirs of Count Grammont*, editions 1888 and Monaco, 1958.

Hayward, John. *Collected Works of the Earl of Rochester*, Nonesuch Press, 1926.

Hayward, John. *The Letters of Saint Evremond*, London, 1930.

Hearne, Thomas. *Remarks and Collections*, ed. C. Noble, Oxford, 1885–1889.

Historical Manuscripts, Reports of the Royal Commission.

Hobbes, Thomas. *The English Works of Thomas Hobbes* (eleven volumes), London, 1889.

Hore, J.P. *The History of Newmarket and the Annals of the Turf*, 1886.

Jaffray, Alexander. *The Diary of Alexander Jaffray*, Aberdeen, 1856.

Journals of the House of Lords.

Kenyon, J.P. *The Stuarts: A Study in English Kingship*, 1958.

Langbaine, G. *An Account of the English Dramatic Poets*, Oxford, 1691.

Lee, Nathaniel. *The Princess of Cleve*, London, 1689.

Longueville, T. *Rochester and Other Literary Rakes of the Court of Charles II*, London, 1902.

Marshall, E. *A Supplement to the History of Woodstock Manor and its Environs*, London, 1874.

Nicol, Allardyce. *A History of English Drama, Volume One, Restoration Drama*, 1952.

Ogg, David. *England in the Reign of Charles II*, 1963.

Parsons, Robert. *A Sermon Preached at the Funeral of the Rt. Honourable John Earl of Rochester*, Oxford, 1680.

Pepys, Samuel. *Diary*, various editions but mainly The Globe Edition, London, 1924.

Pinto, Vivian de Sola. *Enthusiast in Wit. A Portrait of John Wilmot Earl of Rochester 1647–1680*, London, 1962.

Prinz, Johannes, *John Wilmot Earl of Rochester. His Life and Writings*, Leipzig. 1927.

Prinz, Johannes. *Rochesteriana*, Leipzig, 1926.

Savile, Henry. *Letters to and from Henry Savile*, Camden Society, London, 1858.

Sedley, Sir Charles. *The Poetical and Dramatic Works*, ed. V. de Sola Pinto, London, 1928.

Smith, Captain Alexander. *The School of Venus*, 1716.

Vieth, David. *Complete Poems of John Wilmot Earl of Rochester*, 1968.

Wilson, J.H. *Court Wits of the Restoration*, Princeton, 1948.

Wilson, J.H. *The Rochester-Savile Letters, 1671–1680*, Ohio, 1941.

Wolseley, Robert. *Preface to Valentinian*, London, 1685.

Worden, Blair, Ed. *Stuart England*, Oxford, 1986.

INDEX